An Introduction to Contemporary Fiction

An Introduction to Contemporary Fiction

International Writing in English since 1970

Edited by Rod Mengham

Polity Press

First published 1999 by Polity Press
in association with Blackwell Publishers Ltd.

Editorial office:
Polity Press
65 Bridge Street
Cambridge CB2 1UR, UK

Marketing and production:
Blackwell Publishers Ltd
108 Cowley Road
Oxford OX4 1JF, UK

Published in the USA by
Blackwell Publishers Inc.
Commerce Place
350 Main Street
Malden, MA 02148, USA

ISBN 0–7456–1956–8
ISBN 0–7456–1957–6 (pbk)

A catalogue record for this book is available from the British Library and has
been applied for from the Library of Congress.

Typeset in 10½ on 12 pt Sabon
by Ace Filmsetting Ltd, Frome, Somerset
Printed in Great Britain by MPG Books, Victoria Square, Bodmin, Cornwall

This book is printed on acid-free paper.

Contents

Notes on Contributors

Maud Ellmann lectures in English at Cambridge, where she is also a Fellow of King's College. She has written *The Poetics of Impersonality* (1987) and *The Hunger Artists* (1991) and is currently working on a study of Elizabeth Bowen. She has also edited Bram Stoker's *Dracula* and *Psychoanalytic Literary Criticism* (1994).

Geoff Gilbert is a Lecturer in English Literature at the University of Cambridge, where he writes and teaches on early twentieth-century literature, critical theory, and contemporary Scots fiction. He is currently completing a book on the culture of modernism.

Sophie Gilmartin is a Lecturer in English at Royal Holloway, University of London. She has published articles on Victorian literature and culture and is the author of *Ancestry and Narrative in Nineteenth Century British Fiction* (1998). She is currently researching a book on Victorian widowhood. She is also Director of the MA in Narrative, Literature and Culture at Royal Holloway.

John Harvey lectures on English Literature at Cambridge. His first novel, *The Plate Shop*, won the David Higham Prize in 1979, his second, *Coup d'Etat* (1985), deals with a military dictatorship in a European country. His third, *The Legend of Captain Space*, appeared in 1990. His non-fiction writing includes *Victorian Novelists and their Illustrators* (1970) and *Men in Black* (1995). He has published studies of Beckett, Blake, Cruikshank, Shakespeare and Tolstoy, and has reviewed new fiction extensively in the *London Review of Books*, the *Sunday Telegraph* and the *Sunday Times*.

Rod Mengham lectures in the Faculty of English at Cambridge, where he is also Director of Studies in English at Jesus College. He has published books on Charles Dickens, Emily Brontë and Henry Green, as well as *The Descent of Language: Writing in Praise of Babel* (1993). He has edited the short stories of E. M. Forster, and has co-edited with Jana Howlett *The Violent Muse: Violence and the Artistic Imagination in Europe 1910–1939* (1994). He is the editor of the Equipage series of poetry pamphlets and his own poems have been published under the title *Unsung: New and Selected Poems* (1996).

Drew Milne is the Judith E. Wilson Lecturer in Drama and Poetry, University of Cambridge, and a Fellow of Trinity Hall. He edited *Marxist Literary Theory: A Reader* (1996) with Terry Eagleton and was the editor of the journal *Parataxis: Modernism and Modern Writing*. His books of poems include *Sheet Mettle* (1994) and *Bench Marks* (1998). In 1995 he was Writer in Residence at the Tate Gallery, London.

Adrian Poole is Reader in English and Comparative Literature at the University of Cambridge, and a Fellow of Trinity College. He has written on Greek and Shakespearean tragedy, and on novelists including Dickens, George Eliot, Hardy and Henry James; he has also co-edited with Jeremy Maule the *Oxford Book of Classical Verse in Translation*.

Ato Quayson is a Lecturer in English and Director of the African Studies Centre at Cambridge. His teaching interests include Post-colonial Studies, Magical Realism, African American Literature, Shakespeare, and Tragedy. His book *Strategic Transformations in Nigerian Writing* was published in 1997 and he is currently completing *Postcolonialism: Theories, Problems and Practices*. He is a Fellow of Pembroke College.

N. H. Reeve is a Lecturer in English at the University of Wales, Swansea. He has written *The Novels of Rex Warner* (1990), *Nearly Too Much: The Poetry of J. H. Prynne* (with Richard Kerridge, 1995), and numerous articles and essays on nineteenth- and twentieth-century fiction and poetry. He edited *Henry James: The Shorter Fiction – Reassessments* (1997), and was the founding editor of the *Swansea Review*. He is currently working on a book on Lawrence and a book of essays on the fiction of the 1940s.

Kiernan Ryan is Professor of English Language and Literature at Royal Holloway, University of London, and a Fellow of New Hall, Cambridge. He is the author of *Shakespeare* (1989, 2nd edn, 1995) and *Ian McEwan* (1995), and the editor of *King Lear: Contemporary Critical Essays* (1993), *New Historicism and Cultural Materialism: A Reader* (1996) and *Shakespeare: The Last Plays* (1999).

Geoff Ward is Professor of English at the University of Dundee. He has lectured widely in Europe, North America and Japan. His chief publications include *Statutes of Liberty: The New York School of Poets* (1992), and *Language Poetry and the American Avant-garde* (1993). He is editor and co-editor respectively of *The Bloomsbury Guide to Romantic Literature* (1993) and *Re: Joyce. Text. Culture. Politics* (1998). He is an editor of *The Cambridge Quarterly*, and has also published several collections of poetry, most recently *Rilke's Elegies, Barbarously Recast* and *Translations from the Finish* (both 1998).

Kathleen M. Wheeler is a Fellow of Darwin College and University Teaching Officer in the English Faculty at Cambridge. Her most recent books include *A Guide to Twentieth Century Women Novelists* (1997), *Explaining Deconstruction* (1998) and *Modernist Women Writers and Narrative Art* (1994). She has published books on Romanticism and Modern Theory (German, French and Anglo-American), and two on Coleridge. Most recently, she is preparing a book on Greek scholarship in the eighteenth century and its influence on the rise of Romanticism.

Mark Wormald is Fellow and Director of Studies in English at Pembroke College, Cambridge. He has written on George Eliot, Dickens and Hopkins as well as contemporary poetry and fiction, and has edited *The Pickwick Papers*. He is currently working on a book entitled *Watermarks: An Element of Consciousness in the Modern Literary Imagination*.

Introduction

Rod Mengham

The essays in this volume provide a comprehensive introduction to the state of fiction in the English-speaking world during the period from 1970 to the present day. This particular chronological period has been chosen because of the sea-change transforming fiction in English during that time. It was during the 1970s that British fiction began to interact more readily with the modes of foreign (chiefly French, Eastern European and Latin American) writing practices; and it was from the late 1970s onwards that the mutual dependence of fiction and critical theory began to figure largely in the production and reception of numerous texts. In particular, the emergence of postmodern, postcolonial and gender-specific concepts of literature has had a crucial effect on the understanding of the social and cultural role of fiction writing and reading. Perceptions of history, the environment and the politics of culture have all undergone major alterations, and there have been corresponding reappraisals in fiction of modes of narration, point of view and temporal and spatial coordinates; an accelerating interest in certain genre-bound preoccupations has meant a relative loss of interest in others. This introduction will provide a survey of the main preoccupations of the fiction, and of the key issues in the cultural and critical agenda. It will refer not only to the authors discussed in the essays that follow but also to a range of works that could not be given such detailed attention.

The fall of the Berlin Wall, the disintegration of the USSR and the installation of new regimes in Eastern Europe have provided dramatic and often highly symbolic instances of a breakdown in the narrative of history. But what kind of history? What precisely governs our sense of the historical process and how do our imaginations cope with the often barely perceptible nuances of cultural change? According to

Muriel Spark, in her novel *The Takeover* (1976), an equally significant 'sea-change in the nature of reality' had already occurred in the
period 1973–4, in the shape of 'changes in the meaning of property
and money' and in the degradation of the language of values: transformations which in the capitalist world might have implications even
more serious than the momentous collapse of communist regimes.
Across the world, historical time in much of the post-war era has also
converged with the 'time of the disaster'. Military strategy has been
overshadowed by the time-scale implied by the nuclear threat; the
political process has been devalued by the realization that democracy
is inoperable within the period of the four-minute warning. Political
control has been confined, ultimately, to the split-second decision-
making of supreme commanders. 'The present feels narrower, the
present feels straitened, discrepant, as the planet lives from day to
day', claims Martin Amis in a statement discussed by Kiernan Ryan in
his essay on the work of Amis and Ian McEwan. Given this contraction of the time available for significant action, and the sense of
meaninglessness it produces, we should not be surprised that the last
thirty years have seen a remarkable surge in the growth of millenarian
and apocalyptic religious sects, since these provide a framework for
the disaster which turns it into the most significant event in history,
rather than a means of ensuring the failure of history altogether. The
deep imprint left by this model of history as curtailment has survived
the withdrawal of the nuclear threat and is reflected in popular enthusiasm for the Hollywood disaster-substitutes of invading aliens,
volcanic catastrophes and impacting asteroids. In a sense, the real
catastrophe is the irreversible social and psychological damage occa-
sioned by the mere existence of nuclear weapons. This is the point
Ryan makes in turning to Amis and McEwan for indications of how
'the depth at which we have buried their presence in our subconscious
is the exact measure of our subjection to their silent terror'.

The need to restore a comprehensible human dimension to historical experience is perhaps the chief reason for the phenomenal popularity of old-fashioned, highly individualized accounts of moments of
extreme crisis. One particularly striking example of this trend is Andy
MacNab's narrative of Gulf War operations, *Bravo Two Zero*. While
the dominant image of the Gulf War was the screen on which targets
were located, aligning the situation of the combatant with that of the
television viewer, and while the time of the disaster seemed to have
edged nearer, with the spectacle of Scud missiles landing on Israeli
cities, it was the profoundly traditional account of the individual soldier, eclipsing the technological novelty of the war, that appealed most
vividly to a reading public strangely consoled by episodes of solitary

heroic struggle of a kind that would have been recognizable in any war at any time in history.

The demise of state Marxism and the associated 'grand narratives' of European modernity has not been succeeded by a historical vacuum. A growing internationalism of economic culture has been accompanied by a progressive dislocation between national outlooks with their different models of history. The crude identifications on offer in this situation have been complicated and challenged by the procedures of historical fiction, which has seen a remarkable upsurge during the period under review. Whereas historical fiction in the nineteenth century frequently was associated with the formation of national identity, in the contemporary scene it has been used as a means of practising an archaeology of the imagination; writers such as Peter Ackroyd have been concerned to explore the historical layering of experience that has accumulated in a particular place: for Ackroyd, in London. In novels such as *Hawksmoor* (1985) and *The House of Doctor Dee* (1993) he has invested in a form of 'psychogeography', a method of divining the aura possessed by a place in which energies have been discharged by intense individual experience, whose imaginary sedimentation over centuries has become the foundation of true historical meaning. This description could apply equally well to the novels of Iain Sinclair (*White Chappell, Scarlet Tracings* (1981), *Downriver* (1991), *Radon Daughters* (1994)), except that for Sinclair the notion of time folding up like a concertina remains at the level of a working hypothesis, a means of conjuring up powerfully unorthodox perspectives on a set of contemporary social phenomena that form the critical focus of an authorial project with strong documentary impulses. Ackroyd's historical elisions are usually literary conceits, fictional projections, representations of the experience of characters whose sensibility is separate from that of the author's, despite the family resemblances between characters from different books. Sinclair's language is the vehicle of a distinctive personal style, whereas Ackroyd's writing is frequently drawn to the use of pastiche.

Pastiche has been employed widely in the historical fiction of the last three decades – see Robert Nye's *Falstaff* (1976) for a particularly bravura example – and it has been identified by Fredric Jameson as one of the besetting vices of postmodernism. In an admonitory review of the American novelist E. L. Doctorow, Jameson stresses that 'this historical novel can no longer set out to represent the historical past; it can only "represent" our ideas and stereotypes about the past.'[1] Jameson is right to be nervous about ventriloquism; language encodes historical experience in the evolution of its forms and styles, but it ceases to be a true index of historical change in the linguistic equivalent of costume drama. To be fair to the novelists, neither Ackroyd nor Doctorow is unaware of the problems of pastiche or more generally of the issues of representation and interpretation involved in narrative reconstructions of the past. The dilemma of the historical novelist is encapsulated in one of the ruminative, meta-textual passages interspersed between the chapters of Ackroyd's biography of Dickens: 'I was lost in some time between the mid-nineteenth century and the late twentieth century, and I could not speak. I was adrift between two worlds which now seemed to exist simultaneously – or, rather, had become one world.'[2] The extent to which modern narrators have projected back onto the past a reflection of their own modern preoccupations has been no less of an issue for historians themselves. The work of Hayden White has illustrated the degree to which modern history-writing has been conditioned by the same demands of narrative unity and authorial point of view that we expect to find more readily in works of fiction.[3] Novelists who deliberately introduce a historical perspective into their work are only making an architectural principle out of circumstances that affect the reading of any writing, since writing is always issued to the reader from a moment of composition necessarily in the past. Reading operates through a tension between the modes of thought and feeling that obtain at the moment of composition, and those that obtain at the moment of reading (what Reception Theory refers to as the moments of 'production' and 'reception'). No matter how close together these moments are, there will always be a discrepancy between the two sets of conditions. Some of the most serviceable and rewarding of contemporary narratives have aimed at exploring the nature and repercussions of this historical tension.

In the fiction of Graham Swift this tension is a central concern of characters, narrators and readers, as Adrian Poole argues: 'all Swift's fictions move between a remembering present and remembered pasts'. Poole notes the recurrent focus in Swift's work on historical depth, and particularly on the legacy of the Second World War; he argues that this period has a special resonance through association with the idea of shared experience and collective memory: the last war was 'the last great collective ending the English have known'. Projections of social unity onto wartime experience have been authorized by acts of reading, by acknowledgements of those images and stories that have seemed to define the experience of the 1940s. Most people's sense of the war has been constructed, as a form of cultural memory that may or may not coincide with the testimony of individuals. Swift investigates the advantages and disadvantages, the losses and gains, that arise from being caught up in this process of construction.

Jonathan Coe's brilliantly satirical condition-of-England novel *What a Carve Up!* (1994) uses the same historical time-frame in exploring how identity is shaped by cultural myths and forms and stereotypical patterns of organization. For the writer-protagonist Michael Owen, memory and desire are both anchored in 'collective' experiences that he becomes fixated on. Owen is obsessed with the flight of Yuri Gagarin, the first man in space, and with the stylized denouement of the popular film that the novel takes its title from. In a sarcastic alternative to Salman Rushdie's observation that the ties of a generation bind more closely even than those of race, gender, caste or religion, Coe imagines the extent to which the shared experience of the Thatcher years is one of cultural psychosis. In the work of Swift, Spark and Coe the individual's sense of relationship to the movement of history is familiarized, rendered intelligible through the medium of inherited stories and myths.

In the post-colonial sphere, this situation is complicated by the dramatic manner in which narrative accounts of origins are transmitted; there are stories that are inherited and stories that are imposed, introduced from outside. In Sophie Gilmartin's essay in this volume, the resistance to colonial forms of relationship and methods of relating is seen at work within the British Isles themselves, in the confrontations between the Celts and their invaders. Here the historic importance of topography, of the mapping and naming of conquered territory, represents the scope of language, the potential force of narration, the violence implicit in speaking for others, that overshadow the post-colonial agenda. In Brian Moore's *Catholics* (1972) and John Fuller's *Flying to Nowhere* (1983), the language of the invader fails to capture the nature of what it seeks to translate, as the properties of these Celtic landscapes evade their given meanings in a process of transformation, or, more pertinently, transubstantiation. The clash of cultures is explored through oppositions of rational and spiritual, science and the miraculous; ultimately, these island-stories suggest a Catholic response to the Protestant myth of Robinson Crusoe.

Mark Wormald argues for a similar motivation in the work of Jeanette Winterson; both *Oranges are not the Only Fruit* (1985) and *Sexing the Cherry* (1989) are set during the reign of Charles II, whose Catholic, royalist England, with its associations of sexual liberty and freedom from dogma, is contrasted with the Puritan epochs that preceded and followed it. Wormald connects Winterson's libertarian heterodoxy with Salman Rushdie's battles against fundamentalism. Both writers are interested in mixing traditions, in devising styles of narration that can accommodate different beliefs and modes of thought. Rushdie's priority is very clearly the production of a hybrid form that blends and 'chutneyfies' his various sources in an act of revisionary story-telling that brings into relation the traditions of colonizer and colonized. He understands history in terms of a 'perpetual oscillation' between consolidation and fragmentation, in the process of forming and re-forming cultural, racial and religious identities. The most celebrated example of this paradox comes at the end of *Midnight's Children* (1981), when the protagonist appears to be breaking up into millions of constituent parts at the precise moment of India's national self-realization.

'Perpetual oscillation' is a phrase borrowed from Maud Ellmann and used by Ato Quayson to make sense of an equivalent manœuvre in African fiction. The oscillation between wholeness and dismemberment in the texts that Quayson looks at concerns states of disability, both actual physical conditions and cultural symptoms. Recent fiction has focused crucially on the disabled as figures of national or cultural identity in post-colonial societies, and this reflects tellingly the extent to which colonialism has disabled the colonized, as Quayson puts it, 'from taking their place in the flow of history other than in a position of stigmatized underprivilege'.

Kathy Wheeler's essay extends the analysis to show how formal experimentation in recent English and American writing has been used to undermine received notions of subjectivity, particularly with reference to gender and ethnicity. She explores the relationship between literary technique and the conviction that 'heterogeneity, not homogeneity or unitariness, impurity and mélange, nor originary purity' are the defining characteristics of identity. Among the authors she discusses, Walter Abish demonstrates the use of 'metaplasm', which involves the repeating and rewriting of material from his own texts and those of others, in order to question the distinction between pure and impure, original and secondary, states of being. Kathy Acker deploys a more energetically overt method of plagiarism in order to claim that all social identity is irrevocably 'metaplastic'. For Cynthia Ozick the equivalent operation includes the renovation of 'midrash', the ancient Hebrew procedure for textural analysis. The fundamental principle of this is multiplication: the supplementing of new readings that make the Bible 'polyvocal' rather than held to the authority of a single tradition of interpretation.

The violence of spokesmanship, and the violence that is used to prevent others from speaking for themselves, is the subject of Maud Ellmann's essay, which considers the literary history of rape and its bearing in the fiction of Alice Walker and Toni Morrison. The double burden of suffering and silence, the prohibition against testimony that would shatter the illusion of a workable society, shifts the responsibility for destructively anti-social behaviour from the rapist to his victim.

Ellmann meditates on how women's writing originates, paradoxically, from an inability to speak, from the lack of a position in which women are not already inculpated in the process of their own victimization. She points to the non-existence of a comprehensive history of rape, of a means of accounting for its structural role in existing social relationships.

In other respects crime, and the systematic accounting for its agents and motivations, has sustained the growth of one of the most lucrative branches of the fiction industry. Both the detective novel and the spy thriller, with their related emphases on covert practices and withheld meanings, provide a means of locating transgression, rendering it intelligible, and defining the boundary between the licit and the illicit. This may be one sphere of cultural activity in which British and American procedures are sharply disjunctive. In the American tradition, stemming from Hammett and Chandler, and maturing in films like *Chinatown* and the novels of James Ellroy, it is the private investigator who holds the key to American culture. By no means a representative of the law, he (it is nearly always a he) is nonetheless the instrument of a forensic process which accentuates his independence and his occupancy of a private space and a life-style that is the pared-down quintessence of defensive urbanism. By contrast, the archetypal British equivalent is the Le Carré secret agent, a fully integrated member of an elite group in a world where espionage lives in easy proximity to the central traditions of British culture. The basic codes of literary detection are often powerfully subverted, in terms of gender in the novels of Sara Paretsky, and in terms of genre in the brilliantly eccentric fiction of Derek Raymond. At its most ambitious, the spy thriller has produced some of the most powerful and complex articulations of contemporary history; James Buchan's *Heart's Journey in Winter* (1996), set in the last decade of the Cold War, is an exceptionally subtle examination of social and psychological patterns in Eastern and Western Europe that do not reflect one another directly, but which bear on the same issues of conspiracy and paranoia.

The literature of conspiracy theories and paranoid systems has also become immensely popular during the last three decades. It encompasses several genres and media and has been particularly evident in recent films; in fiction it ranges from the fantasies of Pynchon, particularly *Gravity's Rainbow* (1973), in which twentieth-century history is revised to conform with an attempt to decode and render coherent its alleged hidden meanings to the obsessional fictions of Iain Sinclair, which attempt to reconstruct the unofficial and encrypted histories of a specific terrain. In the middle ground, as it were, are novels of a basically more realist colouring which concentrate on the hidden

persuasions of an advanced media culture, on the corrupt machin-
ations of a secret society and on the insidious displacement of political
power by commercial influence. These concerns are all preoccupations
of the American writer Don DeLillo, whose novel *Libra* (1988) is the
subject of Neil Reeve's essay. *Libra is* a text which hovers around the
Lee Harvey Oswald/Kennedy assassination story; at its centre is a quest
for or approach towards the catastrophic defining act which organizes
into meaning the field of forces that surrounds it. The book addresses
head-on the political and market value of coherent testimony within
the conditions of information overload, of an inexhaustible pile of
random information awaiting the stories that will be attached to it
and that it will defy. DeLillo interrogates radically the kind of fiction
that sees itself as grounded upon the authority of factual events and
'real' people, and investigates the culture of what has become known
as the 'simulacrum', literally an identical copy for which no original
has ever existed. The term 'simulacrum', which has been given cur-
rency by the theoretical writings of Jean Baudrillard, refers to phenomena such as life-style models that bear little relation to actual
social existence but which are produced and reproduced throughout
the media and in particular the entertainment industry.

Among British writers, perhaps the most impressive grasp of the
scope of simulacra has been evidenced in Gordon Burn's novel *Alma
Cogan* (1991), which enquires into the ways in which subjectivity is
shaped under the influence of advertising and publicity, film and popular music. Burn's crooner protagonist, the eponymous Alma Cogan,
half-recognizes the degree to which the publicity shot effaces the 'state
of upheaval' behind the public mask, displacing a sense of individual
development with the reproduction of images that 'were out there somewhere, circulating, multiplying, reproducing, like a spore in the world,
even when you were sleeping'.

There is a curious parallel to this global outreach of simulacra in the
culture of eco-politics. There has been a wide range of recent expressions of the view that sees the planet as a single organism, the natural
environment as a medium for a creative agency immanent within
life as a whole. The variety of literary responses to this prospect
has included the recent work of J. G. Ballard, whose *The Day of
Creation* (1987) proposes a jarring overlap between certain aspects
of the simulacrum and certain directions within the ecological movement; where too much stress is laid on the relationship between
humankind as species and the rest of creation, this can lead to the
eliding of social relations and the local politics of everyday life. At one
point in Ballard's novel his protagonist Mallory recalls sitting exhausted
in a junior doctors' common room in a London hospital, watching a

broadcast by his antagonist Sanger, a 'sometime biologist turned television popularizer' who holds forth in the 'rootless international style of an airline advertisement' about the presence of 'extra-sensory powers distributed throughout the biological kingdom'.

Ballard's text argues rather cynically for the view that anti-capitalist protest is always amenable to absorption by the 'society of the spectacle'. However, certain aspects of counter-cultural resistance have been less easily assimilable to this process than others. Since the 1960s fiction has reflected various expressions of a powerful tradition of alienation that has taken the forms of insanity, psychedelia, drug cultures and related addiction phenomena. R. D. Laing's and David Cooper's invention of 'non-psychiatry' as part of a campaign to diffuse so-called madness throughout society 'as a subversive source of creativity, spontaneity, not "disease" ',[4] might be counterpointed with drug-based experiments in 'consciousness raising' promoted by Timothy Leary but satirized by Hunter S. Thompson in *Fear and Loathing in Las Vegas* (1972). The prodigious overdrive of Thompson's prose communicates a kind of self-perpetuating relish at more and more different kinds of experience of excess, but it also discloses the negative repercussions of the drug culture and begins to explore the kinds of structures of addiction and control that are detailed so exhaustively in the works of William S. Burroughs.

The burden of Geoff Ward's essay in this volume is that Burroughs remains an incorrigible deviant, a permanent outsider who has operated as a major influence on subsequent novelists such as Angela Carter, Kathy Acker, Irvine Welsh and Will Self. Ward stresses the structural ambivalence of his writing, an elusiveness that prevents his work from being assigned a clearly identifiable role in cultural debate, and which provokes renewed attention to the intricacies of his text. In this respect it may be that the Scottish writer Alan Warner has effected the most comprehensive development of Burroughs's strategies and preoccupations, in his morally opaque, stylistically delirious and telepathic account of contemporary social derangements, *Morvern Callar* (1995). According to Ward, it is Burroughs who has effectively written the mission statement for 'our ongoing collective narrative of the modern city as site of decadence/apocalypse'. He has also provided the most scrupulous of analyses of disempowerment. Burroughs's understanding of control systems as fundamental to all contemporary societies conflates the operations of technological and biological structures, particularly in the amenability of both to viruses. His crucial perception of language as the most significant virus of all ('no control machine so far devised can operate without words'[5]) raises questions about the limits of personal agency in language whose implications have been developed in the work of Avital Ronell. Her *Crack Wars* (1992) explores the ways in which literature itself creates a system of dependencies, implicating readers in a structure of addiction (at the centre of her book is a reading of *Madame Bovary*).

The relationship between reading and power is considered by Geoff Gilbert in his study of the reception of James Kelman's Booker Prize-winning novel *How late it was, how late* (1994). Kelman's own attitude towards cultural institutions has aligned them with more obviously political embodiments of state authority. However, as Gilbert points out, the history of the Booker Prize has been a history of negotiations with this kind of adversarial stance, 'transforming journalistic debate, disbelief, and even scorn into a form of cultural legitimation'. The main difference between Kelman's experience of winning the prize and that of his predecessors has been the non-convertibility of this symbolic capital into market value: *How late it was, how late* has simply failed to achieve the level of sales expected. Gilbert identifies 'bad language', execration and obscenity, as the crucial factor in this commercial nose-dive. 'Bad language' has been a successful strategy in ensuring some degree of aesthetic autonomy – it has been the instrument of Kelman's refusal to connive in the process of salvaging a respectable literary status from a condition of social ostracism. A similar dilemma must have faced Samuel Beckett after the award of the Nobel Prize in 1969. Drew Milne's essay starts from the premise that everything Beckett wrote between 1970 and his death in 1989 'does not so much attract as repel the resulting glare of publicity'. More than any other contemporary writer, perhaps, Beckett found the means to 'resist contextualization within the cultural or national interests of Irish, French or English writing'.

It is the thematic and formal emphasis within Beckett's writing on exhaustion, inanition and immobility which tests to the utmost the limits of narrative as a form that, as John Harvey's widely ranging essay demonstrates, is tied fundamentally to the experience of movements as both subject and method. It is in the tension between Beckett's idea of stillness and the varying rates of flow that Harvey discusses that the most rewarding of contemporary fictions are produced: novels that acknowledge the movement of history, its direction, rhythm and change of pace, even when they disavow it – that movement within the field of forces that requires a constant adjustment of the ratio, both to respond to and to resist.

Notes

1 Fredric Jameson, *Postmodernism, or, the Cultural Logic of Late Capitalism* (London: Verso, 1991), p. 25.

2 Peter Ackroyd, *Dickens* (London: Sinclair-Stevenson, 1990), pp. 1059–60.

3 Hayden White, *Metahistory: The Historical Imagination in Nineteenth Century Europe* (Baltimore: Johns Hopkins University Press, 1973); *The Content of the Form: Narrative Discourse and Historical Representation* (Baltimore: Johns Hopkins University Press, 1987).

4 David Cooper, 'The Invention of Non-Psychiatry', in *Semiotext(e)*, 3/2 (1978), p. 66.

5 William S. Burroughs, 'The Limits of Control', in *The Adding Machine* (London: John Calder, 1985), p. 116.

Part I

Issues

1 Constructions of Identity in Post-1970 Experimental Fiction

Kathleen M. Wheeler

The 'question of the subject' is one of the most overt and recurring concerns of twentieth-century fiction, perhaps in part a result of the influence of psychological writings from James and Havelock Ellis to Freud, Lacan, Kristeva and Foucault.[1] Characterization in fiction, authorship and intention, readership, narrative point of view, style, genre and thematics all reflect the concern with this 'question', in post-modern, magic realist, realist, and other experimental types of writing. Modernists had also questioned the subject's unity, identity, autonomy, sometimes emphasizing its embeddedness in language, sometimes its dialogic character, sometimes its warring, conflicting aspect, sometimes its historical contingency. The construction of identity and individual-ity, its nature, its possibility, has always interested writers, yet after such texts as Robert Louis Stevenson's *Dr Jekyll and Mr Hyde* in the 1880s, and after the growth at the turn of the century of political movements challenging attitudes to sexuality, women's status and racism, literary investigations into representations of the subject gained in intensity and diversity. Gertrude Stein, James Joyce, Djuna Barnes and Virginia Woolf in England were some of the more experimental writers in a tradition of European and American artistic explorations of innovative forms for questioning the nature of individuality, which continued into the mid-century with Roth, Nabokov, Heller, Marguerite Young, Ann Quin, Susan Sontag and many others. The self, portrayed as a network of values, attitudes, or acts – with no substrate (or soul) behind it, no essence – had been a familiar representation since the beginning of literature, whether we call this a Bakhtinian dialogism, a (Kenneth) Burkean belief that the telling of stories is the defining characteristic of human identity, a Cervantes-like construct from read-ing too many romances, or a relatively existentialist humanness, as potentiality through acts, not reality through essence. The self as a rhetorical position, a site from which to exercise power or be victimized, a sociological construct, together with other portrayals, politicized the concept of the self, since it was no longer natural and substantive, but constructed and changeable. Consequently, knowledge and values of all kinds were also politicized; for they were seen as results of self-positionings and consequently never neutral or objective, but expressive of social relations and structures. Who is speaking becomes an issue, not just what is spoken. And how this who as subject is constituted by discourse led to an awareness of the variety of discourse available and to the need to resist the hegemony of any one specific discourse as limiting and even victimizing.

Freud's problematizing of the distinction between madness and sanity, between animal and human, even more than his theoretical constructs of the unconscious, the id, ego and superego, captured the modernist and surrealist imagination, and influenced literary representations of the subject. His method of dream interpretation emphasized, moreover, the idea later vividly illustrated by Proust, amongst others, that the story of the telling is the notional core: it is the textuality of the dream, its rhetoric, which is analysed. That textuality includes the gaps, the silences, the spaces between what is said, and these indicate what is specifically not said. Ideally, Freud's analytical approach functioned to empower his patients by helping them to reveal the ideologies and social pressures making them ill and marginalized, as modernist and other literatures of the period did. The subject was portrayed in literature, following psychoanalysis, as not so much stable and essentialist, but in process, 'other'-determined and over-determined. Consequently, gender, sexuality, ethnicity, class and race also fragmented under this analysis of the subject; they too were shown to be constructs, networks, rhetorical positions, and constructed out of discourse. Heterogeneity, not homogeneity or unitariness, impurity and mélange, not originary purity, was shown to be the character of these aspects of identity.[2]

The cultural story (let us remember that it is just one possible version) that this involved a denial of humanist, Enlightenment meaning through the decentring and de-essentializing of the subject, so that meaning is provisional and social, and knowledge is always perspectival and contextual (not transcendent or objective and neutral), had precise applications to art and culture. No longer conceived of as representational, art and culture were also politicized and empowered when no longer institutionalized in museums, asylums or aristocracies. Art and culture, restored to their social, political and historical realm, no longer exiled from the marketplace, could not so easily be divided into high or low, mass or elite. Equally, culture could not be conceived as a superstructure on a base of economic/historical reality, since culture participates in the production of that reality. After Nietzsche, an emphasis upon sensuous experience as the material of intellectual response permeated fiction, poetry, and the other arts. The wilfully anti-representational and even primitivist techniques of many artists in the twentieth century deliberately frustrated the search for thematic interpretations, as well as a too strict attention to form, in order to express the belief that art and language do not merely represent the real, the unified, or any originary experience or transcendent truths in some mimetic or copying way. Rather, culture participates in the creation of the real, while signs take the place of objects, whether material or cultural, of consumption. This 'hyperreal' realm of codes and simulacra, where the world is an effect of the sign, must be analysed to reveal the programming of desire if we are to escape the tyranny of one system over diversity and 'dissensus'. Notions that modernism, postmodernism or deconstruction were degenerate because apolitical arise from forgetting that to question representation and thereby expose hegemonies is a subversive political strategy. The resistance to established practices and beliefs characteristic of these three movements empowered those at the margins, while central values and universal principles passed off as facts were demoted to local, tribal status. Rationality was not rejected for irrational Nietzschean excess, so much as redefined as strategies for engaging with or adapting to the social context (constituted by a plurality of discourses and structures of power).[3]

These strategies empower the individual and the community since the process of revealing unconscious ideologies is the most effective stimulant for new forms of behaviour, new ways of sharing and distributing goods. The conception of the subject as embedded, like society, in language and discourse works to undo the binary opposition between individual and society, between objectivity and relativism. It also challenges other dichotomies involving gender, sexuality and ethnicity, race and class. These characteristics are analysed as forms of behaviour rather than natural essences. Humanly generated principles of identity can be challenged and superseded; their applications to various domains of endeavour can be rejected. Many writers have tried to portray attitudes to gender and ethnicity as dependent upon socialization and education for their construction within the individual psyche, in order to explore what we might become, if we were socialized differently, and what present processes of socialization do to our potentialities, our self-regard and the regard of others.[4] The belief that a variety of forms of rationality exist, and that human identity is not final and natural, but 'processual' and made up of social fields and narratives, suggests the power to change, even to change economic hegemonies through cultural awareness, and through the communication of heightened awareness of possibilities. That such communication involves struggle with prevailing ideologies suggests that art is also agonistic, and that reading (and writing) must include an analysis of the effects of our stores of expectations and inferences that we bring to everything we read. Divergent readings are the result of the creative role played in all our readings, and are never just divergent, but always involve shared experience too. Characters in the text intermingle and struggle not only with each other, but with author and reader, and this new frame, which breaks through the traditional boundaries of the work of art to include reader and author, is depicted overtly by many twentieth-century writers by means of both old and new conventions, since art has always framed reader and author.

Since the mid-century, literature has subjected questions of subject, gender and ethnicity to scrutiny in more overt ways, perhaps, than much prior literature, which often veiled or posed such questions more decorously. These issues have not been allowed by imaginative writers to remain at the level of thematics, because they go to the heart of literary conventions and of language as the means by which identity, social roles, gender and sexuality, and ethnicity or race are created. Writers demonstrate – enact for us as readers in their narrative strategies and stylistic devices – that story-telling, whether spoken or thought in our daily lives or written down in literature, is the constitutive force in all identity creation. Much post-1970 fiction has refined earlier techniques and made its central objective the idea that we create our selves out of the stories we tell ourselves and each other, and the stories told by our parents, teachers, and friends.[5] This literature rarely asks the badly posed question, what is the relation of art or literature to life, what is the relation of language to reality? For reality is embedded in art and language, while they are the driving forces which give it meaning and intelligibility. Our selves and our societies, treated as texts, as books to be read, interpreted and rewritten, can be changed according to new ideas and imaginative innovations. Our reality (and our history) has been shown to be a magic one, partly because it can be constructed in new and previously unrealized ways, by altering the words and phrases we value and privilege, thereby challenging history, life, and even nature as traditionally conceived. Art has always done this, though it is one illusion of our times that such practices are new, postmodern, and enact crises.

Writers such as Sontag, Marguerite Young, Nabokov, Bellow, Roth, Heller, Pynchon, Muriel Spark, Janet Frame, Jane Bowles and Barbara

Pym prepared the reader for the more overt and excessive postmodernist experiments. Often dumbfounded by the humourless responses of reviewers and critics to their efforts to find new and imaginative formulations for human experience and changes in 'structures of feeling', these writers explored the nature of human particularity as a function of community. Often they turned to sophisticated forms of comedy and wit, joke and pun, parody and satire. They named their characters Scheisskopf (shit head), or Philip, after themselves (as in Roth's *Operation Shylock* (1993)), to confuse the fictional/factual realms. Mock-autobiographical fiction proliferated, as authors mixed themselves into their texts, thus drawing the reader in after them. Saul Bellow is one example of an ambivalence toward the self and its properties (gender, ethnicity), when he wrote of the endless theatricality of the self, the illusory nature of the self as a unitary being. A prolixity of characterization – as characters endlessly explain themselves, then express anxiety about being boring, prolix, moralizing or irrelevant – leads to self-referentiality as the author is confused with characters, and reader with characters too. Roth, in a Bakhtin-like manner, suggested that the test of novelists' worth is the degree to which they can challenge their own beliefs and expose them to destruction in Socratic tests of dialogic agonistics. His self-cannibalizing structures are not avant-garde or postmodern: Roth located them in familiar life practices by showing that we all write fictitious versions of our lives. These mutually entangling stories may be falsified either in subtle or gross ways, but they do constitute our hold on reality, and are the nearest to what we call truth.

In *My Life as a Man* (1974), Roth created three different versions of a writer/character, who gets inextricably mixed up with Roth. One of the most revolutionary and politicized aspects of art is its ability to show the reader that, when you stop separating literature and reality, you begin to be able to act in more imaginative ways than your prior accounts allowed. Accounts of reality, whether regarding nature, gender, morality or ethnicity, are narratives which only fear and anxiety prevent us from altering. Pynchon portrayed this anxiety in *The Crying of Lot 49* (1966), while Heller used humour to chart the dehumanization of institutions in *Catch 22* (1961) and *Good as Gold* (1979), for which he was endlessly criticized by reviewers and readers, whose *gravitas* seems incredible today. Pynchon used labyrinthine, Borges-like plots, endless deferral, theme as an allegory of reading; he created competing realities, blurred borders between reality and fiction, sanity and madness. His novels, like those of Robert Coover, Leslie Marmon Silko, Bobbi Ann Mason or Mari Sandoz, are often rewritings of history, especially American history, exposing the ideologies which pass for fact. All these writers attacked the literary conventions of fictional representations as themselves politically and culturally ideological, shoring up specific, entrenched attitudes to art, identity and society. Disrupting accepted modes of fiction or art reveals their contingency and constructedness, and, since fiction is such a central part of our story-constituted lives (and an emblem of art generally), such disruption is political.

Pynchon's 'allegories of reading' chart the anxiety involved in trying to make sense of literature. Characters struggle to figure out the meaning of situations, to interpret the actions and thoughts of other characters, to determine the action, to get to the end of something. Reading is shown to be an allegory of perception, too, an example of our processes of ordering and stabilizing experience. Whether we can be said to find meaning or create it, the reader is still dragged into the text, actively to participate in the quest. Before Barthes, Pynchon was characterizing reading as an erotic experience of seduction and often betrayal. Betrayal because the end is never satisfactory. One plot gives way to another, one game to another, one metaphor to another, as characters move from one puzzle and situation to another, imagining they are on the track of a final word, a solution, a glimpse of the other, the lover. Constant frustration of this revelation, as repetition never ends, often leads to violence, when characters and readers are confronted with endless, playful pleasure instead of justifications of art by truthful representations.[6] Woolf's *Between the Acts* (1941) and Bowen's *House in Paris* (1935) are obvious precursors of such toyings with anti-representational techniques, but Marguerite Young's *Miss Macintosh, My Darling* (1965) was a mid-century Joycean epic of erotic reading. Less well known even than Young is Ann Quin's fiction, and it is to her and Kathy Acker's treatments of gender, Cynthia Ozick's and Walter Abish's handling of ethnicity, and Christine Brooke-Rose on identity in general in her incredible pyrotechnic novels, that we now turn.

Both Ozick and Abish are American, but their cultural and historical reconstructions involve, overtly at least, European contexts, whereas Pynchon and Acker direct their attention to the USA. Ozick and Abish make constant reference to the Second World War and Nazi Germany, embedding their fiction in this specific moral and historical context, and then turning its familiar content inside out by means of postmodern strategies, to raise more general issues about ethnicity and gender. In *How German Is It?* (1980), Abish challenges the belief in the historical reconstruction of Germany as basically free now from the Nazi prejudices of the 1920s and 1930s. His fiction tests the idea that the prejudices and attitudes which led to genocide and war are actually hidden under a thin facade of modern regeneration. Most of all, he questions how German these prejudices are, and whether the alleged Germanness of Nazism is not perhaps a characteristic of many societies, such as American or British or French. The central character, Ulrich, is a novelist, and the progress of his present book is a constant theme of the novel, as is the growing confusion that his alleged relations with a terrorist group whom, in an example of typical analepsis, he exposed at a trial before the action of the novel begins. The theme of Ulrich's book is a love-affair in Paris which went wrong, and which raises questions about his fidelity and reliability. A complex web of characters and events woven throughout the novel still results in a plotless intricacy. Like Pynchon's and Ozick's texts (especially *The Crying of Lot 49* and *The Messiah of Stockholm*), the emphasis is on the impossibility of any character knowing the identity of others, or whether the other characters are spies, terrorists, or uninvolved 'ordinary' people. Borgesian themes of treachery and duplicity and impersonation are taken to extremes. The characters, then, are constantly trying to read and interpret each other, while also struggling to interpret events as significant or insignificant. An aura of paranoia is encouraged as characters meet coincidentally and turn out, unexpectedly, to know, or at least to know of, each other. The effort to crystallize meanings or solve mysteries about the identity of characters and the meanings of events is also disrupted in the text by a whole range of illusion-destroying devices, including analepsis.[7]

For example, constant self-referentiality recurs; what is said of Ulrich's novels is clearly applicable to Abish's: 'one reads your books, always feeling some vital piece of information is being withheld' (p. 52). Reading and writing are said to be like trespassing (p. 36), while the 'spy', Daphne is described as not being able to tolerate the ambiguity and uncertainty of Ulrich's texts, which 'remained somehow inaccessible to her', she wanted to have specific meanings. Reading is said to be about the Forbidden City (p. 48), and Ulrich is described as reading a French book about someone wanting to penetrate into the City, to observe all that had been previously withheld from him. An Elizabeth Bowen-like compulsion to know, a need for clarification, is portrayed. ('The wish to know, what else is there?' *The House in Paris*, yet, Bowen shows, what we can know is precisely nothing.) While Ulrich explains to an impatient journalist that he is still searching for the ending to his novel, Abish's novel ends by throwing us into complete doubt about Ulrich's patrimony, which had focused meaning in the novel, and Ulrich as main character, from the outset. Is he Jew or is he Nazi, is he German or something else? How germane are these questions? Other techniques Abish uses are 'metaplasm', or the idea of repetition and plagiarism from himself and others, with slight variation, a favourite technique of Acker and Quin. Metaplasm is a play on its opposite, protoplasm, the original, living matter in all cells, while the former is a different kind of matter, which fills up the rest of the cell, is secondary not pure, not original. Abish shows that protoplasm may be a myth; what is proto from one point of view may be meta from another, and this infects the Germanness of things. There may be no pure Germanness after all, no before, just after. Constantly enquiring about the progress of the novel, sometimes rhetorically, sometimes directly to the reader, the narrator destroys the aesthetic illusion and the fiction/fact borders, as reading becomes, like writing, an overt subject matter, thus making impure the text's content. Themes of forgetfulness and repression are reinforced by insinuations of sinister things lurking behind the surface (Brumholdstein, a new model city, is, it turns out to the horror the unsuspecting inhabitants, built on top of a concentration camp, full of the skeletons of *its* inhabitants; the present is thus literally embedded in the past).

Cynthia Ozick's *The Messiah of Stockholm* (1987) puts gender as well as ethnicity under analysis. Combining overtly Jewish elements of, for example, the 'golem' (a man or woman created out of magical art, sometimes also meaning as yet unformed matter), with postmodern techniques, she analyses gender or sex differences as decisive for art or life, and invokes ideas of the 'epicene': belonging to or partaking of the characteristics of both sexes (from the Greek *epikoinos*, meaning common). Characters in her fiction display this epicene quality, indeed, epicene is an apt word for describing Ozick's commitment to a common humanity. The emphasis is on overcoming barriers of both sex and ethnicity, as well as religion, and she laments the exclusion of Jewish women from their own culture and religion, arguing that their second-class status has made them 'born to have no ancestry and . . . no progeny'. Postmodern techniques which question issues of gender and ethnicity are illustrated most impressively in *The Messiah*, though there were already evident in 'Rosa' and 'The Shawl', as well as *Cannibal Galaxy* (1983). Ozick's interest in a 'new culture-making' suggests the creation of a Jewish liturgical fiction via the rejuvenation of 'midrash', or the ancient method of textual exegesis. This involves interpreting the Bible in a way that allows for several coexisting accounts, leading to polyvocal commentaries which prevent the Bible from becoming a set, static, unalterable text. The method of midrash also fills in the written text with oral, living traditions. Thus the Bible never becomes exiled from the historical and temporal settings of its different readers. Productive of new meanings, the text is never closed or final. New interpretations, Ozick suggested, preserve the text rather than destroy it. What has been previously missed out or disregarded (women, for example, in Jewish culture and ritual) can be filled in; the text can be augmented, expanded and enriched.[8]

The Messiah uses many typical devices, such as recursive embedding, mixing of ontological levels, radical undecidability, disruption, labyrinthine plot. The quest for a missing manuscript involves a text entitled 'The Messiah'. Identity and authority are problematized in a protagonist who is an orphan, who has made up his name, having lost his own, and who claims nevertheless to be the legitimate son of Bruno Schultz, the author of the missing 'Messiah'. When the manuscript finally turns up in extremely suspicious circumstances, its very authenticity is in doubt, though never actually disproved. Moreover, the bringer of the 'Messiah' is a rival protagonist, Adela, who claims implausibly (to our anti-hero) not only to have rescued it from a cellar in Poland, but also to be the daughter of the author; therefore, the authentic messenger of the word, the text, is a woman. So threatened by her advent is the hero that he destroys the manuscript in a violent act of arson after trying unsuccessfully to read it:

> What was in The Messiah? Lost! Chips of dream. It was nearly as if he had stumbled into someone else's dream. Whose? ... He could not remember what he had read five minutes ago. A perplexity ... fragments of some vague insubstantiality, folklorish remnants; a passage of oxygen-deprivation perhaps. It had receded, whatever it was – he retained nothing ... only the faintest tremor of some strenuous force ... Lamentation remained, elegy after great pain. (p. 115).

As with Abish's novel, Ozick's refers constantly to the Holocaust; insistent references to a persistent 'smell of something roasting' disturb the reader, as do frequent remarks regarding events in Poland. This mélange of history and fiction leaves the reader in a borderland of uncertainty, as the narrator raises questions of plagiarism, authenticity and originality of manuscript, characters and events. History depends more on artefacts and manuscripts than literature does on history or reality; sincerity and objectivity are overturned by duplicity and deceit. The author is possibly only an impersonator anyway, Ozick suggests, while gender roles are overturned as the Son becomes a woman, ethnicity is disrupted when Jew and Christian collide, and the novel ends as indecisively as the quest for the original began.

The English novelist Ann Quin, who died of drowning aged 37 in 1973, anticipated Philip Roth's *My Life as a Man* by eight years with her second novel, *Three* (1996), in which the characters lose their distinctiveness, though *Berg* (1964) and later novels such as *Passages* (1969) and *Tripticks* (1972) also explore character fragmentation and narrative disruption. (A portion of an unfinished novel, 'The Unmapped Country', was published in *Beyond the Words*, ed. Giles Gideon, 1975.) From the start, Quin dispensed with any realist conventions in order to show that familiar order and logic are much less native to our experience than we normally realize, whether we mean inner mental experience (stream of consciousness) or the apparent order of nature and the 'external' world. Quin's novels focus intently on questioning both individual identity and its construction (as well as breakdown) through gender, especially, but also through other categories and constructions. Yet the novels also function to relate this human focus to the individual identity of works of art, and a continuous analogy between the two runs throughout her writing. Like her famous predecessor Jane Bowles, in *Two Serious Ladies* (1943), Quin toyed not only with gender categories, but with stereotypes within gender, which she saw as limiting individual creativity and even preventing genuine individuality itself. She analysed the way characters impose on themselves and others roles and clichéd forms of behaviour, whether in manners, dress, sexual conduct, or thought and feeling.

Starting with *Berg*, Quin began unravelling fantasy and reality, past and present, memory and perception – all are eroded as separate categories through Quin's merging of characters into each other and the world, her rejection of plot, and her radical disruption of thematics. In *Passages* the narrative proceeds literally by passages in both senses of the word: short passages from a diary and marginal notes, and journeys and quests for a dead brother. A radical alternation between chapters composed of first/third person mixed authorship, one a woman, the other a man, presumably lovers, exacerbates the indeterminacy of events and relations, when the reader realizes that numerous passages are taken verbatim from writers such as Coleridge, passages from his notebooks on dreams, consciousness and perception. The object of the quest is never achieved, and the reader is invited to lose faith in the characters' commitment to success, anyway.[9]

Tripticks, with its wonderfully effective use of pop art scattered throughout the novel (drawings in the margins, at the centre, sometimes the whole page) anticipates Acker's pop art tone. Unconscious (or conscious? it is impossible to tell) fantasies of sex and violence invade the minds of the characters while the narrative point of view becomes completely indeterminable. In this novel, consciousness (whether conscious or unconscious!) *is* the only reality, while, for the reader, the ongoing passage of language, with its resistance to any familiar representations, *is* the content. The analogy between art and life is reinforced in opposition to the mimetic or representational view of art. Reading and writing are themselves seen as forms of life, as processes of perception ordering and patterning our lives and giving them meaning. Quin's novels give us new views on our lives, from perception itself as something different, to identity as a fragile, constructed artefact. Modes of organization, categories and concepts are shown to be mere conventions which can be altered with imagination and will. Language can be the tool for revealing experience in fresh, less stereotyped ways, but only if we are prepared to see it pulled apart and used anti-representationally, so that its materiality and richness, its sounds and looks, its etymological and semantic resources are exhibited. For Quin there is no meaningful separation of art and life: to be concerned as a novelist about language, forms, conventions and modes of articulation is not to ignore life or be apolitical. Our most central values and beliefs about life and about identity, from gender and class to nationality and race, are dependent on our grasp of language, logic and other conceptual forms of order shaping our experience. Quin's novels go to the heart of how we cope (or fail to cope) with life and make it meaningful through values, and those values are subjected to intense linguistic and conceptual analysis. *Tripticks* concludes its verbal dimension with an admonition: 'I opened my mouth, but no words. Only the words of others I saw, like ads, texts, psalms, from those who had attempted to persuade me into their systems. A power I did not want to possess. The Inquisition.' Six drawings of portions of a building end the novel; the last portion is a staircase disappearing upwards into a wall.

While Rose Tremain in *Sacred Country* (1992) uses less overtly experimental narrative techniques to thematize issues of sex change and explore the role of gender in identity and widowhood and age in *Sister Benedicta* (1979) and *The Cupboard* (1981), other writers have embraced magic realist strategies, which involve defamiliarization of varying degrees, rewritings of history, border crossings of all kinds, and often intense use of nature as a landscape of the mind. Writers from Jeanette Winterson to Angela Carter, Bessie Head, and Rachel Ingalls focus on gender construction, while Toni Morrison, Alice Walker, Gloria Naylor and Gayl Jones focus on race construction, and Patricia Grace, Keri Hulme, Anita Desai and Jennifer Johnston look at specific ethnicity, though in less magic realist terms. Maxine Hong Kingston, in *Tripmaster Monkey: His Fake Book* (1989), Leslie Marmon Silko in *Ceremony* (1977) and *Almanac of the Dead* (1991) and Louise Erdrich in *Tracks* (1988) and *Beet Queen* (1986) are mistresses of magic realism as a strategy for debunking not only notions of ethnic or gender purity, but also for revealing the ideologies inherent in both historical and literary accounts of Americanness. Alterations in our perceptions of reality are at the heart of magic realism; such fiction can shock, frighten, or entice us into seeing familiar reality as merely one possible description of the potentially marvellous world which we inhabit. Our ways of perceiving nature are shown to be learned attitudes which drastically reduce imaginative responses and inhibit access to powerful natural forces (see, for example, Atwood's *Surfacing*, 1972). Magic realist novels sometimes focus on stupendous landscape and nature as the means of regeneration; sometimes they use the supernatural to make the familiar strange; sometimes they embed magic into the historical, factual realm to construct a speculative history or to rehistoricize events from a previously marginalized point of view. Imaginary landscapes are used, legends are tapped (as in Ingalls's remarkable *Binstead's Safari*, 1983) to show reality being built out of legends and legends as one-time realities. Altered perception is at the heart of such fiction, and imagination can be a more powerful jolt than any drug for achieving such other realities. While there is much discussion about multiculturalism and syncretism, or the melting-pot effect, versus the preservation of distinct cultures, languages, legends and forms of life, our common humanity may help us to find ways forward which preserve differences without creating hierarchies. Gender considerations apply here too, as feminist theories conflict over views about essential male/female differences versus views about the importance of shared experiences of living, working, dying and so on. The valuation of difference over similarity is probably a result of inequality. Until problems of hierarchy and exploitation are resolved, difference can probably not cease to be treated in too essentialist a way; it will inhibit progress if allowed to dominate.

In a very different vein, Kathy Acker and Christine Brooke-Rose, one American, the other British, have probably explored the outer limits of fiction-experimentation more than any other writers, and make their male counterparts' experiments look positively domestic by comparison. Acker has explicitly stated the importance of shock in awakening her readers from the sleep of familiarity, which stereotypes and makes clichéd all our speech, actions, and thoughts and feelings, she argues in *Hannibal Lecter, My Father* (1991), a collection of writings from 1968 onward. To her nothing is interesting unless it is slightly shocking. Otherwise one is just dealing with old habits, lulled into habits again and again. It is good to be shocked, she insists. Numerous novels from the early 1970s to the present have involved ribald exposures of the forces within and without the psyche which create and dominate identity through gender, social roles and fabricated desires, such as *Kathy Goes to Haiti* (1978, also in the collection *Literal Madness*, 1988, which includes *Florida*, 1988, and *My Death My Life by Pier Paolo Pasolini*, 1984) but Acker is most passionately interested in finding out what liberates us from these habitual fictions. Her 'I' in her fiction is not only mixed up with herself, it is almost always made into an unknown number of individuals, so that narrative personae become a radically destablizing force in the construction of the text as well as the characters. She uses Foucault-like exposés in the dynamics of political and social and psychological power, as in the collection of her first three novels, *Portrait of an Eye* (1992). In *Hello, I'm Erica Jong* (1982), Acker abuses literary 'powers' (conventions and expectations and values) in a satirical rejection of typical feminist novels published during the 1970s. Their reliance on realist conventions and representation undercuts their thematics and disempowers their feminist goals, she suggests. They prop up the structures they allege to challenge.

Acker's techniques of plagiarism, shock, blasts at decorum and literary proprieties, her incoherent thematics, plotless texts and chaotic character-identities, her erotics and criminalities rejecting the laws of literature and authorship in other novels, such as *Great Expectations* (1983), *Don Quixote, Which was a Dream* (1986), *Empire of the Senseless* (1988), and *In Memoriam to Identity* (1990), are aspects of what she called 'decentralization', or the rejection of genital sexuality and phallocentric meaning as the primary sexuality and meaning, for the subversion of autonomous identity, clear gender demarcations, and notions of originality, ownership and property rights. Her exposure of the horrifying dehumanization of many aspects of social life, involving not just work but relationships and roles, is also a search for finding better reasons for living than saving money for a new car, getting married and living happily ever after, or getting that job promotion. Acker's subversions are worked through analogies between social traditions and the traditions of Great Art. By drawing on punk techniques of rebellion in favour of liberating forms of disobedience, Acker reverses all values and in Nietzschean terms suggests that good is bad; crime is the only possible behaviour, for everything in the materialistic society is the opposite to what it really is. Someday there will be a new world and a new kind of woman, she believes, since the world we perceive causes our characteristics. Woman will be strong and free, stern and proud, able to control her own destiny, by unfastening her chains and removing masks.[10]

Christine Brooke-Rose is Britain's most important experimental novelist of the late twentieth century. Influenced by the French *nouveau roman*, though now writing in a completely different mode from it, she pushed further the challenge to realist and traditional novel conventions. Brooke-Rose has drawn our attention to new possible perceptual processes about identity, consciousness, gender and literature itself. Early novels of the 1950s preceded the experimental fiction of her middle period in the 1960s and 1970s but it has been since the 1980s that she has really broken through into fascinating innovative fiction. With *Amalgamemnon* (1984), *Xorandor* (1986), *Verbivore* (1990) and *Textermination* (1991), referred to as the 'Intercom Quartet', she moved beyond the anti-realist experiments of her middle novels into a new mode of writing which questioned traditional forms of representation, life and literature in quite new ways. Through a process of recontextualization, she challenged that last bastion of objectivity, namely science and technology and their 'neutral' discourses, in witty and incisive ways.[11] Brooke-Rose reveals science to be strange, exotic, metaphoric, and just another discourse for experiencing and perceiving the world. She humanizes computers in a hilarious and convincing story of their sensitivity to human technological noise in their airways, and the efforts of some computer-literate children to 'reason' with them about their destructive responses to that noise.

Reconceptualization involves how metaphors function in knowledge and perception, and Brooke-Rose suggests that they function through 'displacement'. Knowledge arises when we relate through displacement one image, idea or metaphor to another. Far from being substantive, knowledge is a process of constant networkings; indeed the elements of the network even turn out to be themselves products or nodes of earlier webs. Cognitive decenterings can occur, but only with great effort, since people are reluctant to change their perceptions and values, whether about their gender and ethnicity or its meaning. Moreover, new words and relations amongst words are often needed to make possible new responses and beliefs. Conventional notions about gender, character, morality and power relations can be changed, she shows, by learning to replace coercion and authority, purity and competition with fraternization, sisterhood, exchange, flow and hybridity. In *Xorandor* and *Verbivore* 'natural' organic computers, which have existed peacefully for thousands of millions of years on earth, begin to intrude into the computer screens of humans to object to the horrific amount of verbiage spewed out by the machines, and which is causing intolerable pollution and noise to the Xorandors' natural world. Consequently, they are disrupting plane communications, radio, television, internet and so on, causing deadly crashes everywhere, terrifying humans into more ecologically-minded attitudes towards words. In *Xorandor*, the novel is entirely 'dialogue',

but reported dialogue, involving children struggling to find a believ-
able way to tell their story to the world and get it onto their computer.
They stumble upon all the problems of narration, especially when
the categories between not only child and adult, woman and man, but
also human and machine, collapse. In *Verbivore*, a sequel, many
narrators tell stories, all interrelated and endlessly, recursively embedded, with constant interruptions from the 'verbivores'. It is impossible
to tell who is narrating what or on which metaphysical loop we find
ourselves, as a playwright creates characters who have encounters
with each other in the real world while he writes them into plays,
they confront him with his 'false' accounts, he becomes a creation of
theirs after all, and boundaries between fact and fiction collapse. In
Textermination, Brooke-Rose created a hilarious novel of novels, as Emma
Bovary falls out of a carriage when it crashes in a near-plagiarized
passage from Walter Scott, and Goethe, Tolstoy, Emma from Jane Austen,
and others attend a literary conference, whose main event is a terrorist
attack. Authors, readers, academics, reviewers all mingle in politics,
literature, talks, debates, romances and jealousy, while the reader finds
herself populating the novel in a range of genders and ethnicities.
Literature cannot remain outside politics, in whatever form it shapes
itself, nor can theory, Brooke-Rose shows in *Amalgamemnon*, *Textermination* and other novels.

People who have been colonized politically or socially (as well as eco-
nomically and culturally) can gain a more incisive historical grasp of
their situation when they develop imaginative and linguistic forms for
articulating that exploitation. For women and marginalized ethnic
groups, the increased access to the control of communication, as well
as to its formation, confers meaning and authority on the experiences
of those who previously were silent, or whose speech was ignored.
Enhanced meaning through literary representations leads to empowerment as courage increases to act on shared, collective experiences. Both
the reading and the writing of literature help to develop imaginative
strategies and more intelligent modes of analysing received opinions,
attitudes and forms of exploitative behaviour. Literature since 1970
has used more overt techniques than ever before for revealing how we
can shift from one way of looking at things to another, thereby shifting entrenched power structures, whether economic, cultural or social. Scepticism about the status quo, with all its authority and prestige,
its ability to silence and intimidate, is a major step towards creating
alternatives and making new realities that surpass the limited reality
which passes itself off as nature or natural. Male as well as female
writers today are developing strategies for exposing the absurdity of

present attitudes to both men and women, not to mention people of various ethnicities, with their ironic, parodic, disruptive, metaphoric, irreverent, and distinctly political deconstructions of prevailing forms in literature, art, media and culture generally, which otherwise perpetuate prevailing attitudes in society. The notion that recent forms of experimentation in literature, such as postmodernism, or in theory, such as deconstruction, are apolitical, because they do not discuss narrow political topics overtly, is an indication of the extent to which those unconsciously committed to tradition (whatever their conscious assertions) will go to perpetuate confusion, inequality and tradition.

Notes

1 For example, see Jerome Klinkowitz, *Structuring the Void: The Struggle for Subject in Contemporary American Fiction* (Durham, NC, 1991). Bakhtin's writings may deal more indirectly in the main with this question, but they are most relevant, as *The Dialogic Imagination*, ed. M. Holquist, trans. C. Emerson and M. Holquist (Austin, Texas, 1981); see also his *Problems of Dostoevsky's Poetics*, ed. and trans. Caryl Emerson (Manchester, 1984).

2 For discussions of these ideas, some of the following are insightful: Werner Sollors, *Beyond Ethnicity: Consent and Descent in American Culture* (New York, 1986), Mary V. Dearborn, *Pocahontas's Daughters: Gender and Ethnicity in American Culture* (New York, 1986), S. Robinson, *Engendering the Subject: Gender and Self-Representation in Contemporary Women's Fiction* (Albany, NY, 1991) and Susan Suleiman, *Subversive Intent: Women, Men and the Avant-Garde* (Cambridge, Mass., 1990).

3 Jean Baudrillard, *Selected Writings*, ed. Mark Poster (Cambridge, 1988), is a good starting point for introducing radical cultural politics. And see his *The Mirror of Production* (1975), *A Critique of the Political Economy of the Sign* (1981) and *In the Shadow of the Silent Majorities* (1983). For further elaboration, see Fredric Jameson, *Postmodernism, or, The Cultural Logic of Late Capitalism* (London, 1991), Pierre Macherey, *A Theory of Literary Production*, trans. G. Wall (London, 1978), Julian Pefanis, *Heterology and the Postmodern: Bataille, Baudrillard, and Lyotard* (Durham, NC, 1990), and Jean-François Lyotard, *The Postmodern Condition: A Report on Knowledge* trans. G. Bennington and B. R. Massumi (Manchester, 1984). Gilles Deleuze and Felix Guattari, in *The Anti-Oedipus*, trans. R. Hurley, M. Seem and H. R. Lane (New York, 1977) are also fascinating.

4 Some ethnic and gender specific studies include P. G. Allen, *The Sacred Hoop: Recovering the Feminine in American Indian Traditions* (Boston, 1986), R. Fleck (ed.), *Critical Perspectives on Native American Fiction* (Washington, DC, 1993), Amy Ling, *Between Worlds: Women Writers of Chinese Ancestry* (New York, 1990), T. Minh-ha Trinh, *Woman, Native, Other: Writing Postcoloniality and Feminism,* (Bloomington, Ind.,

1989), and E. Butler-Evans, *Race, Gender and Desire* (Philadelphia, 1989).

5 A few of the clearest accounts of these and other recent theorizings about experimental fiction include Ihab Hassan, *The Postmodern Turn* (Columbus, Ohio, 1987) and Ihab Hassan, 'Making Sense: The Trials of Postmodern Discourse', *New Literary History*, 18 (1987), pp. 437–59, Linda Hutcheon, *A Poetics of Postmodernism: History, Theory, Fiction* (London, 1988), and see Brian McHale, *Constructing Postmodernism* (London, 1992). However, see also Jürgen Habermas, 'Modernity versus Postmodernity', *New German Critique*, 22 (1981), pp. 3–14.

6 Molly Hite's *Ideas of Order in the Novels of Thomas Pynchon* (Columbus, Ohio, 1983), is a good introduction to Pynchon's fiction, as is Patrick O'Donnell's collection *New Essays on The Crying of Lot 49* (Cambridge, 1991).

7 For an interesting interview, see Maarten van Delden, 'Interview with Walter Abish on *Eclipse Fever*', *Annals of Scholarship*, 10: 3–4 (1993), pp. 381–91.

8 Special issues on Ozick can be found in *Texas Studies in Literature and Language*, 25 (1983), and *Studies in American Jewish Literature*, 6 (1987), with bibliography, pp. 145–61. Elizabeth Dipple's *The Unresolvable Plot: Reading Contemporary Fiction* (London, 1988), discusses Ozick, and books on her include those by E. M. Kauvar (1993), V. E. Kielsky (1989), and L. S. Friedman (1991), with a collection of essays edited by Bloom (1968).

9 Some (rare) Quin criticism includes Philip Stevick 'Voices in the Head: Style and Consciousness in the Fiction of Ann Quin', in *Breaking the Sequence*, ed. E. G. Friedman and M. Fuchs (Princeton, NJ, 1989), pp. 231–9, Brocard Sewell, *Like Black Swans. Some People and Themes* (Padstow, 1982), John J. White, *Mythology in the Modern Novel: A Study of Prefigurative Techniques* (Princeton, NJ, 1971), and Giles Gordon (ed,), *Beyond the Words: Eleven Writers in Search of a New Fiction* (London, 1975).

10 The most thorough study, and a very fine one indeed, is Robert Siegle's *Suburban Ambush: Downtown Writing and the Fiction of Insurgency* (Baltimore, 1989). The *Review of Contemporary Fiction* has a special issue on Kathy Acker, Christine Brooke-Rose and Marguerite Young, vol. 9 (1989). Another helpful approach is Larry McCaffery's 'The Artist of Hell: Kathy Acker and Punk Aesthetics', also in Friedman and Fuchs, *Breaking the Sequence*, pp. 214–30. For thorough bibliographical information on Quin, Ozick, Acker and Brooke-Rose, amongst many others, see K. M. Wheeler, *Guide to Twentieth Century Women Novelists* (Oxford, 1997).

11 Sarah Birch, *Christine Brooke-Rose and Contemporary Fiction* (Oxford, 1994), has developed this and other illuminating ideas in the only book-length study of the fiction.

2 The Power to Tell: Rape, Race and Writing in Afro-American Women's Fiction

Maud Ellmann

I

'And now, Belford, I can go no farther. The affair is over. Clarissa lives.'[1] This is what Lovelace, the villain of Richardson's *Clarissa* (1747–48), writes to his friend Belford shortly after he has raped the heroine, following a campaign of sexual harassment rarely rivalled in literature, except perhaps in the drama of Racine. It is a strangely telegraphic way for Lovelace to express himself – he is seldom given to brevity – and it sits uncomfortably in the middle of this baggy, garrulous epistolary novel, where it takes 900 pages for Clarissa to be raped, and another 800 or so for her to die. Normally Lovelace is so prolix that the molestation of Clarissa serves largely as a pretext for writing letters to his male conspirators. An economy emerges in which Clarissa has to be abused, humiliated and defiled in order to sustain the correspondence between men and to consolidate what Eve Kosofsky Sedgwick has described as 'homosocial' bonds.[2] In contrast to the Freudian convention that writing is a substitute for sex, Lovelace turns to sex only as a substitute for writing letters, a poor and disappointing substitute at that. When Clarissa escapes after the rape, Lovelace mourns the fact that he has 'lost the only subject worth writing upon'.[3] Ostensibly he means that he has lost the inspiration for his pen, the only subject matter worth writing about; but the phrase suggests that Clarissa, as the 'subject' of his writing, is subjected to his pen as to his penis, raped by his writing, written by his rape; that her body is a surface branded by his death-dealing inscriptions. Having 'lost the only subject worth writing upon', he resorts to rape in order to relieve his graphomania, his fatal avidity for ink; and thus he drives his signature into Clarissa's flesh, substituting violence for the letter.

Clarissa is often described as the prototype of the modern psychological novel, and the fact that rape should be its theme suggests that the evolution of this literary form is embroiled from its origins in the representation of sexual violence. As Frances Ferguson has pointed out, the genre developed in the eighteenth century as a form of seduction, a means of overpowering and captivating women readers in particular.[4] Richardson used his writing, whether consciously or not, to tighten his hold over a whole coterie of women, constantly soliciting their judgements and opinions while disregarding most of their advice.[5] In this sense Lovelace's tortuous, elaborate conquest of Clarissa could be seen as a black parody of Richardson's seduction of the female reader through the ruses and rhetorical excesses of his prose. By proposing such analogies, however, I do not mean to reduce the rape to a rhetorical trope, as deconstructive critics of *Clarissa* have been prone to do, some going so far as to assert that the rape does Clarissa good because it violates her naive faith in single meaning, enlisting her instead into the double-dealings of the signifier.[6] On the contrary, one of the historic functions of the novel has been to provide a space in which rape and other forms of violence against the powerless may be exposed, and in this way to compensate for the defects of a judicial system in which rape is notoriously difficult to represent, because the evidence depends upon the victim's word, in a world where women's words, like children's words, have little credibility.[7] Although Clarissa refuses to bring Lovelace to court, for many reasons, most of them self-defeating, the text itself comes to represent a kind of legal dossier for her defence and absolution. By offering a court of appeal for the unsaid, the unbelieved, the unavenged, the novel as a genre reveals the failings of the legal system but also serves to perpetuate that system by providing imaginary compensations for its blindnesses.

II

In *The Color Purple* (1982) Alice Walker recreates *Clarissa* in the context of the American South, borrowing both the theme of rape and the epistolary form from Richardson. But Celie, Walker's heroine, is black not white; poor not rich; ignorant not educated; yet what she has in common with Clarissa is that she is also raped, confined and silenced, and composes letters as her sole defence against her fate. Clarissa is imprisoned, first by her father, then by her molester, and she resorts to writing because she cannot confront her torturers in person: they have forbidden her to speak. Similarly, the man who rapes Celie, whom she mistakenly believes to be her father, robs her of her voice. He is the first person to speak in the novel – or so we infer, for his cruel words, which loom over the text, italicized without quotation marks, present themselves as vatic and impersonal: '*You better not never tell nobody but God. It'd kill your mammy.*'[8] That 'it' is highly charged: is it the knowledge of the crime that would kill her Mammy, or is it Celie's *words*, her act of speech, that would destroy her mother? Through this ambiguity the rapist cunningly shifts the responsibility for the violence on to the victim: it is not *his deed*, but *her words*, that maim, molest and murder. Similarly, in Maya Angelou's autobiography, *I Know Why the Caged Bird Sings* (1969), Mr Freeman, who rapes the eight-year-old Maya, swears her to silence by threatening to kill her much loved brother. When the crime is nonetheless exposed, Freeman is arrested but subsequently acquitted by the jury – much to his misfortune, because he is immediately murdered by the child's uncles. The little girl then conceives the notion that her testimony caused his death, and thus falls dumb for years out of terror that her words can kill.

The connection between rape and women's silence may be traced back to the story in Ovid's *Metamorphoses* in which the barbarous king Tereus rapes his sister-in-law Philomela and cuts out her tongue so that she cannot accuse him of the crime. But Philomela finds an ingenious way of overcoming her dismemberment: during a long year of forced imprisonment, she weaves a depiction of the rape into a tapestry so that her sister Procne, Tereus's wife, can *read* the crime that cannot be *spoken*. Procne, in revenge, feeds her husband the flesh of their own son, Itys, disguised in a stew. When this trick is exposed, Tereus, crazed with wrath, attempts to kill both sisters, but the gods transform the whole bloodthirsty family into birds: Tereus becomes the hawk, Procne the swallow, and Philomela the nightingale.[9] Thus Philomela is compensated for her loss of speech with wordless song, the nightingale's 'inviolable voice' that fills the desert in T. S. Eliot's *The Waste Land*.[10] In Eliot, as earlier in Keats, the task of the male poet is to transform the music of the nightingale into intelligible speech; and the recurrent figure of the nightingale in English poetry hints that the male poetic voice is founded on the mute and violated phantom of the feminine.

In the myth of Philomela, rape is concomitant to silencing: to be raped is to be stripped of voice. But the death of speech brings about the birth of writing: Philomela's weaving, which Sophocles called 'the voice of the shuttle', functions as a text in which the story of the rape may be deciphered.[11] Similarly, Celie and Clarissa resort to writing in order to elude the prohibitions imposed upon their speech. The disturbing implication is that women's writing somehow depends upon their violation, that rape is the means by which they sacrifice their tongues to take possession of their pens. In *The Color Purple* the rapist's law of silence presides over the text and instigates the whole activity of writing; and Celie's rape could be understood as her violent initiation to the written word. It is all too tempting to translate the novel into psychoanalytic terms, whereby the rapist would assume the role of the castrating father who intervenes between the mother and the child, bearing death ('it'd kill your mammy') and the symbolic order ('tell nobody but God'). According to this logic, rape could be construed as the occasion that engenders symbolization, the wound from which the writing issues forth.

Does rape therefore empower the victim by impelling her to write her degradation? The centrality of rape to recent Afro-American women's fiction has provoked the hostile criticism that these novelists are cashing in on white fantasies of black depravity, marketing rape stories much as Trueblood, in Ralph Ellison's *Invisible Man* (1947), peddles tales of rape and incest to white voyeurs.[12] This criticism is unjust: but these novelists do confirm the Kleinian view that the desire to create emerges out of the experience of psychic fragmentation. What they do not confirm, however, is Klein's conviction that the creative process is intrinsically reparative; on the contrary they suggest through the fissures and fragmentations of their prose, that art contrives to re-inflict, rather than assuage the wounds of life. For rape, although it motivates these narratives it cannot be contained by them but reinscribes its violence in a shattering of novelistic form. By exposing rape in its full horror, and by resisting the consolations of aesthetic unity, these novelists attempt to break the age-old silence about rape, to restore speech to the nightingale. In so doing they oppose themselves to an Anglo-American literary tradition of silencing or concealing rape, especially where racial conflict is at issue. It is this tradition of concealment, and the efforts by black women writers to dismantle it, which the remainder of this essay will explore.

III

The word 'rape' originally meant 'theft', and the crime was understood as an offence against male property, a theft of women from their rightful owners. Ancient Hebrew law stipulated that a rapist of an unbetrothed girl pay fifty silver shekels to her father and marry the victim of his crime. Similarly, in Wiltshire in 1745, a woman named Jane Biggs, wife of John Biggs, was assaulted by one John Newman, and the judge, finding Newman guilty, ordered him to pay five guineas damages to the husband and never to molest John Biggs or his wife again.[13] This case reveals that the woman is regarded as a more or less transparent medium through which men insult, assault and prey on other men. In *Clarissa*, Lovelace chuckles: 'And whose property, I pray thee, shall I invade, if I pursue my schemes of love and vengeance?'[14] Since Clarissa has been dispossessed by her father, the rape does not constitute a crime, because she is no longer the property of any man, and therefore cannot be stolen, cannot be violated.

Unlike other offences, rape depends on verbal testimony: the invaded 'property' must repeat the crime in words. A burglary, by contrast, may be reconstructed from the traces that the thief has left behind; but a rapist often leaves no visible, forensic traces – no injuries, no semen. Thus the rape can be corroborated only through the victim's testimony: her word must overcome the word of her assailant. When rape is defined as sexual intercourse without consent, as it is in many jurisdictions, the effect is that the law focuses exclusively on the complainant: it is she who is the object of attention. Did she consent or didn't she?[15] The prosecution has to prove beyond all doubt that she did not consent; and until recent reforms the defence could retaliate by demonstrating that she would have consented because her sexual history proved that she had consented before. As crimes go, then, rape is remarkable for focusing attention on mental states and the way that these are expressed and understood. It is for this reason, Frances Ferguson contends, that the theme of rape is so important to the evolution of the novel, for the novel asserts the supremacy of private psychological experience over the external action of romance.[16] In Richardson, Clarissa's acts suggest that she colluded with her rape, and yet her private thoughts convince us that she did not. Thus the novel privileges the subjective over the objective, the mental state over the external fact.

Rape, then, depends for its existence and its prosecution on the victim's word: it is her 'no', in the first instance, that distinguishes the act of rape from an act of sex, and it is her word in court that proves that she did not consent, or even that the act occurred. A woman's 'no' is not enough, however, to convince some judges of her non-consent. In a notorious case in Cambridge in 1982, Judge Wild put his summary of a rape case to the jury in these terms:

> Women who say no do not always mean no. It is not just a question of saying no, it is a question of how she says it, how she shows and makes it clear. If she doesn't want it she only has to keep her legs shut and she would not get it without force and there would be marks of force being used.[17]

Thus to prove the rape the victim must make sure her assailant physically injures her, producing marks that can be used in evidence. Her spoken word is not enough – only the writing on her body will suffice: her wounds must speak instead of words. Incidentally, the belief that a woman's 'no' really means a 'yes', or that women secretly desire to be raped because they are suffering from sexual frustration, is a recent superstition probably derived from Freud, who claimed that the unconscious was incapable of saying no. Historians of rape have found scant evidence of this belief in other cultures or in earlier stages of our own.[18]

Yet the reason such misconstructions can occur is that rape depends on verbal report; in this sense – and in this sense only – rape is a verbal or a textual phenomenon. That does not make it less real or less repellent; it is dangerous to imagine that the verbal or the textual is magically insulated from the real. On the contrary, rape calls into question the whole distinction between the word and the event, between the world of language and the world of violence. In literary criticism it is striking that the question of rape tends to disrupt the usual decorum whereby text and history, text and politics, are treated as separate and incommensurable spheres. Critical debates about *Clarissa*, for example, read like rape trials, some critics contending that the heroine was forced, others that she desired to be violated: it has even been proposed that Clarissa is distressed only because she failed to have an orgasm.[19] Richardson himself participated in the early years of this debate and ardently defended Clarissa's innocence; yet the debate ensues inevitably from the novel's epistolary form, in which there is no central narrator to adjudicate between competing testimonies. Moreover, Richardson never provides a definitive account of the rape. In Lovelace's brief note of the event, as we have seen, the rape is more or less erased: 'I can go no farther. The affair is over. Clarissa lives.' This statement, as Ferguson observes, sounds more like 'a bizarre kind of birth announcement' than the report of a rape.[20] Richardson's reticence, of course, could be attributed merely to delicacy: the author himself could go no farther, if it meant providing graphic details of the rape. However, when the missing story finally does get told, Lovelace is presented as the henchman of the prostitutes who goad him into rape by taunting him with accusations of effeminacy. In this way Richardson insinuates that women are to blame for rape, and thus absolves his own sex, and himself, of culpability.[21]

IV

This erasure of the scene of rape recurs in many modern novels, particularly where racial conflict is involved. In E. M. Forster's novel *A Passage to India*, published in 1924 though written some ten years earlier, an Englishwoman, Adela Quested, accuses the Indian doctor Aziz of sexually assaulting her in the Marabar Caves. Or so we assume: because the accusation, like the event itself, is either elided completely or referred to vaguely as an 'insult' by the English characters. Later, during the trial, Adela has a moment of vision in which she retracts her accusation against Aziz, but the reader never finds out what, if anything, actually happened in the caves. It seems that Forster created this ambiguity deliberately: in the manuscript of the novel, the reader enters the cave with Adela and feels the hands that push her against the wall and grab her breasts. We also see her fight off her assailant crying, '*not this time*'.[22] In the published version not only the violent attack but the whole scene inside the caves is omitted; and interpreters have subsequently rushed into the gap, armed with Freud, to argue that Adela is a hysteric who imagined the assault because she was suffering from sexual frustration. So Adela really wanted to be raped, and since she was not raped – becuse she was too freckled and small-breasted, Aziz says – she was driven to hallucinate the whole attack.

The effect of Adela's hysteria is to set the English and Indian communities against each other, and most deplorably to break up the budding friendship between Fielding and Aziz. Sexual difference is thus presented as a more divisive force than racial difference: the novel implies that men of conscience could form alliances across the boundaries of race and class and power if only women did not persecute them with their unbridled sexual fantasies. In the first draft, however, Forster gives Adela just cause for her complaint, and it is only in the final draft that he deprives her of her evidence. In this way he transforms the victim into the attacker: Adela becomes the persecutor of Aziz, with all the power of the British empire behind her. For the assault, whether it occurred or not, can be attested only by a woman's word, which in this case bears more weight than the man's word because the man, the Indian, is even more oppressed than she is.

Jenny Sharpe has argued that Adela's words 'not this time' refer to what the British call the Sepoy Rebellion of 1857, and the Indians call the First War of Independence, which was one of the largest insurrections against the British Raj. During the Rebellion, a rumour swept across Anglo-India that Indian rebels were subjecting Englishwomen to systematic rape, mutilation and murder.[23] A letter from a clergyman, printed in the London *Times*, regaled its readers with pornographic fantasies of English women being stripped under their husbands' eyes, flogged naked through the streets, and finally murdered in an orgy of dismemberment: 'To cut off the breasts of the women was a favourite mode of dismissing them to death.'[24] This letter was promptly discredited; yet although no evidence of rape or torture by rebels was ever ascertained, even at Cawnpore, where two hundred British women and children were massacred, the imaginary violation of the English Lady served as an excuse for violent retaliation on the part of English soldiers who, among other atrocities, fired rebels from the mouths of cannons, and hung the corpses of Indian men, women and children from trees to warn the populace against the dire consequences of rebellion.[25]

To the English residents of Chandrapore, Aziz's crime represents 'the unspeakable limit of cynicism, untouched since 1857'. This suggests that the Rebellion of 1857 hovers over the alleged event within the caves, though both events remain – in Forster's words – 'unspeakable'.[26] These caves might be compared to Freud's conception of the 'navel' of the dream, the point at which its meanings grow so multiplicitous that they dissolve in their own density, leaving a black hole in the dream-fabric.[27] Similarly, Forster's caves are the mark of an erasure rather than an absence, an obliteration rather than a gap; they are not so much empty as too full: they represent the point at which the tensions between sexual, racial and cultural politics become too dense to disentangle, leaving a knot or navel in the narrative. This knottedness is disguised by Forster's favourite euphemism 'muddledom', and even more disguised by many of his critics, who sentimentalize the Marabar Caves as the embodiment of the mystique of India. In this way they evade the knotted question of interracial rape in favour of a self-indulgent orientalism. For other critics, the Marabar Caves represent a dark moment of 'modernist' doubt in a resolutely realist novel; their terrible echo, moreover, augurs the collapse of the distinctions that the familiar world depends upon: 'Hope, politeness, the blowing of a nose, the squeak of a boot, all produce "boum"' – a meaningless democracy of noise. 'Nothing in India is identifiable,' Forster writes; and in this novel modernist indeterminacy and the myth of Eastern mystery work together to erase the rape, to relegate it to the undecidable.[28]

V

Richard Wright's novel *Native Son* (1940) also tells the story of an interracial rape that does not happen, but brings about the same calamities as if it did. Bigger Thomas, an angry, inarticulate black youth, is hired as a chauffeur by a wealthy philanthropic liberal. The boss's daughter, Mary Dalton, persuades Bigger to drive her to an assignation with her Marxist boyfriend, who plies Bigger with drink and attempts to convert him to the Communist Party. Mary herself gets so drunk that Bigger, having driven her back home, is obliged to carry her upstairs to bed and finds himself aroused by her half-unconscious, swaying form. The girl's blind mother intrudes into the bedroom just as Bigger is fondling Mary, and in his panic the young man, after the pattern of his literary ancestor Othello, smothers Mary with a pillow in a desperate effort to suppress her drunken moans. When he realizes the girl is dead, Bigger stuffs her corpse into the basement furnace, sawing off her head when he discovers that it doesn't fit. Later on, he deliberately rapes and murders his black girlfriend, Bessie, as if to take possession of the rape that did not happen and the murder that he did not commit.

The rape and murder of the white girl is thus transferred on to the black girl, whose fate appears to be of little consequence to Bigger; or to the white community, for whom it merely corroborates the rape of Mary; or even to Wright himself, who presents it as a necessary stage in Bigger's existential journey to self-awareness, like Raskolnikov's murders in *Crime and Punishment*. The double rape is thus subjected to a double disavowal: the white girl's rape does not happen; the black girl's rape does not signify. However, as Maria Mootry has pointed out, the rape of Mary Dalton does take place, psychologically if not in fact, and there is evidence that Wright, like Forster, deleted the assault from an earlier version of the novel.[29] The effect of this suppression is to emphasize Bigger's victimization: it is Mary, drunk and irresponsible, who provokes the rape and then, by compromising Bigger, provokes the murder; and finally, when her burnt and broken bones cry rape, she unleashes all the violence of racism against the ignorant black boy, who is electrocuted for the crime that he did not commit, rather than the crime he did. As Wright puts it:

> Any Negro who has lived in the North or the South knows that times without number he has heard of some Negro boy being picked up on the streets and carted off to jail and charged with 'rape'. . . . Life had made the plot over and over again.[30]

Bigger is doomed from the moment that he enters Mary's bedroom; although he does not rape her, he kills her because he thinks that the only possible interpretation of his presence in her room is 'rape'. He resembles Oedipus, Barbara Johnson argues, because it is precisely his efforts to *avoid* enacting the forbidden plot that lead him inexorably to enacting it.[31]

Bigger is also victimized by his mother's emasculating taunts: "'We wouldn't have to live in this garbage dump if you had any manhood in you.'"[32] The implication is that Bigger (it is hard not hear bugger) is compelled to rape and murder by his mother's castrating mockery: just as Lovelace is compelled to rape by the derision of the prostitutes, or Macbeth to regicide by the derision of his wife. It seems that Bigger comes to life only dispatching the women in his world to death: his exhilaration after killing Mary is complete only when the failed rape and the accidental murder are repeated as deliberate brutalities on Bessie's body. His crimes are 'an act of creation!'; or so his lawyer Max, with devastating inhumanity, declares. Like Meursault in Camus's *The Outsider*, Bigger has to murder, and to take possession of his unintended act, in order to accede to masculine identity:

> He looked out of the car window and then round at the white faces near him. He wanted suddenly to stand up and shout, telling them that he had killed a rich white girl. . . . he wished that he could be an idea in their minds; that the image of his smothering Mary and cutting off her head and burning her could hover before their eyes as a terrible picture of reality which they could see and feel and yet not destroy.[33]

Bigger must erase or be erased; and his author seems to have experienced a similar compulsion to obliterate his female characters. Mary Dalton was the *nom de guerre* of a Communist Party member in Chicago whom Wright disliked intensely. When a friend objected to his plan to kill off Bessie too, Wright insisted: 'But I have to get rid of her. She must die!'[34] In 'How Bigger Was Born', Wright claims that *Native Son* was written out of his dismay that 'even bankers' daughters' might enjoy his former work:

> I had written a book which even bankers' daughters could read and weep over and feel good about. I swore to myself that if I ever wrote another book, no one would weep over it; that it would be so *hard and deep* that they would have to face it without the consolation of tears. It was this that made me get to work in *dead earnest* [my italics].[35]

Notice that the bankers' daughters must be punished, not the bankers, just as Mary Dalton is destroyed for the injustices of white society, and Bessie Mears for the emasculation of black men. James Baldwin, in a famous essay on Wright, declared that there is a 'great space where sex ought to be', and what fills this space is 'violence'. This violence, moreover, is 'gratuitous and compulsive'. Although Mary's murder is accomplished bloodlessly, her corpse is luridly decapitated and incinerated; Bessie, on the other hand, is brutally murdered with a brick, a gory 'building block' for Bigger's reconstructed consciousness.[36] If Wright replaces sex with violence, moreover, he replaces reading with a fantasy of violation: the wound his book is to inflict on bankers' daughters must be 'hard and deep' and executed in 'dead earnest' (not buggered up, like Bigger's crime).

VI

In *Native Son*, as in *A Passage to India*, it is interracial rape that drives the narrative, but the rape itself is masked in silence, and under cover of that silence a cunning transference occurs whereby the blame is shifted from the perpetrator to the victim. Afro-American women writers, such as Walker, Morrison and Angelou, have tried to break this silence, and to understand the multiple determinations of the crime. Alice Walker takes up the theme of interracial rape, specifically the rape of white women by black men, in an autobiographical anecdote with the curiously contorted title, 'Advancing Luna – or Ida B. Wells' (1977).[37] This story traces the destruction of a friendship between two young women, one white, the other black, who become acquainted through the civil rights movement in the South. The white woman, Luna, confides in the black woman, who narrates the story, that she was raped some months ago by Freddie Pye, a black comrade in the civil rights campaign. The narrator finds this confidence impossible to swallow. 'Suddenly I was embarrassed,' she writes. 'Then angry. Very angry. *How dare she tell me this!* I thought.' The reason for her reaction, she explains, is that 'Whenever interracial rape is mentioned, a black woman's first thought is to protect the lives of her brothers, her father, her sons, her lover. A history of lynching has bred this reflex in her' (p. 93).

The myth of the black rapist, as many commentators have pointed out, is an 'inversion' of the historical fact that black slave women were regularly raped by their white owners.[38] But the violation – real or imagined – of white women by black men served as pretext for the lynching parties which white men used to hold the black community in terror. Ida B. Wells, named in the title of Walker's story, was a black journalist who devoted her career to the struggle against lynching. She discovered that the vast majority of black men lynched were not even accused of rape, while most of those accused were innocent, but that their murderers invoked the fiction of white womanhood defiled to justify their orgiastic persecution of black men. Wells writes:

> To justify their own barbarism they assume a chivalry which they do not possess. True chivalry respects all womanhood, and no one who reads the record, as it is written in the faces of the million mulattoes in the South, will for a minute conceive that the southern white man had a very chivalrous regard for the honor due to the women of his own race or respect for the womanhood which circumstances placed in his power.[39]

According to Nellie Y. McKay, the lynching of black men for rape historically served two purposes: first it intimidated the black community into submission to white power; secondly it instilled in white women the fear of rape which policed their behaviour, limited their freedom and enforced their dependence on white men.[40]

When Luna makes her confession, then, whose side is the narrator to take? Should she take the part of Luna, as a woman and a fellow victim of the culture of rape which means that women of all races are condemned to constant fear? Or should she take the part of Ida B. Wells and defend black men against white women's death-dealing accusations? She writes:

> (And I began to think that perhaps – whether Luna had been raped or not – it had always been so; that her power over my life was exactly the power *her word on rape* had over the lives of black men, over *all* black men, whether they were guilty or not, and therefore over my whole people.) (p. 95)

But Luna herself is all too aware of the murderous power of her word on rape. And Luna is no Adela: she does not accuse. In the most chilling passage of the story, the narrator asks Luna what she did when she was raped. 'What did you do?' she demands. 'Nothing that required making a noise,' says Luna. ' "Why didn't you scream?" ' the narrator cries, adding: 'I felt I would have screamed my head off.' 'You know why,' Luna replies (p. 92). And the narrator does know why: had Luna screamed and made it known that a white woman had been sexually assaulted by a black co-worker, the whole campaign would have been derailed. So Luna protects Pye in order to protect the cause of black emancipation: her silence is tragic, even heroic.

Yet the narrator begrudges her this heroism. Instead she treats the white girl vengefully throughout the narrative, for Luna's words have wrecked her peace and cannot be contained within a rounded or assuaging narrative. Luna's confession does not harm her rapist, but it does erode the bond between the women friends, reducing both of them, the victim and the confidante, to silence: 'We never discussed the rape again,' Walker writes (p. 97). But one night, just before they move apart, the narrator discovers that Luna has just spent the night – voluntarily, it seems – with Freddie Pye. Luna offers no explanation, leaving the narrator – and the reader – to imagine several possible scenarios. One is the unlikely story that Freddie, stranded in the city, prevailed on Luna's pity, and that they spent the night together discussing his past and the sources of his need to rape (pp. 99–101). A further possibility, which Walker does not propose, is that Luna was compelled to re-enact the rape in order to regain her sense of agency. But we never know what really happened, for Luna never speaks; instead the story splinters into fragments entitled 'Afterwords, Afterwards, Second Thoughts', 'Discarded Notes', 'Imaginary Knowledge', and a 'Postscript' from Havana, Cuba, where a friend of the narrator's, having read the story, suggests that Pye might have been hired to rape white women and thus to sabotage the civil rights campaign, confessing that he himself was once offered this kind of 'work' (pp. 103–4). The narrator makes no effort to reconcile these accounts: as Valerie Smith has pointed out, 'It is as if the conflict between her racial and her gender identity has deconstructed the function of the narrator', who abdicates the power to adjudicate between alternative conclusions.[41] The fragmentation of the denouement suggests the shattering effects of rape itself, while the voices and explanations that compete for the possession of the story at the end reflect the struggle for possession of the victim's body. Meanwhile Luna disappears out of the text, leaving nothing but a mute enigma.

It is no wonder that Luna keeps her mouth shut. Walker describes the white woman's word on rape as the 'poison' that destroys the possibility of love between white women and black men, or between black women and white women. Such love is only possible in a society, she argues, in which 'Luna's word alone on rape can never be used to intimidate an entire people, and in which an innocent black man's protestations of innocence of rape is unprejudicially heard' (p. 102). In this story, therefore, as in Angelou and Forster, the words of women are imagined as weapons far more deadly than the rape that forces them to speak. Celie's words (she is told) will kill her mammy; the child Maya, threatened that her words will kill her brother, imagines they have killed the threatener; Adela's words almost destroy Aziz, and terrorize the Indian community; while Luna's words are tantamount to genocide. Given these powers of destruction, it is not surprising that these women resort to silence: the violence that properly belongs to rape itself is displaced on to the victim's accusation, so that it is women who are seen to prey on men, rather than men on women.

VII

In Toni Morrison's fiction the roles of victim and victimizer cannot be apportioned neatly, for both are entrammelled in histories of violence that exceed their consciousness and agency. It is powerlessness, rather than malevolence, that drives Cholly Breedlove in *The Bluest Eye* (1970) to rape his daughter Pecola. He himself was violated by the white men who surprised him having sex with a young woman in a cornfield, and forced him to continue for their titillation; and this event itself was only the traumatic epiphany of a lifetime of impotence and shame. 'A violence born of total helplessness', Cholly's crime is not condoned by Morrison, but neither is it demonized: she prevents the reader from indulging in the luxury of censure.[42] Instead she breaks the narrative into conflicting points of view, thwarting our impulse to take sides, and forcing us to recognize that we are inculpated by the crime. In a recent Afterword to the novel, Morrison writes:

> One problem was centering: the weight of the novel's inquiry on so delicate and vulnerable a character [as Pecola] could smash her and lead readers into the comfort of pitying her rather than into an inter-rogation of themselves for the smashing. My solution – break the narrative into parts that had to be reassembled by the reader.[43]

Thus Morrison smashes the novel much as her narrator, Claudia, smashes white dolls to discover the secret of their beauty, or as Bigger Thomas smashes the white icon, Mary Dalton.[44] These smashings defy conventional notions of aesthetic form: they reveal that beauty, like its opposite, ugliness, does not inhere in novels or in bodies, but belongs to a violent economy of inclusion and expulsion in which the whole community is implicated. Thus Pecola Breedlove, smashed in mind and body, is left with nothing but the town's projections: 'All of our waste which we dumped on her and which she absorbed. And all of our beauty, which was hers first and which she gave to us' (p. 205).[45]

On the surface there is little comfort to be found for feminists in Morrison's work. Her novels conjure up a matriarchal world where mothers and daughters feed on one another, locked in vampiric sym-biosis. Although men enter this world intermittently, as lovers, fathers, sons, predators or casualties, they are rapidly ejected or eject them-selves, breaking the umbilical cord. The only female characters to escape the mother in Morrison's fiction are loners like Sula, who defy familial ties and loyalties, or Pilate in *Song of Solomon* (1977), who is born without a navel, and hence symbolically without a mother and without the scar, the woundedness, that Morrison habitually associates with motherhood. At the centre of her fiction is the image of the wounded mother who destroys her children: there is Pauline in *The Bluest Eye*, with her damaged foot, who brutalizes her black daughter while pampering her white employers' blue-eyed girl; there is Eva in *Sula* (1973), with her amputated leg, who sets fire to her shell-shocked son; there is Sethe, in *Beloved* (1987), whose back is covered with a tree of scars, and who kills her own beloved daughter to save her from the slave-traders.[46] This tree of scars represents a family tree, a living record of the lacerations of the slaves, and also reasserts the perseverance of the past within the present. Morrison describes memory as 'rememory', as something tangible enough to be 'bumped into', and Sethe's ravaged flesh is 'rememory' incarnate: memory dismembered, unappeased and unredeemed.[47]

In Western literature scars traditionally function as signatures of personal identity inscribed into the flesh which bear mute testimony to forgotten histories. In the famous recognition scene of Homer's *Odyssey*, Odysseus returns to Ithaca incognito; but when his elderly nurse Eurykleia bathes his feet, she discovers his scar, and recognizes her long-lost master. At this point a kind of scar or lesion opens up within the narrative itself, when Homer, in one of his rare flashbacks, tells the tale of how Odysseus received his scar.[48] The scar thus marks the seams or rifts within the present in which other stories, other histories, lie in wait, hushed but potent, ready to reopen and repeat themselves, destroying the illusion that the living could be insulated from the dead. In the scar language and violence, the broken story and the broken flesh reveal themselves as inextricable from one another. In *Beloved*, Sethe's scar reopens to release the ghost of the dead daughter who devours the mother who murdered her: a ghost who cannot be exorcized until her obliterated story has been told.

VIII

In Ovid's *Metamorphoses* Zeus assumes a different shape every time he rapes a nymph or mortal woman; he takes the form of shepherd, satyr, eagle, dolphin, ram, bull, horse, snake, flame and golden rain, as if he were transfigured by his own incursions into otherness. In the magic of these metamorphoses the violence of rape dissolves, its brutality exonerated as a catalyst for transformation. This pattern persists in modernist poetry, where rape is forever changing into something else. In T. S. Eliot's *The Waste Land* rape comes to stand for almost everything but rape itself: the fall of cities, the desecration of tradition, and the invasion of the poet's mind by the voices of his dead precursors, violating his original talent. In the third section of *The Waste Land*, 'The Fire Sermon', the woman who raises her knees – 'Supine on the floor of a narrow canoe' – offers no resistance to the man who violates her; but the man, too, seems overpowered by the act, weeping at his own barbarity. Only the woman's silence – 'I made no comment' – and the wordless song associated with the nightingale – 'la la' – convey the poignancy of rape. The woman's body, identified with ravaged London, decomposes into knees, heart, feet, weirdly disorganized – 'My feet are at Moorgate, and my heart / Under my feet'; while the war-torn city fragments into its parts – Highbury, Richmond, Kew, Moorgate – and disintegrates in broken fingernails on Margate Sands (*The Waste Land*, ll. 292–306). If one considers that post-war London was thronged with legless, armless, eyeless, and castrated men returning from the horrors of the trenches, it is strange that Eliot transposes the reality of male mutilation on to the fantasy of violated and dismembered female flesh. It is as if he were projecting on to women the fragmentation all too evident in men; indeed, as Freud has shown, the female body has traditionally served the purpose of representing and externalizing the castration fears of men. The sexual political implications of rape, however, disappear as Eliot transforms the crime into a metaphor for universal human helplessness.

Similarly, the rape in Yeats's sonnet 'Leda and the Swan' (1923) has been read as a metaphor for almost every struggle except for the struggle between women and rapists. The poem tells the story of the 'violent annunciation' whereby Zeus, in the form of a swan, raped Leda the nymph, whose children from this union ultimately brought about the fall of Troy and the murder of Agamemnon.[49] In Yeats's rendering, however, the opposition of oppressor and oppressed is undone; power, no longer fixed in the figure of the god, is transferred along the circuit of synecdoches into which the girl and her attacker decompose: wings, thighs, webs, nape, bill, breast, fingers, heart, loins, beak. By the end of the poem the distinction between victim and violator, slave and master, has been cast in doubt: 'Did she put on his knowledge with his power / Before the indifferent beak could let her drop?' Yeats's version of the rape of Leda has been read as an allegory of the conquest of nature by the supernatural, of the temporal by the eternal, of life by art; or, in political terms, as the violation of Ireland by England, a violation that secretly empowered the oppressed, who absorbed the knowledge and the power of the conqueror. Yeats himself, however, linked the rape to the conquest of liberalism by fascism, the swan therefore embodying the authoritarian spirit of Mussolini trampling on the 'discomposing [sic] body of the Goddess of Liberty'.[50]

Some years ago I audited Geoffrey Hartmann's seminar on Yeats at Yale, in which he argued with great ingenuity and wit that the most important word in 'Leda and the Swan' was 'and'. A Trotskyist snarled, 'I think this poem is about a *rape.*' He was right, of course, but what was needed was an exploration of the ways in which the poem persuades its critics to obscure the brutality of rape in metaphor. In this poem, as in so many of the works considered above, the literal event of rape is surreptitiously displaced, while the responsibility for the assault passes from the rapist to the unresisting and complicit victim, whose 'vague fingers' and 'loosening thighs' suggest her acquiescence to the violence. It is as if the rape could be represented only by a gap or lesion (the typographical abyss, for instance, that separates 'dead' from 'Being' in the eleventh line of Yeats's sonnet), while around this silence metaphors and mystifications grow and multiply.

Sylvana Tomaselli and Roy Porter point out that there is no comprehensive history of rape.[51] And the issue of rape remains also strangely absent from the political scene, in spite of repeated efforts by feminist scholars to expose the misogyny implicit in the crime.[52] Politicians who readily pontificate on matters like abortion, restricting women's rights over their own bodies, are more reluctant to confront the escalating incidence of rape, where men's control of women's bodies is at stake. The effect of this silence is that rape comes to be regarded as a constant of nature, like sex itself, so that it is up to women to protect themselves from rape, just as they should carry an umbrella to protect themselves from rain. A typical example of this attitude: 'It is the height of imprudence for any girl to hitchhike at night. That is plain, it isn't really worth stating. She is in the true sense asking for it.'[53] Research has shown, however, that rape is not a constant in human civilization; there are societies that are virtually rape-free, and other societies that are rape-prone, or even (like American society today) rape-crazy.[54] And the effacement of rape in literature, the metaphors in which its violence is both concealed and fetishized, can only reinforce a blindness or acquiescence to the crime.

Susan Sontag in her essay *Illness as Metaphor* (1978) makes an eloquent plea to free illness from metaphor, so that the ill can just be seen as ill, rather than demonized as sinners responsible for their own suffering – struck down because they smoke or drank or indulged in sexual excesses – or alternatively sentimentalized, like victims of tuberculosis in the nineteenth century, who were seen as radiant and other-worldly spirits singled out for liberation from the flesh.[55]

Similar metaphors imposed on victims of rape have obscured the true dimensions of the victims' pain, and the reasons why this particular offence against the flesh is so traumatic, is so self-shattering. Sontag is mistaken, in my view, to imagine we can do away with metaphor, or indeed that we can do without it. But the Afro-American women writers discussed in this essay insist that traditional metaphors for rape must be dismantled, even at the cost of aesthetic breakdown.

Allen Grossman has defined metaphor as the 'unknown at hand' (the tenor) conveyed by the 'known far away' (the vehicle).[56] Without metaphor, the unknown at hand is often inaccessible to consciousness: it has been shown, for instance, that survivors of the Nazi death camps cannot grasp their own experience if their metaphoric function is impaired.[57] It seems that even the most intimate of agonies requires metaphor in order to be integrated into subjectivity: thus the known without illuminates the unknown within, and memory is restored to consciousness through a shared language. Metaphor can redeem experience, however, only if the known far away is constantly disrupted by the unknown at hand, the speakable by the atrocity of silence. This is the silence that Shakespeare, writing of the raped Lucrece, describes as the 'deep torture' of the violated:

> And that deep torture may be called a hell,
> When more is felt than one has power to tell.[58]

Notes

1 Samuel Richardson, *Clarissa, or, The History of a Young Lady*, ed. Angus Ross (Harmondsworth: Penguin, 1985), p. 883.
2 Eve Kosofsky Sedgwick, *Between Men: English Literature and Male Homosocial Desire* (New York: Columbia University Press, 1985).
3 Richardson, *Clarissa*, p. 1023.
4 See Frances Ferguson, 'Rape and the Rise of the Novel', *Representations*, 20 (Fall 1987), pp. 88–112; and Ian Watt, *The Rise of the Novel* (Berkeley: University of California Press, 1978), p. 194.
5 See Terry Eagleton, *The Rape of Clarissa: Writing, Sexuality, and Class Struggle in Samuel Richardson* (Minneapolis: University of Minnesota Press, 1982), p. 13.
6 See William Beatty Warner, *Reading 'Clarissa': The Struggles of Interpretation* (New Haven: Yale University Press, 1979), pp. 30, 32, 39, 42, 49.
7 Although this essay focuses on the rape of women and girls, this is not to deny that men can also be victims of rape.
8 Alice Walker, *The Color Purple* (New York: Harcourt Brace Jovanovich, 1982), p. 3.
9 Ovid, *Metamorphoses*, tr. Henry King (Edinburgh: Blackwood, 1871),

Bk. 6, ll. 548–892. In Greek tradition the sisters are reversed: Procne becomes the nightingale, Philomena the swallow.

10 T. S. Eliot, *The Waste Land* (1922), in *Poems 1909–1925* (London: Faber, 1932), l. 101.

11 See Patricia Klindienst Joplin, 'The Voice of the Shuttle is Ours', in Lynn A. Higgins and Brenda R. Silver (eds), *Rape and Representation* (New York: Columbia University Press, 1991), pp. 35 and *passim* pp. 35–55.

12 Ralph Ellison, *Invisible Man* (1947; New York: Random House, 1952), pp. 36–55.

13 See Roy Porter, 'Rape: Does it Have a Historical Meaning?', in Sylvana Tomaselli and Roy Porter (eds), *Rape* (Oxford: Basil Blackwell, 1986), p. 217.

14 Richardson, *Clarissa*, p. 757.

15 See Jennifer Temkin, 'Women, Rape and Law Reform', in Tomaselli and Porter, *Rape*, pp. 24–5.

16 See Ferguson, 'Rape and the Rise of the Novel', p. 88 and *passim*.

17 Quoted by Jennifer Temkin, 'Women, Rape and Law Reform', pp. 19–20.

18 See Susan Brownmiller, *Against Our Will: Men, Women and Rape* (1975; New York: Simon and Schuster, 1981), p. 350.

19 John Vladimir Price, 'Patterns of Sexual Behaviour in Some Eighteenth-Century Novels', in Paul Gabriel Boucé (ed.), *Sexuality in Eighteenth-Century Britain* (Manchester: Manchester University Press, 1982), pp. 159–75, claims that Clarissa's desire for orgasm is compulsively pathological!

20 Ferguson, 'Rape and the Rise of the Novel', p. 101.

21 Judith Wilt makes this argument in 'He Could Go No Farther: A Modest Proposal about Lovelace and Clarissa', *PMLA*, 92: 1 (1977), 19–32.

22 E. M. Forster, *The Manuscripts of 'A Passage to India'*, ed. Oliver Stallybrass (London: Edward Arnold, 1978), pp. 242–3. Feminist critics have seen Forster's deletion of the scene in the cave as a symptom of the novel's pervasive misogyny: see *inter alia* Frances Restuccia, ' "A Cave of my Own": The Sexual Politics of Indeterminacy', *Raritan*, 9: 2 (fall 1989), 110–28; June Perry Levine, 'An Analysis of the Manuscripts of *A Passage to India*', *PMLA*, 85 (March 1970), 287–8; Jo Ann Hoeppner Moran, 'E. M. Forster's *A Passage to India*: What Really Happened in the Caves', *Modern Fiction Studies*, 34 (winter 1988), 596–7.

23 Jenny Sharpe, 'The Unspeakable Limits of Rape: Colonial Violence and Counter-Insurgency', *Genders*, 10 (spring 1991), 25–46.

24 Sir Colin Campbell, *Narrative of the Indian Revolt from its Outbreak to the Capture of Lucknow* (London: George Vickers, 1858); cited in Sharpe (n. 21), pp. 33–4.

25 See Pat Barr, *The Memsahibs: The Women of Victorian England* (London: Secker and Warburg, 1976); cited in Sharpe, pp. 29–33.

26 E. M. Forster, *A Passage to India* (1924; London: Edward Arnold, 1978), p. 178.

27 Sigmund Freud, *The Interpretation of Dreams* (1900), in the *Standard*

Edition of *the Complete Psychological Works of Sigmund Freud*, tr. James Strachey (London: Hogarth, 1953–74), vol. 5, p. 525.

28 Forster, *A Passage to India*, pp. 198, 139, 78.

29 Maria K. Mootry, 'Bitches, Whores, and Woman Haters: Archteypes and Typologies in the Art of Richard Wright', in Richard Macksey and Frank E. Moorer (eds), *Richard Wright: A Collection of Critical Essays* (Englewood Cliffs, NJ: Prentice-Hall, 1984), p. 125. Another deletion was a scene in which Bigger, while having sex with Bessie, fantasizes that she is Mary. This scene was retained in the galleys and changed only in page-proof. See Kenneth Kinnamon, 'How *Native Son* was Born', in Henry Louis Gates Jr and K. A. Appiah (eds), *Richard Wright: Critical Perspectives Past and Present* (New York: Amistad, 1993), p. 121.

30 Richard Wright, 'How Bigger was Born' (1940; 1966), repr. in Houston A. Baker Jr (ed.), *Twentieth Century Interpretations of Native Son* (Englewood Cliffs, NJ: Prentice-Hall, 1972), p. 40.

31 Barbara Johnson, 'The Re(a)d and the Black', in Gates and Appiah, *Richard Wright*, p. 152.

32 Richard Wright, *Native Son* (New York: Harper and Brothers, 1940), p. 7.

33 Ibid., pp. 335, 110.

34 Joseph T. Skerrett Jr, 'Composing Bigger: Wright and the Making of *Native Son*, in Harold Bloom (ed.), *Richard Wright's 'Native Son'* (New York: Chelsea House, 1988), p. 138.

35 Wright, 'How Bigger was Born', p. 40.

36 James Baldwin, 'Alas, Poor Richard', in *Nobody Knows my Name: More Notes of a Native Son* (New York: Dial Press, 1961), p. 188. The suggestion that the brick is a building block for Bigger's new identity is made by Trudier Harris in 'Native Sons and Foreign Daughters', in *New Essays on 'Native Son'*, ed. Keneth Kinnamon (Cambridge: Cambridge University Press, 1990), p. 80.

37 Alice Walker, 'Advancing Luna – or Ida B. Wells', first published in *Ms.* 5: 1 (July 1977); repr. in *You Can't Keep a Good Woman Down* (New York: Harcourt Brace Jovanovich, 1981): page references to this story are given in the text. I am indebted to Valerie Smith's perceptive analysis of this story in 'Split Affinities: The Case of Interracial Rape', in Marianne Hirsch and Evelyn Fox Keller (eds), *Conflicts in Feminism* (London: Routledge, 1990), pp. 271–87.

38 See Barbara Johnson, 'The Re(a)d and the Black', p. 152.

39 Ida B. Wells, *A Red Record: Lynchings in the United States*, in *On Lynchings* (New York: Arno Press and the *New York Times*, 1969), p. 13.

40 Nellie Y. McKay, 'Alice Walker's "Advancing Luna – and Ida B. Wells"', in Higgins and Silver, *Rape and Representation*, p. 257.

41 Valerie Smith, 'Split Affinities', (n. 35), p. 282.

42 Toni Morrison, *The Bluest Eye*, with a new Afterword by the author (1970; repr. New York: Penguin, 1990), p. 148.

43 Ibid., Afterword, p. 211.

44 Michael Awkward draws this connection between Morrison and Wright

in 'Roadblocks and Relatives: Critical Revision in Toni Morrison's *The Bluest Eye*', in Nellie Y. McKay (ed.), *Critical Essays on Toni Morrison* (Boston: G. K. Hall and Co., 1988), p. 60.

45 Morrison, *The Bluest Eye*, p. 201.

46 The 'chokecherry tree' of scars is first mentioned in *Beloved* (1987; London: Picador, 1988) pp. 15–17. Mavis, in Morrison's later novel *Paradise* (1997), is another infanticidal mother whose twins, Merle and Pearl suffocate in an unventilated car.

47 Morrison, *Beloved*, p. 36.

48 Homer, *The Odyssey*, bk. 19, ll. 386–475.

49 See the *Variorum Edition of the Poems of W. B. Yeats*, ed. Peter Allt and Russell K. Alspach (New York: Macmillan, 1957), p. 828.

50 See W. B. Yeats, 'From Democracy to Authority' (1924), in *Uncollected Prose*, ed. John P. Frayne and Colton Johnson (London: Macmillan, 1970–5), vol. 2, p. 434; and Elizabeth Cullingford, *Yeats, Ireland and Fascism* (New York: New York University Press, 1981), pp. 148–9.

51 Tomaselli and Porter, *Rape*, p. xii.

52 See esp. Susan Brownmiller, *Against Our Will*; and Susan Griffin, *Rape: The Power of Consciousness* (New York: Simon and Schuster, 1978).

53 Cited in Tomkin, 'Women, Rape and Law Reform', p. 20.

54 See Peggy Reeves Sanday, 'Rape and the Silencing of the Feminine', in Tomaselli and Porter, *Rape*, esp. pp. 93–8. See also Susan Griffin, 'Rape: The All-American Crime', *Ramparts*, 10 (1971), pp. 26–35; and A. G. Johnson, 'On the Prevalence of Rape in the United States', *Signs*, 6 (1980), pp. 136–46.

55 Susan Sontag, *Illness as Metaphor* (New York: Farrar, Straus and Giroux, 1978).

56 For the theoretical context of this remark see Allen Grossman, 'Why is Death in Arcadia? Poetic Process, Literary Humanism, and the Example of Pastoral', *Western Humanities Review*, 41: 2 (1987), 152–88.

57 See Ilse Grubrich-Simitis, 'From Concretism to Metaphor: Thoughts on Some Theoretical and Technical Aspects of the Psychoanalytic Work with Children of Holocaust Survivors', *Psychoanalytic Study of the Child*, 39 (1984), pp. 301–29; cited by Jacqueline Rose, 'Daddy', in Maud Ellmann (ed.), *Psychoanalytic Literary Criticism* (London: Longman, 1994), p. 229.

58 Shakespeare, *The Rape of Lucrece*, ll. 1287–8.

3 Looking Awry: Tropes of Disability in Post-colonial Writing

Ato Quayson

Mr Jeremy Beadle, host of 'You've Been Framed' and 'It Could Be You', parried criticism made against a televised practical joke he seems to have once made on a disabled person. The comic potential in any disconcerting scene was because the spectators always heaved a sigh of relief that it was not them at the receiving end of the confusion or discomfiture. And this, he continued, applied in any situation where someone was alone in being confused about something that to others around was plain to see. The fact that they were disabled was not directly relevant to the comic potential of such scenes, he thought.[1]

It is obvious that Mr Beadle's definition of comedy ignores the fact that, when it is at the expense of the disabled or of the weaker in society, it achieves its effect partly because these weak ones cannot 'strike back', as it were. There is an implicit privileging of the strong versus the weak in any comedy that depends for its effect on putting the weak, or the disabled, or the racial minority for that matter, in a position of discomfort. Highlighting some of the obviously misguided media treatments of the disabled in opening an essay on tropes of disability in post-colonial writing, however, is not of interest in itself; rather its aim is to suggest that there is a curious affinity between what I am going to describe in greater detail as the primal scene of the literary encounter with the disabled and attitudes that pertain to disabled people in other contexts. To begin in this way is also to take a cue from Slavoj Žižek in *Looking Awry* (1992), who, apart from providing the first part of the title of this essay, re-routes popular culture through the works of Jacques Lacan and shows how paradoxically 'looking awry' at an object (with a specific philosophical or ideological interest) allows it to come into focus and gain shape. Furthermore, Žižek demonstrates in his methodology the productiveness of juxtaposing the highest spiritual products of culture alongside the most common, prosaic and mundane. In doing this he suggests a fruitful way of understanding the tropes of disability that we are going to attend to in this essay. A looking awry at such tropes throws the subtle evasions of literary discourse into sharp relief.

I will be making three critical moves: the first will be to explore a Lacanian conceptual apparatus for theorizing what happens in the encounter with the disabled. This will be done through a strategic reading of two essays, namely 'The Mirror Stage as Formative of the Function of the I' and 'Aggressivity in Psychoanalysis', both in *Ecrits* (1966; 1989). The second will be to attend to the various discursive ways in which the disabled are figured in post-colonial writing, with particular reference to J. M. Coetzee's *Waiting for the Barbarians* (1980), Keri Hulme's *The Bone People* (1986) and Ben Okri's *The Famished Road* (1992). The third will be to conclude by arguing that these primal scenes may be useful for grasping traumatic post-colonial histories, especially when these are 'littered with disembodied pasts' as is the case in some African countries riven by present and past wars. What, in other words, does it mean for the reconstruction of civil imagining when history itself has to be seen through a trope of disability?

The disabled, Lacan and the primal scene[2]

Defining disability is fraught with problems. As Whyte and Ingstad note, 'any attempt to universalize the category "disabled" runs into conceptual problems of the most fundamental sort.'[3] Furthermore, they note that the category is often used to refer to a broad range of phenomena, covering manifest physical disability, less manifest forms, such as deafness, and insanity. More significantly, they join others in highlighting the need to see disability as a cultural as well as physical problem. However, it is in the seminal work of Erving Goffman, suggestively entitled *Stigma: Notes on the Management of Spoiled Identity* (1963) that the complex issue of the cultural dimension to disability is raised more fruitfully. In an illuminating account of the nature and sources of social stigma, Goffman points out that physical disability produces its own gestalt and that those confronting the disabled often have a whole range of attitudes based on stereotype.[4] More disturbingly, these stereotypes often work on the psyches of the disabled themselves, generating problems with their self-esteem, as Robert F. Murphy shows from personal experience.[5] Physical disability, then, may be said to be constitutive of social and psychological relations in a very troubling way.

But how does this come to be as it is, and in what terms do we describe the primal scene of the encounter of the able-bodied with the disabled through a Lacanian reading? Without actually attempting to discuss Lacan in full (something which most commentators agree is easier said than done), I want to interleave my own ideas with his conceptions so as to indicate his line of thinking while at the same time distinguishing my own reasoning from his. To summarize the argument in 'The Mirror Stage': when children are between six and eighteen months, they enter a curious phase in which they begin to recognize themselves in a mirror and start a long-term process of subjectivity that continues through life. The salient points of this mirror stage may be stated schematically as (1) the baby learns to recognize its image and gestures in the mirror; (2) the baby discovers that the image in the mirror has its own properties (pun intended) and, furthermore, that it is whole; (3) the baby develops an attachment to this specular image, which, though reflecting a unified object back to it, is actually deluding the baby with a sense of wholeness. The phase is attended by signs of triumphant jubilation and playful discovery. As Malcolm Bowie puts it: 'At the mirror moment something glimmers in the world for the first time. . . . The mirror image is a minimal paraphrase of the nascent ego'.[6] But that the baby's sense of identification is delusional is seen in the fact that even as it requires the support of parental hands or of some artificial contraptions, it has begun to imagine itself whole and powerful. For Lacan the ego is formed on the basis of an *imaginary* relationship of the subject with this specular image. Because this stage is actually not a phase but a stadium (*stade*), the mirror stage rehearses a lifelong process by which the ego, as Maud Ellmann succinctly puts it, 'constantly identifies itself with new personae in the effort to evade division, distance, difference, deferral, death'.[7] The result, she continues, is a 'wilderness of mirrors in which self and object oscillate perpetually, each eclipsed under the shadow of the other'. Ellmann's notion of perpetual oscillation is an interesting one to which we will return.

In translating Lacan's conceptions into a definition of the primal scene of the encounter with the disabled, it is crucial first of all to take away the mirror while still keeping it in mind. One significant difference between the gaze of Lacan's baby and that of the able-bodied as he or she gazes at the disabled is that in the second case there is flow of affectivity. This affectivity relates to a multiplicity of emotions, which include guilt, bewilderment and even fear. Robert Murphy points out that the disabled serve as 'constant, visible reminders to the able-bodied that the society they live in is shot through with inequity and suffering, that they live in a counterfeit paradise, and that they too are vulnerable'.[8] But these often contradictory emotions arise precisely because the disabled are continually located within a multiple frame of significance that is activated through the culturally regulated gaze of the able-bodied. My use of the word frame in this context is not idle. It is useful to think of such a frame in the light of physical coordinates as if thinking of a picture-frame. The frame within which the disabled are continually placed is one in which a variety of concepts of wholeness and completion structure the disabled and place them at the centre of a peculiar conjuncture of conceptions. At the same time, and quite paradoxically, this frame always harbours behind it the earlier frame of the mirror phase of childhood. It is a conflation of the mirror phase of identification with a culturally structured set of stereotypes about wholeness and personhood that gives this primal scene its particular intensities.

But how are we to attend to this contradiction? How does the new frame of wholeness and completion palimpsestically, as it were, overwrite the mirror stage of childhood? To clear this point, we have to turn to the second essay. In 'Aggressivity and Psychoanalysis', Lacan notes the degree to which the analyst becomes an object of cathartic resolution for the aggressivity inherent in the analysand's self-imagining. But the aggressivity is often captured in what he describes as *imagos*, tropes, as literary critics might call them, some of which 'represent the elective vectors of aggressive intentions, which they provide with an efficacity that might be called magical'.[9] These *imagos* are the images of 'castration, mutilation, dismemberment, dislocation, evisceration, devouring, bursting open of the body, in short, the *imagos* that I have grouped together under the apparently structural term of *imagos of the fragmented body*'.[10] As he further points out, aggressivity is in the early stages inextricably linked to the images of fragmented bodies:

> One only has to listen to children aged between two and five playing, alone or together, to know that the pulling off of the head and the ripping open of the belly are themes that occur spontaneously to their imagination, and that this is corroborated by the experience of the doll torn to pieces.[11]

Crucially, however, he also notes that 'in itself, dialogue seems to involve the renunciation of aggressivity' (p.12). He has in mind the role of the analyst in establishing a dialogic context within which the analysand's repressions may be brought to the surface. But, unlike in the case of Freud, Lacan maintains that the analyst is never completely detached from the unfolding process of psychoanalysis but is inextricably involved in its very discursive composition. Transposing these insights into the primal scene of the encounter with the disabled, it may be argued that it is precisely the enframing within normative assumptions of personhood that disenables a liberated 'dialogue' or 'dialogic' encounter with the disabled. This represents the fact that the encounter is always overdetermined by stereotypes of wholeness. And, paradoxically, the notions and stereotypes of wholeness are grounded on the repressed *imagos* of the fragmented body. The primal scene of the encounter with the disabled may then be described as always being crossed by a problematic aggressivity. The aggressivity, however, can rarely be expressed in its own terms, but is diverted in different direc tions and manifests itself as guilt, bewilderment, fear and, in a happy moment of sublimation, as charity.

If the mirror stage is taken as metaphorically extending throughout life, it is possible to argue that this phase represents for any growing subjectivity the figure of wholeness as normative. For the disabled caught in the mirror stage, it is not only their own reflection that they see. As many commentators have noted, there is an endless internalization on their part of the images that define wholeness.[12] The mirror is populated endlessly with the reflections of 'whole' people and a world in which things are made with such people in mind. At the primal scene, there is a whole series of double visions at play: the able-bodied see a totality that is themselves reflected back to them along with an anxious fantasy of dismemberment. For the disabled, the vision is of what is normative crossed with their own sense of fragmentation. Finally, and even more uncannily, they are both being made the objects of gaze of the frame of wholeness and completion whose repressed Other is all the figures of dismemberment that play across the mirror stage. The 'perpetual oscillation' in the making of the ego that Ellmann remarked in discussing the mirror stage may then be said to be hyper-inflected in the primal scene of the encounter with the disabled.

The anxieties of literary discourse in the encounter with the disabled

It is now time to test these formulations against some post-colonial texts.[13] The first thing to note in the literary primal scene of the encounter with the disabled is that the narrative is often marked at such points by signs of what we might term 'discursive nervousness'. This is reflected in a variety of ways, either in a sudden effusion of violence and chaos accompanied by a change in the texture of the language, or by a general reversion to images of primary sensations, or even of a subliminal unease with questions of identity.[14] Coetzee's *Waiting* is an interesting illustration of the last of these points. Coetzee's novel is about a character called the Magistrate through whose eyes the entire novel is narrated. At the opening of the novel he has been a dutiful functionary of the Empire for many years. Now, however, a propaganda frenzy has led to the arrest and torture of members of barbarian tribes who live at the edges of the Empire. One of these barbarian girls, blinded in torture and with broken ankles and sundry scars, is taken in by the Magistrate. His motives seem to be altruistic at first, but it does not take long for him to begin desiring her sexually. It is a relationship, however, which for a while is doomed to remain unconsummated, owing partly to the Magistrate's mental struggle to erase the scars from off her body. At one point in the narrative, he is watching her eat while thinking about how much pain she must have suffered:

> I watch her eat. She eats like a blind person, gazing into the distance, working by touch. She has a good appetite, the appetite of a robust young country woman.
> 'I don't believe you can see,' I say.
> 'Yes, I can see. When I look straight there is nothing, there is—(she rubs the air in front of her like someone cleaning a window).
> 'A blur,' I say.
> 'There is a blur. But I can see out of the sides of my eyes. The left eye is better than the right. How could I find my way if I didn't see?'
> 'Did they do this to you?'
> 'Yes.'
> 'What did they do?'
> She shrugs and is silent. Her plate is empty. I dish up more of the bean stew she seems to like so much. She eats too fast, belches behind a cupped hand, smiles. 'Beans make you fart,' she says. The room is warm, her coat hangs in a corner with the boots below it, she wears only the white smock and drawers. *When she does not look at me I am a grey form moving about unpredictably on the periphery of her vision. When she looks at me I am a blur, a voice, a smell, a centre of energy that one day falls asleep washing her feet and the next day feeds her bean stew and the next day – she does not know.* (Coetzee, *Waiting*, p. 29; my emphases)

Because this novel is narrated entirely from the viewpoint of the Magistrate, the nervousness is as much his as that of the narrative in general. Particularly significant in this regard is the fact that, at the end of this extract, he shifts into a free indirect discourse that seems momentarily to conflate his own perceptions with those of the barbarian girl. In describing how he appears to her – like a grey form moving peripherally, or a blur, a voice and a smell – he seems to be uncannily 'seeing' himself through her eyes. This self-seeing, which folds into itself a self-unseeing, defines the precise space of an unnameable anxiety for the Magistrate. It is the anxiety of being effaced and disembodied in the partial gaze of the girl even as he thinks himself whole and in control of her immediate destiny. This is illustrative of the primal scene of enframing that we elaborated earlier, but with the added dimension that here the disabled girl is actively gazing back. The barbarian girl is a mirror that reflects back to the Magistrate his potential dissolution on its surface. Curiously enough, this uncanny moment of dissolution comes after the Magistrate's careful location of the girl in a stereotypical frame of reference. He notes matter-of-factly that 'she eats like a blind person, gazing into the distance, working by touch'. In addition that 'she has a good appetite, the appetite of a robust young country woman.' What is this about blind people gazing at the distance while they eat, and what is it that sustains these broad generalizations? It is simply the fact that he feels himself empowered to enframe and name her, as one who controls the tools of such procedures as well as one who regulates the movement of the narrative in the first place. It is therefore highly ironic that he finds himself later in the passage an object of effacement in the eyes of the girl.

Later on in the novel, the Magistrate makes an admission to himself that shows the extent to which the framing of the blind barbarian girl is a desperate attempt at stabilizing a sense of wholeness that would liberate his libidinal impulses:

> No more than before does my heart leap or my blood pound at her touch. I am with her not for whatever raptures she may promise or yield but for other reasons, which remain as obscure to me as ever. Except that it has not escaped me that in bed in the dark the marks her torturers have left upon her, the twisted feet, the half-blind eyes, are easily forgotten. Is it then the case that it is the whole woman I want, that my pleasure in her is spoiled until these marks on her are erased and she is restored to herself; or is it the case (*I am not stupid, let me say these things*) that it is the marks on her which drew me to her but which, to my disappointment, I find, do not go deep enough? *Too much or too little: is it she I want or the traces of a history her body bears?* (Coetzee, *Waiting*, p. 64; my emphases)

The Magistrate seems to be in an odd position of psychological denial. On the one hand, he asserts that he is not with her for any possibility of rapture, but he cannot identify the real reason for his attraction to her. More important, however, is his admission that he simultaneously desires her without the marks of torture as well as seeming to be attracted to her because of them. The oscillation in his mind is nothing other than a figuring of the uneasy dialogical relationship he has attempted to establish with the disabled barbarian girl. He desires a dialogue with her as an equal and struggles to understand her historical position in the brutal narrative of empire. And yet, contradictorily, he finds himself frustrated from doing this not only because she is a barbarian (his view of her table manners reflects this sense) but also because her disability reflects to him all the negations of personhood which, as a liberal humanist, challenge unconscious assumptions he has held all his life. His problems are additionally compounded because he also recognizes that her body has been sacrificed by an imperial history to which he has somehow contributed. Her disability exceeds its frame of reference to envelope him in an embrace of complicity and guilt.

If the main features of the primal scene of the discursive encounter with the disabled may be seen in the bounded interaction of such scenes in Coetzee's novel, Keri Hulme's *The Bone People* illustrates a far more complex configuration of the primal scene in that the entire text rehearses the perpetual oscillation of the encounter. There are three main protagonists in the novel: Kerewin, an artist who lives by herself on a South Island beach in New Zealand; Simon, a dumb child; and Joe, his adoptive father. The first encounter with Simon is fruitful in the way in which it reproduces the contours of the primal scene:

> She stands over by the window, hands fistplanted on her hips, and watches the gathering boil of the surf below. *She has a curious feeling as she stands there, as though something is out of place, a wrongness somewhere, an uneasiness, an overwatching.* She stares morosely at her feet (longer second toes still longer, you think they might one day grow less, you bloody werewolf you?) and the joyous relief that the morning's hunting gave ebbs away.
>
> .   .   .   .
>
> There is a gap between two tiers of bookshelves. Her chest of pounamu rests in between them, and above it, is a child. A thin shockheaded person, haloed in hair, shrouded in the dying light.
> The eyes are invisible. It is silent, immobile.
> Kerewin stares, shocked and gawping and speechless.
>
> .   .   .   .
>
> *She doesn't like looking at the child. One of the maimed, the contaminating. . . .*
> She looks at the smoke curling upward in a thin blue stream instead.
> 'Ah, you can't talk, is that it?' (Keri Hulme, *The Bone People*, pp. 16–17; my emphases)

Keri Hulme's novel is marked by a highly poeticized mode of writing. Though it is essentially a third-person narrative, there is a constant integration of the thoughts and feelings of individual characters. From these extracts, however, two things are worthy of note in relation to our argument. The first is that Kerewin has a sense of a 'wrongness somewhere, an overwatching' when alone in her house; its source is not clearly formulated till a little later. Though this eerie feeling of being watched might be said to be a natural intuitive reaction to being the object of an undisclosed person's gaze, it is important to note that later the notion of a vague 'wrongness' is given a specific location when she thinks of the child as one of the 'maimed, the contaminating'. Significantly, though, she thinks of him in this way *before she fully discovers he is dumb.* Is this momentary foreknowledge attributable to Kerewin's heightened intuitions or does its significance lie elsewhere? At this point the issue is undecidable but, as the narrative progresses, it is clear that Simon's proleptic framing as a maimed and contaminating factor in Kerewin's mind even before she discovers he is disabled resonates at a more complex level of the narrative's discourse.

As the novel progresses, one senses a certain struggle to avoid a full disclosure of what it is that seems to be constantly disturbing Simon. Though, as I noted before, the novel frequently reflects the innermost thoughts of individual characters, what goes on in Simon's mind is rigorously withheld from us. All we get is his momentary sensations and reactions to events, not his thoughts on his own condition. In fact, for much of the time, the novel reads almost like a psychological mystery thriller in which we are constantly made to wonder at what possibly might have happened to Simon. We are shown signs of physical abuse, but led in a circuitous way to suspect various people other than Joe of harming the boy. When Kerewin arrives at a fair conviction that Joe is responsible for the boy's abused condition, her subliminal sensual attraction to Joe initially prevents her from dealing with him as ruthlessly as she would have wished and from reporting his actions to the Social Services. The moment of the explicit disclosure of Joe's responsibility for Simon's abuse is a moment of great violence and bloodshed. It is also paradoxically the moment when Simon strikes back and we are allowed to grasp the intensity of his delayed response. In reaction to being beaten yet again by Joe for some misdemeanour, Sam launches wildly at Joe with a glass splinter, stabbing him in the stomach and almost killing him (pp. 306–9). It is only at this point that we are forced to reinterpret all the coded signals provided earlier in the text about the ambivalent looks that he often gave Joe, his strong attachment to Kerewin and reluctance to go to his own home, and the tense behaviour that he often displayed in the presence of the two of them. Strangely enough, however, shortly after this explicit articulation of the boy's response to his abuse the three characters are separated and the text falls apart. Joe's confession to Kerewin and her subsequent reactions to the full disclosure are particularly relevant in this regard:

> 'You know what?' he asks yet again, on the last recital, and she shakes her head tiredly. She has become more and more sober as the night has worn on. 'I think I was trying to beat him dead,' says Joe. 'I think I was trying to kill him then.'
> *   *   *
> He says something in passing that Kerewin wishes he had never revealed. A few words, but they make for horror.
> He says, 'I don't think I'm the only one that's hurt him. He had some bloody funny marks on him when he arrived.'
>
> .   .   .   .
>
> She stowed her backpack into a large suitcase, added a few clothes, all her remaining smokes, the last of the bottle of Drambuie, Simon's rosary and three books.
> One is the Book of the Soul, the one she normally keeps under lock and key.
> One is the Concise Oxford Dictionary.
> The last is peculiarly her own.
> It is entitled, in hand-lettered copper uncials, 'Book of Godhead', and the title page reads,
> 'BOG: for spiritual small-players to lose themselves in.'
> It contains an eclectic range of religious writing.
>
> .   .   .   .
>
> It was a book she had designed to cater for all the drifts and vagaries of her mind. To provide her with information, rough maps and sketches of a way to God.
> *She has a feeling her need for the numinous will increase dramatically from now on.* (Hulme, *The Bone People*, 328; 329; my emphases)

We notice, first of all, that Kerewin refuses to pass judgement on Joe. This is especially odd, as she had been shown in the novel to be very strong-minded and forthright with her opinions. What is even more strange, however, is the fact that, immediately after this confession, she decides to pack bag and baggage and leave her lovingly created spiral home. The books that she decides to take along are also significant in this respect: a dictionary and several spiritual books. But it is not for nothing that she senses an increasing 'need for the numinous'. The novel itself subsequently becomes highly religious and esoteric in tone, following Joe on a visit to a shaman in a quest for atonement for his cruelties and, sporadically, Kerewin, on a journey that seems not to have any clear direction. All this narrative 'falling apart', however, has to be understood in the light of the novel's special discursive location of Simon and the contradictions involved in his rebellion against oppression.

Simon is frequently described with an array of quasi-religious significations. His age is undecidable. He seems to be simultaneously five years and ten times that. His eyes are 'seagreen' (p. 22), and he is said by Joe to have come on shore as part of the jetsam of a shipwreck a few years earlier (pp. 51, 83–8). When she first sees him, Kerewin describes him as a 'thin shockheaded person, haloed in hair, shrouded in the dying light' (p. 17). He makes a gift to Kerewin of a magnificent rosary of semi-precious stones which seems to be some kind of heirloom. Looking at how his hair falls across his face, she is reminded of 'the skirts of dervishes as they spin to ecstasy' (p. 68). Later in the novel, when he is hospitalized following the brutal final encounter with Joe, his hands are said to be marked by a network of pink scars and his feet are described as being wrapped in bandages, covering 'what feels like holes' (p. 387). His hair is shown to be 'gone to a fine gold fuzz' (p. 389). And, to top it all, Simon claims with great conviction to be able to see people's auras in the dark (p. 93). What all these quasi-religious references suggest is that Simon is a sort of sacrificial figure and is made to carry, *pace* Shakespeare's Hamlet, the 'slings [stings] and arrows of an outrageous fortune'. The point, though, is that this outrageous fortune is not only the fact of being the adopted child of an abusive parent; it is also the fact of carrying a disability that makes him the butt of insults and the suspect of contamination and, at a more complex discursive level, that operates so as to render him silent, spoken-for and misunderstood in the narrative. It is therefore significant to note that despite Kerewin's growing friendship with him, she consistently thinks of him in terms of negative epithets, repeatedly extending in different directions what she earlier defines intuitively as 'contaminating'. The novel rehearses the contours of the primal scene at several levels of its discourse. Much as in Coetzee's novel, the disabled in this text, though located within a particular frame, exceeds its regulative parameters and is seen to affect the boundaries of the entire narrative itself. It is almost as if the text is nervous about the disabled, its nervousness displaying itself in ways that undermine its narrative stability.

If Keri Hulme's novel can be said to produce a sense of discursive nervousness that spreads throughout its narrative, Ben Okri's *The*

Famished Road is crucial for grasping the significance of surrendering the entire universe of discourse to a figure that is not only traditionally thought of as disabled but, additionally, is believed to be liminal, existing between the interstices of this world and the next. Okri's novel is a bold experiment with narrative form in which the entire novel is narrated in the first person through the eyes of Azaro, an *abiku* child. The *abiku* is a child believed to be a 'born-to-die', one that has an umbilical connection to the otherworld and, trapped in a restless cycle of rebirth, is born only to die again and be reborn to the same mother. Belief in the phenomenon is common in southern Nigeria and has figured prominently in Nigerian literature.[15] The key difference between Okri's use of the concept and its treatment by others is that, in his novel, there is a free interaction between the real world and that of spirits that disobeys all notions of boundaries or of a clear narrative teleology.

At various points in the novel, Azaro encounters disabled people who also seem to be lunatic:

> There was a man standing near me. I noticed him because of his smell. He wore a dirty, tattered shirt. His hair was reddish. Flies were noisy around his ears. His private parts showed through his underpants. His legs were covered in sores. The flies around his face made him look as if he had four eyes. I stared at him out of curiosity. He made a violent motion, scattering the flies, and I noticed that his two eyes rolled around as if in an extraordinary effort to see themselves. (Okri, *The Famished Road*, p. 17)

> He had on only a pair of sad-looking underpants. His hair was rough and covered in a red liquid and bits of rubbish. He had a big sore on his back and a small one on his ear. Flies swarmed around him and he kept twitching. Every now and then he broke into a titter.
> . . . He had one eye higher than another. His mouth looked like a festering wound. He twitched, stamped, laughed, and suddenly ran into the bar. (Ibid., p. 84)

In the case of the first one, encountered early in the novel when Azaro is lost in a market and struggling to find his way home, the lunatic is strange in that the already bizarre nature of his eyes is further complicated by the flies that seem to multiply them. The second one, encountered much later when Azaro is tending Madame Koto's palm-wine shop, recalls the earlier lunatic, but with the crucial difference that this one is shown to be potentially more violent. But, because Azaro is constantly shifting between the real world and that of spirits, he regularly meets characters who match these two lunatics in grotesqueness.

It is as if to suggest that in the dispossession and destitution of the poor, whose conditions of existence are central to the novel, the anxiety-generating potential of the esoteric realm is equally at play in the real world. If it is remembered that the novel is being narrated by a figure thought of as liminal and disabled, we see how the entire universe is produced through a trope of disability.

A further complexity introduced by Okri's text is that the *abiku* child is also meant to stand for the fractious post-colonial history of his native Nigeria:

> Things that are not ready, not willing to be born or to become, *things for which adequate preparations have not been made to sustain their momentous births*, things that are not resolved, things bound up with failure and with fear of being, they all keep recurring, keep coming back, and in themselves partake of the spirit-child's condition. They keep coming and going till their time is right. History itself demonstrates how things of the world partake of the condition of the spirit-child (*The Famished Road*, p. 487; my emphases).

In this linking of a national history with the condition of the *abiku*, Okri echoes a suggestion made by Wole Soyinka in *A Dance of the Forests*, which was commissioned specifically to commemorate Independence in 1961. At a moment in Soyinka's play, the nation is figured as a half bodied *abiku* child, challenging the substance of Independence. Reproducing the trope thirty years on, Okri destablizes the relation between history and progress by centralizing the liminal *abiku* child and making it the (counter-)productive point of narrative unfolding. Unlike the previous examples we have looked at, in Okri's work the contours of the primal scene mark the potential dissolution of any certitudes that we might have had concerning the boundaries or hierarchized relationships between the able-bodied and the physically disabled. The perpetual oscillation in the primal scene of the encounter with the disabled is marked in this text by a restless oscillation between the real world and that of spirits, mediated through the liminal *abiku* figure of Azaro.

Conclusion: post-colonial history in a trope of disability

The presence of disabled people in post-colonial writing marks more than just the recognition of their obvious presence in the real world of post-colonial existence and the fact that, in most cases, national economies woefully fail to take care of them. It means much more than that. It also marks the sense of a major problematic, which is nothing less than the difficult encounter with history itself. For colonialism may be said to have been a major force of disabling the colonized from taking their place in the flow of history other than in a position of stigmatized underprivilege. The devastating effect of colonialism on the psyches of the colonized has been written about by Frantz Fanon and need not detain us here.[16] What is important to note, however, is that the encounter with the disabled in post-colonial writing is as much a struggle to transcend the nightmare of history.

But it is a nightmare which is also as much a product of warped post-colonial national identities as it is of the traumatic processes of colonialism. This is particularly the case in Africa, where wars and rumours of war succeed in proliferating disability on the streets daily. Angola, Mozambique, Liberia, Rwanda, Sierra Leone: in all these countries reckless wars have ensured that the disabled are a part of everyday life. In any attempt to create a civil imagining in these countries, the problem will always be how to confront a traumatic history of disability at the personal as well as social level. Though it is not wise to venture any answers, we may yet add that there will be a perpetual oscillation between the painful past and the vital present that will make civil societies in such contexts liminal and riddled with emotional contradictions. A crucial step, perhaps, would be to recognize this for a fact and to account for it as a *process of becoming*, one that needs to be grasped in its full complexity before it can be overcome, requiring patience, fortitude, hope and, above all, dialogue. A ceaseless dialogue.

Notes

I wish to express special thanks to Jo Emeney, who, as a student of mine at Pembroke College, Cambridge, in 1995/6 first drew my attention to the proliferation of disabled figures in post-colonial literature. Thanks are also due to Kate Huntington and Bibi Jacob of King's College, Cambridge, who in the Lent term of 1997 had to sit through what I think was an interminable supervision at which I struggled with great enthusiasm but little coherence to explore my ideas on Keri Hulme's *The Bone People*; also to Mark Wormald, my colleague at Pembroke, for reading and commenting on a first draft of this essay. Finally, I want to dedicate the essay to my father, a great story-teller who had one leg shorter than the other.

1 This was in a BBC television talkshow called 'Esther', aired on 20 March 1997 and hosted by Esther Rantzen. The show was concerned with finding out what might be said to constitute comedy for a British audience.
2 Contrary to how the term is applied in Freudian usage, 'primal scene' is used here not to denote the child's witnessing of the sexual encounter between parents, but rather with the sense of being basic, primary, and fundamental.

3 Susan Reynolds Whyte and Benedicte Ingstad, 'Disability and Culture: An Overview', in *Disability and Culture* (Berkeley: University of California Press, 1995), p. 5.

4 Erving Goffman, *Stigma: Notes on the Management of Spoiled Identity* (Englewood Cliffs, NJ: Prentice-Hall, 1963), p. 6.

5 Robert F. Murphy, *The Body Silent* (London: Dent, 1987), pp. 96–115.

6 Malcolm Bowie, *Lacan* (Cambridge, Mass.: Harvard University Press, 1991), 96–115.

7 Maud Ellmann, *Psychoanalytic Literary Criticism* (London: Longman, 1994), p. 18.

8 Murphy, *Body Silent*, p. 100.

9 Jacques Lacan, *Ecrits*, trans. Alan Sheridan (London: Routledge, 1989), p. 11.

10 Ibid.

11 Ibid. An example of this childhood fascination with dismemberment is reflected in Disney's *Toy Story* (1995). In this film about toys coming to life, fragmentation is continually represented in the figure of Mr Potato Head, a toy potato with detachable limbs and facial components. Not only does Mr Potato Head regularly detach parts of his body to stress his arguments or gain some advantage, at three different points in the film he suffers complete fragmentation on collision with fast moving objects.

12 See Goffman, *Stigma*: Murphy, *Body Silent*; Joan Ablon, *Little People in America: The Social Dimensions of Dwarfism* (New York: Praeger, 1984), pp. 23–30. In a racial context, it is interesting to note how often racial stereotypes get internalized by racial minorities and constantly become the objects of struggle. A very interesting tragic account of this is offered by Toni Morrison in *The Bluest Eye* (1970; London: Picador, 1990).

13 Though I will be looking mainly at the three texts I have already mentioned, the general thesis may be tested and elaborated in relation to a variety of post-colonial texts in which the disabled appear either peripherally or centrally. A useful list of such works could include Ngugi Wa Thiong'o's *Petals of Blood* (1997), Bapsi Sidhwa's *The Ice-Candy Man* (1989), J. M. Coetzee's *The Life and Times of Michael K.* (1983) and even earlier works such as Wole Soyinka's *Madmen and Specialists* (1971) and Naguib Mahfouz's *Midaq Alley* (1947) among others.

14 An excellent illustration of these features is provided in Nayantara Saghal's *Rich Like Us* (1987) in an encounter with a cripple beggar who is a completely peripheral character to the main action. See especially the account of the attempt to seize the beggar for an enforced vasectomy on pp. 89–90.

15 I explore this idea more fully in *Strategic Transformations in Nigerian Writing* (Oxford and Bloomington: James Currey and Indiana University Press, 1997), pp. 123–39.

16 Frantz Fanon, *Black Skin, White Masks*, trans. Charles Lam Markham (New York: Grove Press, 1967); idem, *The Wretched of the Earth*, trans Constance Farrington (Harmondsworth: Penguin, 1967).

References

Literary Sources

Coetzee, J. M., *Waiting for the Barbarians* (London: Secker and Warburg, 1980).
—— *The Life and Times of Michael K.* (London: Secker and Warburg, 1983).
Disney, *Toy Story* (1995).
Hulme, Keri, *The Bone People* (1983; London, Picador, 1986).
Mahfouz, Naguib, *Midaq Alley*, (1947; London: Doubleday, 1992).
Morrison, Toni, *The Bluest Eye* (1970; London: Picador, 1990).
Ngugi Wa Thiong'o, *Petals of Blood* (London: Heinemann, 1977).
Okri, Ben, *The Famished Road* (London: Cape, 1992).
Saghal, Nayantara, *Rich Like Us* (1983; London Sceptre, 1987).
Sidhwa, Bapsi, *The Ice-Candy Man* (Harmsworth: Penguin, 1989).
Soyinka, Wole, *A Dance of the Forests* (1963), in *Collected Plays*, Vol. 1 (Oxford: Oxford University Press, 1973).

Critical Sources

Ablon Joan, *Little People in America: The Social Dimensions of Dwarfism* (New York: Praeger, 1984).
Bowie, Malcolm, *Lacan* (Cambridge, Mass.: Harvard University Press, 1991).
Ellmann, Maud, *Psychoanalytic Literary Criticism* (London: Longman, 1994).
Goffman, Erving, *Stigma: Notes on the Management of Spoiled Identity* (Englewood Cliffs, NJ: Prentice-Hall, 1963).
Fanon, Frantz, *Black Skin, White Masks*, trans. Charles Lam Markham (1952; New York: Grove Press, 1967).
—— *The Wretched of the Earth*, trans. Constance Farrington (1961; Harmondsworth: Penguin, 1967).
Lacan, Jacques 'Aggressivity in psychoanalysis' (1948) in *Ecrits* trans. Alan Sheridan (London: Routledge, 1989).
—— 'The Mirror Stage as Formative of the Function of the I as Revealed in Psychoanalytic Experience' (1949), in *Ecrits*.
Murphy, Robert F., *The Body Silent* (London: Dent, 1987).
Quayson, Ato, *Strategic Transformations in Nigerian Writing: Orality and History in Rev. Samuel Johnson, Amos Tutuola, Wole Soyinka and Ben Okri* (Oxford and Bloomington: James Currey and Indiana University Press, 1997).
Whyte, Susan Reynolds and Ingstad, Benedicte, 'Disability and Culture: An Overview', in Susan Reynolds Whyte and Benedicte Ingstad (eds), *Disability and Culture* (Berkeley: University of California Press, 1995).
Žižek, Slavoj, *Looking Awry: An Introduction to Jacques Lacan through Popular Culture* (Cambridge, Mass.: MIT Press, 1992).

4 Movement in Fiction

John Harvey

I

In collecting for this volume, Rod Mengham was kind enough to ask if I would contribute as a 'practitioner'. To my regret, my own novels are not so celebrated that I can count on the reader knowing them: so I shall refer only incidentally to *The Plate Shop* and its successors. But there is an issue, which I find important in my practice, which I hope will provide a useful angle of general approach. The issue is that of movement.

The crucial point for me, in the writing of a novel, is that moment when the novel finds its movement. There are various 'findings' a novel requires – the nub of situation, the characters' voices, a particular 'flavour'. And one's draft can have these, but still want tension, direction, rhythm, the sense of a current, both fluid and electric, that draws the narrative and the reader on. But at a certain point, as one reworks and haunts the text, the novel finds its 'movement', its way of advancing, its pace but even more its 'gait'. It is partly a matter of economy and emphasis, of giving this and eliding that; and it is not a movement in a single line, rather a balance of 'contrary motions' (to use Sterne's phrase), a product of tensions, both a pushing and a pulling to resolve, or explode.

Novels after all are 'movies', they *were* the 'movies' before the 'movies' came. And if one looks from one's own novels, to the novel in general, one cannot, I think, fail to see the importance, for its success, of the whole movement of a novel, the rhythm and increment in its convergences, which in popular fiction is felt as 'pace', and in 'literary' fiction often follows the principle, which Italo Calvino celebrated, of *festina lente* – of hurrying slowly.[1]

This 'whole movement' is an impetus in the prose, a kinesis in the conflicts, an impulsion within the characters who often have an important want. But also, often, the movement is physical: geographical movement is important in fiction. It has been so in all fictions, in Gilgamesh, Homer, Virgil, in Dante's spiral through great cones. And again it has been important in the novel; witness the role, in shaping whole books, of questing journeys (*Don Quixote, Pickwick*), of outward journeys and journeys home (*Tom Jones, Joseph Andrews*), of journeys with a river, like *Huckleberry Finn*, or against the current, to a dark source (*The Heart of Darkness*), and more at large of voyages (in Defoe, Verne, Conrad, in Woolf, Hughes, Golding) and of vessels (most famously the *Pequod*). But even a novel with no physical or social movement at all – as in a Beckett monologue, where the 'hero' may be a cut-off trunk in a pot – still talks itself *forward*, with the impetus of unstoppable speech: I can't *go on*, I'll *go on*,' announces the voice of *The Unnamable*, attaining his last full stop (the first in many pages of tumultuous speech). For chiefly the movement and the travel is inner, the track of a Blakean mental traveller. The current is 'the current of the poet's imagination' (in Johnson's phrase). The movement is mental and emotional, for finally what is important is the connection between the felt 'movement' of the novel, and the reader's experience of being 'moved' – moved emotionally.

These remarks are very general, but, if one looks at famous novelists of the past, it is clear that a certain character of movement is part of their most intimate quiddity as authors – the relaxed, improvisatory unfolding of Stendhal, the accelerating oscillation of Dostoevsky. A distinctive movement is the signature of a novelist: which is not to say that the movement is the same in each novel, or the same at the beginning and at the end of a career, or that it is unrelated to those realities outside the fiction, which the fiction reflects. In a sense the work that novels do is to translate value into movement. To take the most patent example, in the old novel a certain sort of marriage – of man with woman, but also of property with charity, and of morality with fertility and beauty – is not explicitly preached and exhorted: rather, it is made the destination of a journey. Or journeying with no destination is the value, if one is Kerouac 'on the road'. Or the failing of values – like the lack of money (one of the potent motors of fiction) – translates into constant motion. It is a feature of Hardy's late novels, especially, that his characters are always unhappily in motion. And this seems the expression both of their social and their moral placelessness, and also of a bitter restlessness in Hardy himself, which finally carried him clear of the novel form entirely.

The question of 'movement' is, I believe, pertinent for all novels at all times: but certainly it is pertinent to the present period. The twentieth century as a whole has famously been associated with movement and with rapid movement: the age of the car, the plane, the missile; of jazz and quickstep; of the moving film; of headlong social change; and of refugees in numbers never known before. But fiction, in the first half of the century, did not notably travel further faster than it had in the nineteenth century: and in some ways experimental fiction and the *nouveau roman* worked to slow time, developing almost a rotary motion. But since the 1970s, there has been a preoccupation with motion and speed. Especially in the fabulatory, magic-realist novels, people travel and even fly, covering continents and periods of decades, while also travelling both in body and in spirit, along 'fast tracks' of metamorphosis. Many novels are road novels. The heroes of J. M. Coetzee, Paul Auster, John Banville, Martin Amis, Thomas Pynchon, are seldom still, either in place or in psyche: and in their novels language also flies, and technique shifts and rapidly evolves. We have a fiction of journeys, and technical journeying, alike in the novels of revivified fantasy, and in those in the most hard-bitten, realist mode: Naipaul circles Trinidad or traverses his 'Free State', Patrick White drives into iridescent desert. The heroes of Raymond Carver's stories regretfully move on. People 'change places' steadily, in fiction since 1970, possibly out of some deep homelessness, but also they are at home in movement: whereas the old novel, with all its internal circulation, frequently recurred to one city, one region.

It does therefore seem to me that movement is an issue now: and one that deserves discussion the more because the bent of our more scientific criticism has been to resolve the immediate movement of the text into tensile structures. Paul Ricoeur notes in *Time and Narrative* that 'the major tendency of modern theory . . . is to "dechronologize" narrative'.[2] Roland Barthes said in *The Structural Analysis of Narrative* that 'analysis today tends to "dechronologize" the narrative continuum and to "relogicize" it' and that 'the task is to succeed in giving a structural description of the chronological illusion'. Structures are there and important, but still one may also agree with Peter Brooks, when he says in *Reading for the Plot*:

> I am convinced that the study of narrative needs to move beyond the various formalist criticisms that have predominated in our time: formalisms that have taught us much, but which ultimately – as the later works of Barthes recognized – cannot deal with the dynamics of texts as actualized in the reading process.[3]

Peter Brooks speaks of the 'dynamics' and 'energetics' of texts, and refers also to the 'drives' and the 'motors' of narrative. The main motor of fiction he sees to be desire – he cites Susan Sontag's 'we need an erotics of art'. And it could be said that the more recent criticism, which stresses the role of desire in art, has connected literary theory to the prime motor of movement in human life itself. The difficulty with desire-theory is that a psychological construction may be placed on 'desire' which separates it from the kinds of desire we are normally capable of feeling. And Peter Brooks, as he develops his argument, comes to associate narrative 'desire' with the 'thanatos' concept of Freud – with the Death Wish. But is it really because of a Death Wish that we read books to the end? It is true there can be a fascination in a fiction circuitously approaching a death, but not all absorbed reading is a kind of vicarious dying.

This essay will try to tabulate some kinds of movement that may be identified, directly, in the reading process. Because it seems to me that movement is under-discussed, I shall first briefly try to resume the main forms of movement that have characterized the novel, as the form itself has moved from romances and old tales to be what it is today.

II

The dominant movement of the early novel was picaresque, a loose, rapid aggregation of episodes, prodigal with short-lived characters. This rhythm persisted through the eighteenth century, and dominates Fielding, even the elaborately planned *Tom Jones*. It is still there as the favoured locomotion of Smollett, long after the development of the epistolary novel – in the hands of Richardson above all – had allowed a more deeply breathing development. In Richardson's novels, with their powerful irregular epistolary rhythm, a mutual fascination builds incrementally towards its completion: marriage for Pamela, and marriage with her second lover, death for Clarissa.

Even after Jane Austen, whose novels move by scenes and stages, a little like an updated form of Shakespearean comedy, the picaresque movement remains robust. It is the starting style of Charles Dickens; and it is Dickens in his later novels – still working to the underlying, episodic beat – who develops the larger wonder of novel-movement, the integral coordination of many characters, and indeed several narratives, to serve a single, embracing theme. Where is there in fiction a more poetic and significant profusion than in the cornucopia outpouring at the opening of *Bleak House*? Its poetic fog, its Rowlandson lawyers all noses and wigs, the Lord Chancellor in his chambers as real as in Tolstoy, its lost young people, jaded aristocrats, *distrait* philanthropists, and the surreal Mr Krook in his warehouse of waste are all reflections of the reactionary, British 'dedlock'. But still it can seem, by the middle part of the novel, that beneath the active surface the imaginative current stagnates – a sense one may connect with the fact that each individual in it is actually of limited interest. At the end, Dickens depends on the contrivance of the hunt for Lady Dedlock to *mobilize* his closing chapters (the hunt or chase being another of the great motors of fiction, most notably for *Moby Dick*). If Dickens's late great novels suggest the power of an 'orchestral' movement, still we may feel a more satisfying movement would depend on the presence of lives with a larger, more complicated interior space.

Such lives are offered by George Eliot: and the unhurried momentum of her novels reflects the steady living forward of her more subtly understood personalities. The same is true – to range more widely – in the slow, big novels of Richardson and Proust. For what is remarkable about the truly long great novels is that their principal cast is very small: chiefly Clarissa and Lovelace in *Clarissa*, and Marcel, Swann and Charlus in Proust (for the beloveds are more phantasmal beings). It would be hard to overstate the primary importance, as the main motor principle that sustains massive fictions, of the merest handful of intricate personalities, involved in a close, absorbing relationship. What the longest novels, *Clarissa* and *A la recherche*, share, is the dominance of an obsessive love – and fascination with the intricacy of obsessing love – which brings us back again to the importance of *desire* for moving fictions.

At the same time, both *Clarissa* and *A la recherche* are tragic, with a darkness in their representation of love, so that they need to end in death. And without doubt, finally, the most powerful current in fiction has been the tragic current: the pull of the inescapable, the sense, that held ancient audiences rapt, that something inevitable and terrible is going, in an unpredictable way, to occur immediately before us. It was not to be supposed that an ever-more ambitious rising form like the novel would leave outside its endeavours tragic art, and in fact the history of the novel, up to about 1900, is the history of the steady growth of the tragic movement. Even *Don Quixote*, which began as a satire to the picaresque rhythm, moved finally into the tragic register; and Richardson conceived of *Clarissa* as a tragedy in acts. By the mid-nineteenth century, a novelist was likely, in a large, ambitious novel, to *include* a tragedy, and even the comedic Dickens does so: *David Copperfield* includes the tragedy of Steerforth, *Bleak House* the tragedy of Lady Dedlock, *Little Dorrit* the tragedy of Old Dorrit. Often, at the core of big novels, there is a double movement, with a benignly opening, productive story set beside a fated, closing life: as Dorothea's story is beside the tragic Lydgate in *Middlemarch*, Levin beside the tragic Anna in *Karenina*. This generous breadth, placing tragedy within a larger flow, is itself forsworn, at the century's end, as the novel finally becomes High Art, with the result that the most ambitious novels aim to be poetic and tragic throughout, as with Hardy, Meredith, James.

Without doubt the tragic movement was assisted by the development, through the mid-century, of a remorseless *causal* drive. For the novel was necessarily affected by the great change in mental perspective, which led many forms of discourse – historical and political as well as geological and biological – to trace minutely, in a linear logic, the determination of things. In the process the happy prodigality of the 'old' novel, where caricature eccentrics and idealized lovers rubbed shoulders with 'real' people, was subdued to the momentum of cause-and-effect. 'Characters' become more similar to each other, and more quotidian, living out their fates in the style – but it is especially a movement – we call 'realist'. The result, in George Eliot, is a rapt determinism of the moral life – I will show you how your soul works. It is this especially that gives her fiction its distinctive grave power of movement. A more social and 'mass' determinism is the engine of the novels of Zola. It may be symbolized by the 'train' of passion, a chain of cars running on rails, in novels of doomed adultery both by Zola and by others – *La Bête humaine, Dombey, Anna Karenina*.

At the end of the century, as enquiry works inward, there is a slowing, and a diversion from the 'linear' advance. In George Meredith, and even more in Henry James, sentences lengthen and complicate as the momentous and the subtle come to be equated, and in velleities of interrogation within closed chambers large moral weights invisibly shift. The author who most gives himself to the ever-slower and more tarrying hesitation is of course Marcel Proust, in whose coiling, retrospective art time may stop altogether, as a part of the past arrives, and expands to be coterminous with the present.

This rocking, eddying movement of Proust signals a change, in the relation of fiction to time. In Conrad the dislocation of time seems related to the bitter extent of his irony (his unironic fictions are smooth forward voyages). Or time may slow to slow-motion or a freeze-frame, while text proliferates laterally in the twenty-four hour novel: the minutely ticking clock of *Mrs Dalloway*, the enormous diurnal rotation of James Joyce's *Ulysses*.

For the great change in twentieth-century fiction has been in the degree of dissociation between the movement of the narrative and the movement of the action narrated. Of course there was always a distinction to be made, between the pace and itinerary of the narrating voice and the pace and the track of the imagined events, and not only

Sterne, but Smollett in *Humphrey Clinker* and Dickens in (again) *Bleak House*, develop complex movements of narrative that have quite a different shape from the lives of the protagonists. But clearly novelists have been interested in the twentieth century, more than previously, in the movement of narrative as something with a separate dynamic and rhythm, enhanced and charged by cuts and jumps from 'shot' to 'shot' in effects that Richard Pearce, in *The Novel in Motion*, has compared to 'montage' in the cinema.[4] The result can be a form of movement which may run athwart the movement of time. Especially in the French *nouveau roman* of the 1950s, the linear is replaced by incremental variations, repetitions and returns. Once out of time, the tendency is to music, and some of the novels of Claude Simon move like an intricate, rapid quartet, where motifs made from parts of a tragic experience are woven in a rhythmic unfolding pattern. The qualities of pace, strong linear narrative, accelerating 'gripping' action, were largely reserved to popular, lowbrow genres – thrillers, detective novels, science fiction.

And there was something transcendent in the escape from time in the *nouveau roman:* as if the novel itself attained a kind of Nirvana, an escape not only from time but from society. This was also the period in which there was most talk of the death of the novel. The movement not of novels, but of The Novel itself came into question. *Where*, after the *nouveau roman* could the novel go?

III

But time never stops, nor did the novel die. And in coming to the present period – the years since 1970 – it is time to consider, precisely, time. For the movement of the novel has brought it ever more to gaze into the face of Time. In mathematics, movement resolves into distance and time – which is two sorts of distance, in space and in time. Phenomenologically however we might regard movement as prior to time, since time is only known through some form of motion. Especially in fiction time is movement: we may think of novels as containing years, but also they are vehicles that cover years quickly. Time itself is often called a river, and it is hard not to think of time as an enormous invisible movement, or as a medium or current in which things move. Time has, for instance, a direction, a *forwardness*, and cannot ever go back, though still we are haunted by the thought that everything that has been in some way still is, and may, in strange moments, seem to revisit us.

In the world of art, especially, time is motion. Even still artworks move: we walk round statues and scan and build paintings. Some art forms depend on motion – the 'movies' do – but can still exist frozen, as in a 'still'. Yet other arts vanish if there is no motion: a note of music is moving air; it would not exist if the air could be paralysed. The novel is perhaps like a film – or, even more, a video – since we can only experience it by reading forward through it, though we also skim, or jump forward, or back. Also, like a film, there is a kind of double movement, since as we proceed through the narrative a sense of the whole trajectory collects.

Fundamentally the novel's interest in time is an interest in the deeper motion of life. Especially in the twentieth century, the novel has become an instrument with which to examine underlying movements. This was of course very much D. H. Lawrence's idea, achieved most dramatically in *The Rainbow*, where the protagonist is not Tom or Anna but the relation between them, swooping and curving in warring love, a little like those speeded-up films of sky, in which we see the clouds ferment. In more modest style, many twentieth-century novels have aimed to be life-shaped, novels of growing up, the first half of the pilgrimage, novels moving outward to an inderminate bright place, like Naipaul's *Mr Biswas* (1961) or David Storey's *Saville* (1973). The grief and wisdom of the twentieth century is that, though the journey starts so, there is no destination. Our further movement is to emptiness and loss, our larger journey ends in a void, and the recent years especially have seen the development of a bright-coloured, almost jaunty fiction, which records a lonely losing and fading. In Auster the losing movement has an elegiac beauty, with a slight Beckettian playful pedantry. In the novels of Peter Ackroyd the losing movements may be multiplied and coordinated, as for instance in *Chatterton* (1987), where in different periods Chatterton dies, Meredith's wife leaves him, the present-day hero succumbs to cancer. In J. M. Coetzee's *The Life and Times of Michael K.* (1983), Michael K. progressively reduces to a minimal, in some way blessed subsistence, lowering a bent teaspoon down a shaft for water – 'and in that way, he would say, one can live'. Perhaps these novels return to an ancient poetry, of the basic human sentences of mutability and mortality. But clearly also they embody a sense of the movement of life in our time – of a sad current under the urban jostling – and it is perhaps hard not to relate this movement to the isolation of these novels' protagonists, to the absence or thinness of the relationships round them. Frequently they are parentless and partnerless, childless too, bonded to no one and outside joint endeavours, while 'society' seems disintegrated and spectral. One might then think of their dying diminutions as the translation *into* movement of a social texture atomized and attenuated to the point where both the human community, and the person, fade. They achieve, as it were, a still, sad music of alienation.

In relation to Time, the most dominant of our movements has surely been the return to History. There are historical novels as such, like John Banville's brilliantly visualized novels about astronomers. That distinguished genre, the novel of classical history, practised by Robert Graves and Marguerite Yourcenar, has been revived with distinction by Alan Massie. Many contemporary novels include historical narratives alongside the present-day ones, of which the best-known and best is perhaps A. S. Byatt's *Possession* (1990), others are Peter Ackroyd's *Hawksmoor* (1985) and *Chatterton* (1987). But also the whole movement associated with the term Magic Realism has largely been a matter of Magical Historical Realism. The forerunner, Günter Grass's *Tin Drum* (1959), was a part-fantastic take on Hitler's Third Reich. Marquez's *Hundred Years of Solitude* (1967) was one hundred years of fantasy history. Salman Rushdie's *Midnight's Children* (1981) is early twentieth-century history, as also is the great American fabulatory fantasy, Thomas Pynchon's *Gravity's Rainbow* (1973).

Thus, even at its most fabulatory and fantastic, fiction in recent decades has chosen often to synchronize its movement with the huge forward linearity of history. Indeed, in a number of novels, the *significant* movement is that of history, while individual lives zigzag aimlessly, at the mercy of the greater currents. And this perhaps chimes with the modern sense of fate: for seeing history as fate is another way, for us, of seeing politics to be fate. A large change that has occurred over the century, in the more philosophical kind of fiction, is that, whereas in the existential novels of Sartre, Camus and Beckett the individual was perceived to hang in a void, in our fiction the individual is rather a moving atom in history (which may, again, be of dark or no meaning).

One might argue that, for many novels, History has replaced Society, as the context within which novels live. This change can give novels a larger dynamic: they are small movements within a great sweep of movement, rather than disturbances within the static medium of Society. The other side of this argument would be that 'history', in our novels, is researched and imagined, not experienced, and thus cannot have the density of life of a 'society' known shrewdly through and through.

Most characteristic of contemporary attitudes is the 'split-time' novel, set in two or even more historical periods – but normally one is the present day – where the narrative movement of the novel as a whole is a weaving or plaiting of different narratives – as it were a meta-movement, or movement of movements, placing two histories in a

Greater History. The principal examples are A. S. Byatt's *Possession* of 1990, and the split-time novels of Peter Ackroyd, set in two periods in the case of *Hawksmoor* (1985) and in three in *Chatterton* (1987). Barry Unsworth's *Stone Virgin* of 1985 is also in three periods, as is Alan Garner's *Red Shift* (for younger readers). Both the novel, and film, version of Ruth Prawer Jhabvala's *Heat and Dust* (1975) were set in two separate decades of twentieth-century India. A theatrical analogue to these is Tom Stoppard's *Indian Ink* (1995), and he had earlier set his *Arcadia* (1993) both in the Romantic period and in the present day. A verse analogue is Geoffrey Hill's set of poems in prose, *Mercian Hymns* (1971), juxtaposing the Mercian rule of Offa with the poet's contemporary and family experience. Other novels of some relevance are Thomas Pynchon's *V* of 1963, which has some chapters set in earlier years of the present century; Graham Swift's *Waterland* (1983), which slides back and forth between the present and several pasts; Julian Barnes's *Flaubert's Parrot* (1984), which moves between a scholar's trip in the present and the historic Flaubert's life and travels; Michael Ondaatje's *The English Patient* (1992), which moves between wartime Italy and a pre-war Cairo-based group of desert cartographers, who cooperate happily though of different nationalities. I imagine the reader will easily think of other split-time or many-time novels – and perhaps films – which I have omitted.

One is wary of generalizing about a phenomenon which will have different values for different practitioners. A more particular point about these split-time novels is that it is passion, passionate acts, and especially passionate love – things that might seem the heart of life – that are located in history (as the tragic love affairs are in *Possession*, *The English Patient*, *Heat and Dust* and the play *Indian Ink*). The effect of this relocation of passion further off is to dissociate the movement of the novel from the movement of the passion itself, which an earlier school of fiction would have endeavoured to follow closely. At the same time, this passion in the past seems not something behind us, but something which we are groping towards: it is in the fictional past, but in the reader's futurity, so that even after the last page we are still piecing together the tragedy. Which is perhaps to say that History, in these novels, may after all also be, as in older literature, the realm of Romance and Tragedy. One could thus see the split-time novel as practising a marriage of the novelistic (for the novel, as a form, is still associated mainly with its own present time, however many historical novels there may be) with the romantic and the tragic. It is precisely this contrast that A. S. Byatt develops in *Possession*, where the intense passion, and tragic loss of it, are located in a past brought vividly into the present, partly with the aid of tragedy's traditional language, poetry – for the two lovers are two different kinds of poet, as it were Robert Browning in love with a poet made half-and-half of Emily Dickinson and Christina Rossetti. Byatt has been criticized for offering, as novelist, to write the poetry of poets of genius: but the body of poetry given in the novel is small, and the point is rather that verse is one among a variety of different modes and resources – imaginary letters, fairy tales, journal entries – which separate the 'past' passages from the straightforward narrative of the present day, and work together to construct a more charged, and genuinely more poetic, mode in which to render passion and loss. And a poetic intensity is certainly achieved in Byatt's prose, for instance in the passage where the woman poet and her companion imagine their house haunted and prowled round by a menacing masculine animal.

Putting aside, however, the question of double and multiple time, the great figure, in the relation since 1970 of movement and fiction and history, must be the American novelist Thomas Pynchon, whose *Gravity's Rainbow*, in 1973, signalled at the start of our period, a change in innovative fiction from the relatively enclosed involutions of the New Novel to a fiction of massively energetic flight, a fiction soaring and diving in both local and enormous arcs of movement, geographically spanning Europe and Africa with an eye at times towards both Asia and West-Coast America; historically superimposing on the close of the Second World War the greater bomb fears of the nuclear decades, with a backward eye also to much of world history, especially Western colonial history; its large cast kept spinning in constant hurry, farcical, tragic, fantastical, in a prose that is now supple poetry, now comic-strip burlesque, now social detail and now an exuberant-preposterous flight to the limits of celestial or scatological fantasy: a novel of colossal dynamic, which for all its exuberant push beyond all known forms of limit is no mere rumbustious carnival, since all its arcs of misadventure, intrigue and fantasy end both accelerating and breaking towards death. Its title gives its theme: the curve followed by all ascending machines (including civilizations), as they span the sky splendidly but gravitate to destruction, a fate shared with the novel's hero, who in the latter part 'scatters' and disappears. Pynchon's central metaphor of the rocket gives him a way of investing the process he sees occurring generally – the process of entropy, of dissipating, of running down – with an accelerating speed. In the run of broken short sections that close the novel, narrative splinters while themes converge, and past Germany and present America unite, as the rocket, grown now from a V2 to a ballistic missile to the rocket of humanity's end, accelerating to a speed of a mile a second, heading for the old cinema of the novel and its readers, reaches the last split-second before impact: which Pynchon leaves in a freeze-frame as an image for eternity. More signally than any other novelist writing since 1970, he has found a new movement in fiction.

It is a novel that can sum up the whole new launch of fantastic, exuberant, fabulatory fiction that came in the late 1960s and early 1970s, with the complicating paradox that all the movements of the novel are presented by its author as disintegrative and death-bent, and indeed this huge arching novel seemed not to launch its author on any sort of productive arc, since it was followed by nothing new until *Vineland* in 1990. *Gravity's Rainbow* can thus represent both the large impulsion in innovative fiction since 1970 and also the attendant question mark, as to where the new flight was heading. And that question has been sharpened and perhaps answered by the appearance in 1997 of an equally extensive historical novel, which shows us where after all Pynchon has been travelling, *Mason and Dixon*. It is, even more, a novel of both history and movement, since it traces the lives of the two British astronomers who travelled to the ends of the earth to observe the pattern of the heavens, before travelling to America to rule a dividing line in history.

Mason and Dixon shows, moreover, that Pynchon's view has, over the years, become more subtle and more benign. But a more complex understanding of life does not necessarily translate into a clear forward impulse of fiction: and one might criticize *Mason and Dixon*, for all its exhaustive research and craft, as being governed by an impulse intricately to turn back on itself. Where the prose of *Gravity's Rainbow* is precipitate, projective, the prose of *Mason and Dixon* is oddly verbless, with a pausing, eddying, recurring swirl. From *Gravity's Rainbow*:

> But out at the horizon, out near the burnished edge of the world, who are these visitors standing . . . these robed figures – perhaps, at this distance, hundreds of miles tall – their faces serene, unattached, like the Buddha's, bending over the sea, impassive indeed, as the Angel that stood over Lübeck during the Palm Sunday raid, come that day neither to destroy nor to protect, but to bear witness to a game of seduction.[5]

At the level of the sentence, movement in Pynchon's fiction often involves a syntactical slippage, whereby, through a coil of clauses, the subject and the dominant verb are replaced and maybe replaced again. But the windings also tease forward the reader's curiosity, and are perhaps the very form of 'hurrying slowly' at the level of the sentence. And from *Mason and Dixon*:

Believing he has walked away from the Cape and successfully not looked back, to see what Plutonian wife, in what thin garment, may after all have follow'd, – tho' none of them is anyone's Eurydice, he knows well enough who that is, – or would be, were he Orpheus enough to carry a tune in a Bucket, – Mason continues to wonder, how Dixon has brought himself to turn, and then, to appearance imperturbable as a Clam, go back in, – back to Jet, Greet, Els, Austra, Johanna, the unsunn'd Skins, the Ovine Aromas, the Traffick to and from the Medicine-Cabinet at all hours, the Whispering in the Corners, the never-ending Intrigues, – whilst coiled behind all gazes the great Worm of Slavery.[6]

There is again the slippage, as the subject, who for some lines seems to be Mason, seems liable after all to prove to be Dixon, only to be replaced in the last six words by 'the great Worm of Slavery'. As writing it is surreal, poetic, 'special', but the sentence changes course repeatedly, and though it ends with the strong surprise of Slavery, it is hard to follow on a first reading. And it seems to me that most of *Mason and Dixon* is like this, and is so again at the level of the sentence, the paragraph, the chapter, and the 'Part'. There is so much careful *lente* that *festina* is lost. In other words, though it is a wonderful book – a book full with wonders – it is liable, I suspect, not always to be finished, since it lacks what *Gravity's Rainbow* had in so many sorts, and at all levels. It lacks something novels have to have. It lacks movement.

IV

In discussing modern novels moved by history, I have not meant to suggest that their way of moving is *the* way of moving in fiction now, or that any one form of movement is. We want novelists to be different from each other, and the novel at any time has many movements. There is the further complication that movements, in the modern novel, are especially numerous. The novel has existed for three centuries now (at least), and it seems that no active impetus of fiction is ever wholly superseded. Through the century, and through recent decades, the diverse progressions of picaresque, of the slow incremental *Bildungsroman*, of the converging accelerating tragedy, of the ironic novel stepping forward like a subtle well-made play – these may all be found, each bearing a new inflection for our times, but also moving with an ancient impulsion. The expansive, fabulating magical novel may extend encyclo-paedically, satirically, incorporating rhythms one could trace back to Rabelais. And while some big 'magic' novels may have moved most noisily, the most formidable form of advancing has perhaps all the time been the vigilant, unkind-eyed, penetrating tracking of nearly soulless modern living in the 'realist' fiction of the early 1970s – in Patrick White (*The Vivisector*, 1970), V. S. Naipaul (*Guerrillas*, 1975), David Storey (*A Temporary Life*, 1973). It is a movement recovered again in the recent, less experimental fiction of Walter Abish (*Eclipse Fever*, 1993).

Categories apart, I wanted to examine more closely the movements of two novelists. The first is Don DeLillo, whose *White Noise* (1984), a novel in the 'campus' genre, is an unusually harsh and penetrating satire. Its hero is a mediocre academic, Jack Gladney, who resolves to revive his flagging career by founding a school of Hitler Studies: and the novel proceeds to contemplate, in various more contemporary forms, the entry of death into life.

The second section ('The Airborne Toxic Event') is the turning to narrative of an eco-disaster, as what seems a relatively minor spillage in the goods yards develops, in a surreal or nightmarish way, into a vast carcinogenic cloud, 'a roiling bloated slug-shaped mass'. The chapter proceeds according to the advance, changing with the veering wind, of the toxic cloud across the country; and at the same time according to hectic human movements. There is the hurry of panic and flight, which often turns in circles, and in the end makes slow advances, stuck in a gridlocked exodus of cars. The emergency services both race with stretchers, and, clad 'in bright yellow Mylex suits . . . moved slowly through the luminous haze'. But especially there is verbal and linguistic movement. In the emergency announcements, the toxic spillage itself is lifted through an escalation of euphemisms. It is first 'a feathery plume', then a 'a shapeless growing thing', then 'a black billowing cloud', till finally it is upgraded to 'an airborne toxic event'. Instructions to the populace come in an alien officialese no-speak, 'Abandon all domiciles. Now, now. Toxic event, chem-ical cloud.' The talk of Gladney's family spins through crazy loops at repartee-speed, and is itself unpredictably interrupted by media messages – 'The radio said: "It's the rainbow hologram that gives this credit card a marketing intrigue" ' – and by excursions into the paranormal, and indeed the whole gamut of cult, health and after-life lunacies. The touch stays light and quick, even in its closest encounter with death, when Jack is told by a medic he has suffered 'actual skin and orifice contact' with the cloud: ' "Am I going to die?" "Not as such," he said.' All the time the cloud and people are following tracks which, at the last, intersect:

Through the stark trees we saw it . . . immense almost beyond compre-
hension . . . It seemed to be generating its own inner storms. There were
cracklings and sputterings, flashes of light, long looping streaks of chem-
ical flame. . . . The helicopters throbbed like giant appliances . . . It moved
horrible and sluglike through the night.[7]

Which visually is an image of the chapter too, with its gradual gathering of alarm and its turbid frightened flow, its sparks and loops of
wit and satire, all returning to a poetry of death, with an aptness as
nemesis for the guru of Hitler studies.

The chapter is an incident, not the climax of the novel: there is a
further, more intimate nemesis for Jack. In the novel's long third section, 'Dylarama', it transpires that his wife Babette has been having an
affair with the man who has been supplying her with the 'Dylar' capsules on which she now is hooked. 'Dylar' is the product of a secret
group which was 'working on the fear of death . . . trying to perfect a
medication'. In a dingy motel room, his Zumwalt revolver in his hand,
Jack creeps up on the supplier, Willie Mink. Jack is acceleratedly aware
of each 'move' he makes – 'I was advancing in consciousness. I watched
myself take each separate step.' He discerns a figure, slumped in the
flickering glare of the television: 'Information rushed toward me, rushed
slowly, incrementally.' That precisely, is the movement of the chapter
– the movement of human consciousness in crisis, a vast slow rushing,
with much of the feel of those passages in films where a rapid and
crucial action is shown in extreme slow-motion, partly to express the
importance of these movements, and partly to represent the way that,
in a crisis, perception itself races so events seem to drag. We are at
once at the quick, and at the slow, of human awareness. As they talk
crazily, Mink throws capsules in the direction of his mouth, till Jack
shoots him, and, in the hallucinatory flicker from the television, watches
the blood inscribe 'a delicate arc'. Still with visionary slowness, he
puts the gun in Mink's hand to make it seem he killed himself – and
Mink comes round, and shoots him. At this point both men somewhat
wake, and, with a different form of slowness, help each other to Jack's
car. At the hospital, Jack tells the attendant nun, ' "We're shot." "We
see a lot of that here," she answered matter-of-factly.' What the chapter has achieved, none the less, in the flickering strobe of its sound-off
telly, is a hectically slow-motion modern *danse macabre*. The novel as
a whole shows the power of Calvino's motto – Hurry Slowly – which
is an apt motto too for the movement of death through life.

The other work whose movement I wanted to signal is the *Regeneration* trilogy by Pat Barker. I concentrate on the third, Booker-
winning novel, *The Ghost Road* (1995), because the main movements

in it are exceptionally distinct. The trilogy is concerned with those soldiers suffering shell-shock in the First World War, who were treated by the doctor-anthropologist W. H. R. Rivers: the patients described include Siegfried Sassoon and Wilfred Owen, but the principal patient is a fictional figure called Billy Prior, a dashing and partly bisexual man whose sensibility may strike us as being somewhat contemporary. His crises have been extreme, but in *The Ghost Road* he does resolve to return to the front. The war is very near its end, and for many of its pages the novel's movement is coordinated with Billy Prior's journey across France, to catch up with the Allied army, which itself is now advancing through the German lines. Prior's life hangs on the question of whether he will reach the army, or the war will reach its end, first. The other movement in the novel concerns Rivers himself, who is moving across a moral terrain – one of the ironies of the novels, to the modern reader, has been the fact that Rivers, who is so patient and helpful in dealing with the minds most damaged by war, has himself so far believed in the war. He becomes ever less able to do so. But also he is remembering his years as a young anthropologist, long before the war, in Papua New Guinea, when he was studying a tribe of headhunters. In successive excerpts we follow his journey to a central shrine or Skull House, accompanied by the witch doctor-chief Njiru: and this also is a mental journey. The headhunters have been prohibited by the British colonial authorities from their traditional lifelong habit of waging war, not for territory but for honour. And what Rivers comes to see is that the tribe is suffering, indeed is dying, and dying in its psyche, from this infliction of peace. Life expectancy has shrunk, and couples are not marrying, or are having fewer or no children. They are deeply demoralized, from the loss of the pursuit that for them gave life meaning. The novel examines the complexities of war: as, in 'the present', it records both the unbearableness of trench conditions and also the compulsion of soldiers to return to them. Billy Prior finds he *wants* not to miss the final assault, even though he knows he is almost certain to be killed.

Rivers, in Papua New Guinea, arrives at the Skull House, and clambers into the pitch-dark interior cavern, where he drops his torch, 'then the walls lifted off and came towards them'. The cavern is solid with bats. 'The cave mouth disgorged fleeing human beings; behind them the bats streamed out in a dark cloud that furled over on to itself as it rose, like blood flowing from a wound under water.' Inevitably, in the context, one connects this unfurling cloud of bats with the lost lives, ghosts, the countless dead, both of the headhunters' wars, and of war. And in 'the present', in his hospital, Rivers is attending the horribly long-drawn-out death of a young man catastrophically wounded in the head. His gathered family cannot help praying for him to die. He keeps repeating a word they cannot understand, 'Shotvarfet', till Rivers realizes 'He's saying, "It's not worth it."'

'"Oh, it is worth it, it is," Major Hallet said, gripping his son's hand.' It is not a claim that Rivers, at this point, can assent to.

In the meantime Billy Prior's company, the Manchesters, have attacked, standing little chance. 'He saw Kirk die. He saw Owen die, his body lifted off the ground by bullets, describing a slow arc in the air as it fell. It seemed to take for ever to fall, and Prior's consciousness fluttered down with it.' Movement at the crucial point is physical movement, *and* inner, psychic movement: for this final curve, in the novel's many movements and maneouvres of war, is the declining curve of Prior's own life, as he dies also.

In the hospital ward, at dawn, following Hallet's death, Rivers, trying to stay awake, sees briefly an apparition:

> And there, suddenly, not separate from the ward, not in any way ghostly . . . but himself in every particular, advancing down the ward . . . came Njiru.
> *There is an end of men, an end of chiefs . . . then go down and depart. Do not yearn for us, the fingerless, the crippled, the broken. Go down and depart, oh, oh, oh.*
> He bent over Rivers, staring into his face with those piercing hooded eyes. A long moment, and then the brown face, with its streaks of lime, faded into the light of the daytime ward.

In these final movements the past comes to meet the present, the other war-world enters Rivers's war-world, and the arrival of the witch doctor is a reunion and a parting, and a lamentation and a benediction: *Requiescant in pace.* It is certainly 'moving', but I hope I may also have suggested, even in summary, how this powerful novel depends on different, coordinated movements, which converge with intense cumulative poignancy at the close. It is of the effect that Njiru does not simply appear, but *advances, comes* to meet Rivers, and joining him departs and disappears.

Movement in space, when recorded in fiction, is almost invariably both psychological and symbolic, a passage from state to state as well as from place to place. And, on the psychological level, no novel is still. Writing advances: a novel is not an epigram. The final question, perhaps, is to what extent movement is also inward, carrying us to the heart of issues of death and love, where one feels one attends at a final realization, a movement forward of human spirit, even if this is at last a kind of illumined turning to the dark.

V

There is a further form of movement I have not so far discussed, because it is to be found in very few works: but they are some of the most distinguished and original novels. It might be designated 'formal movement'. For there are certain novels where the conventions the novel has proposed for itself undergo radical alteration as the novel advances. The great prototype is James Joyce's *Ulysses*, where successive chapters may be written in substantially different techniques and styles. Operating at a more local level, there are the 'cut-up' novels of William Burroughs, which jump abruptly from narrative to narrative within a paragraph (for present purposes, I am treating successive jumps as amounting to movement, rather as successive frames make movement in film). A notable instance in the mid-1960s was John Fowles's *The Magus* (1966), which continually changes genre, and imagined level of literary 'reality', as the strange events on the island come to be explained by almost one thousand and one different stories, which also are different *kinds* of story. In a more basic way, one might include change of tense, change of person, and change of narrator, though change in this area often has only two or three possibilities to shuttle between, and there is no great gain in calling these changes 'movement'. The term 'movement' seems more appropriate to a work such as *Ulysses*, which might be said to be progressively moving, through its stylistic metamorphoses, towards more audaciously 'different' languages, culminating in the unpunctuated monologue of Mollie. Burroughs and Fowles – and Italo Calvino, in his novel made of beginnings, *If on a Winter's Night a Traveller* (1981) – might similarly be said to have covered a technical and formal distance between the beginning and the end of their novels, in a way that is unusual in the form, and exhilarating. Another case would be Walter Abish's early fiction, notably *Alphabetical Africa* (1974), which begins its narrative using only words beginning with 'a', then 'a' and 'b', until the full alphabet is available; and then reverses the process, shrinking back again to the confinement of 'a' words.

I have not discussed formal movement more extendedly because the great cases of it are so remarkable and particular that generalization is perilous (and the instances already given are clearly very different from each other). It is also true that the use of the term 'movement' in this context is somewhat metaphorical. But still there is a taste in contemporary fiction for a novel which, as it progresses, seems also in some way to become a different *kind* of novel. The novels of Paul Auster, which in any case travel often from region to region, are likely to be of this nature. In closing a discussion of movement in the novel, it may be apt to end with a form of movement that is especially open, and open especially to difference.

One further postscript: having mentioned my own novels at the start, I should perhaps not close without making some attempt to say where I see them figuring, among these many movements. I shall do this briefly.

My first novel, *The Plate Shop* (1979), was in part based on my experience of several temporary jobs in an engineering works, and certainly it incorporates some events there that 'made an impression' – the unjustified sacking of a not English worker, insufficiently supported by his union; an industrial accident; the decision of an ageing disabled worker in the drawing stores to go on strike. In the form it finally took (after the many rewritings that can attend a first novel), the book moves from person to person, both outwards through the workshops to paint shop and foundry, and upwards through the factory's hierarchy, through the white-collar offices and managerial types, to a summit that proves to be an empty place, with disaster (asset-stripping) pending. But still it constantly returns to the central figure, the foreman of the plate shop, Edward Clyde, who has come over the years to be something like a father to both men and machines. There are narratives within narratives like wheels within wheels, and maybe the novel itself has features of a big live machine (though a point of the book is that, where men work with machines, it is not so much that the men become mechanical, as that the machines develop kinds of personality). I suppose I see the movements of grief and anger given stress, and counterpointed, by the movements of machinery in the workshop – an enormous weigh hopper hovering slowly into sunlight, or the overhead crane returning, with the hand of its hook hanging loosely down.

Something of the machine idea carried into my second novel, *Coup d'Etat* (1985), which is set in Greece through the seven-year period of the colonels' dictatorship (1967–74). The novel chiefly tells the story of members of an extended family – politically extended and divided, as Greek families often are – caught in one of those periods that recur in history, when life in a country comes to move like a grim machinery, cog turning cog inescapably on. The recent development of the Yugoslav break-up had something of this feel, of cruel wheels turning in a process which was both unpredictable and inescapable, and which *must* proceed onwards, with a kind of fatality in its movements. The Greek dictatorship was not so catastrophic, but it affected the course of many lives. Various characters in the book have their own coups, and falls, and there is some sense, I hope, of successively rising personal waves, within the big graph of the Junta's rise and rise and smash.

Other lives follow other lines entirely, some sublimely indifferent to politics: there are many 'contrary motions', and actually the happy solution for the country is an unhappy solution for the lovers in the book, who have followed their own curve in the shadow of the Junta, but would not have been together had there been no coup d'état. Not that the movement of the book is smooth. It is surprises that ring true which give fiction an impetus, and make the movement broader while it advances. And it is the unpredictable way in which the inexorable occurs that enables terrible events to hold one rapt. But I must leave it to the occasional reader, who may yet venture into this novel, to see whether it has surprises of this character.

In the case of my third novel, *The Legend of Captain Space* (1990), it will, I think, be pretty clear to the reader what kind of correlation I have wanted between the elliptical prose and the contrasted 'fast tracks' the separating husband and wife are on. He is in long-distance haulage driving, slowly moving nearer to his dearest wish, the racing-circuit, she turns on the momentous mill-wheel of London, while also following a longer loop, to return to the child from whom she has run away. I suppose I felt that behind their restlessness there was a national restlessness, soul-searching in a world that has made soul hard to find.

The novel I am at the present time completing – and of which a chapter has appeared in *New Writing*, 6 (1997) – is to some extent another split-time novel, though one working through distinctly visual means. A present-day painter crosses a divided emotional terrain, while working on a suite of prints, which follow Rubens in his journey to England, in 1629–30, when he believed he could make peace among the nations. But Rubens's journey too will bring him back to questions of marriage. Whether I can truly find a fresh locomotion, between the times and themes, is all undecided at this instant; but I may perhaps say that I do in this novel make my own attempt at formal movement, to see not only through changing eyes and in changing light, but through successively different kinds of eyes. I know this statement may not be clear, but still I hope it may be fit to end this disquisition on the movement of a literary form which is itself in mid-flight, progressing we know not where, to close with a freeze-frame of an author turning from the critical task to attempt, in all uncertainty, to remount, and seek to spur, his unfinished novel heading . . .

Notes

1 Italo Calvino discusses 'Quickness' (and slow quickness) in the second of his *Six Memos for the Next Millennium*, trans. Patrick Creagh (London: Cape, 1992).

2 Paul Ricoeur, *Time and Narrative* (Chicago: University of Chicago Press, 1984), vol. 1, p. 30. For Ricoeur's discussion of Barthes on the subject see ibid., vol. 2, pp. 31ff.

3 Peter Brooks, *Reading for the Plot* (Oxford: Clarendon Press, 1984), pp. 35–6.

4 Richard Pearce distinguishes extendedly and subtly 'the novel of motion' (the novel recording physical travel) and 'the novel in motion' (the novel of moving point of view); see esp. *The Novel in Motion* (Columbus, Ohio: Ohio University Press, 1983), pp. 3–10.

5 Thomas Pynchon, *Gravity's Rainbow* (1973; London: Picador, 1975), pp. 214–15.

6 Thomas Pynchon, *Mason and Dixon* (London: Cape, 1997), ch. 14, p. 147).

7 Don De Lillo, *White Noise* (New York: Viking, 1984), p. 157.

Part II

Key Texts and Authors

5 The Dissident Imagination: Beckett's Late Prose Fiction

Drew Milne

More than any other writing of the second half of the twentieth century Samuel Beckett's writing embodies the fate of fiction. His developing critical reputation was publicly recognized by the award of the Nobel Prize in 1969, but the works he wrote from 1970 till his death in 1989 do not so much attract as repel the resulting glare of publicity. Instead, these works find new and distinctive ways of reworking the ends of fiction reached in his earlier works. The internal consistency in Beckett's work is remarkably resistant to conventional modes of reading and criticism. Written in both French and English, his fictional worlds resist assimilation within conventions of narrative, and resist contextualization within the cultural or national interests of Irish, French or English writing. Beckett's refusal to participate in the culture industry of self-promotion also made him a very public example of the private writer, an iconic figure of the dissident imagination. This essay introduces some ways of reading Beckett's late prose by exploring how the negativity integral to his prose fiction affords not an insistent nihilism of 'lessness', but a sustained articulation of the dissident imagination.

The difficulty is to specify how Beckett's dissidence sustains its aesthetic autonomy as a determinate negation of the society which it is mediated by. The estrangement of his later work from the conventions of realism involves a marked absence of reference to contemporary society, almost as if capitalist relations of production were taboo, subject to the secular aesthetic of an image ban. With a playful imagination which cannot quite free itself from the compulsion to go on with its work, the writing registers estrangements from work, sexuality, language and national identity: estrangements Beckett experienced in his 'own' life. His writing, however, reflects such structures of experiences not as private properties, but as fictions shaped by narrative structures such as the fictions of biography and autobiography.

Beckett's earlier trilogy of novels – *Molloy, Malone Dies* and *The Unnamable* – appeared to bring such resources of fiction to an implacable impasse. *The Unnamable* concludes: 'in the silence you don't know, you must go on, I can't go on, I'll go on.'[1] This restless movement through silence, ignorance and pronouns ends on a resolution to continue. But the text stops where it says it will not, without naming either the agency which impels the narrative voice to speak, or that which allows it to stop. Minimal conditions for the development of fictional narrative seem unreconciled but exhausted. The inability to stay put, forced to go on while saying no, motivates Beckett's subsequent prose fiction. The final words of *Worstward Ho* (1983) – 'Said nohow on'[2] – provide the title for Beckett's late trilogy *Nohow On* (1989). In this prose-scape of 'no' and 'on', 'nohow on' plays on the denial of 'know-how' as the 'no' which nevertheless goes 'on'. 'On', the flip side of 'no', is a command to 'go on' simultaneously imagined as a description of a journey which knows no 'how' to get on with.

The exploration of this narrative terrain forms a continuous and reflexively self-cancelling oeuvre. On such famished and slender means, however, it would seem that Beckett's writing can offer little but an autopsy on the ends of fiction, a post mortem inquiry into abstracted formal conditions rather than an exploration of the social conditions which prompt such fictions. Fiction in denial, it might be said, is the enemy of imagination. But the process of denial in Beckett's writing is not static. Each new work works itself out of the impasse of the preceding work, developing word and sentence anew. As *Texts for Nothing* puts it: 'No, something better must be found, a better reason, for this to stop, another word, a better idea, to put in the negative, a new no, to cancel all the others, all the old noes . . . '[3] Each new work tries to free itself from the tyranny of its precedents and its place within Beckett's oeuvre, recognizing fiction's lies and 'the screaming silence of no's knife in yes's wound'.[4] Negativity is developed not as an abstract problem with narrative as such, but as a question of particular words, stories, memories and imaginings. Beckett's late prose fiction is constituted by this tension between his oeuvre and the autonomy of word and imagination.

Beckett was pressed by publishers to cash in on the publicity generated by the Nobel Prize; the first new prose text which he allowed to be published in English was *Lessness* (1970). Beckett's blurb describes *Lessness* as having:

to do with the collapse of such refuge as that last attempted in *Ping* and with the ensuing situation of the refugee. Ruin, exposure, wilderness, mindlessness, past and future denied and affirmed, are the categories, formally distinguishable, through which the writing winds, first in one disorder, then in another.[5]

Ping was written after *Texts for Nothing*, part of a series of short prose texts including *Lessness, All Strange Away* and *Imagination Dead Imagine*, the longest of which is *The Lost Ones* (1972).[6] These texts offer curtailed, almost clinically estranged descriptions of places which lack stable social identities. As if to compensate, *The Lost Ones* has been likened to a report by a Civil Service commission into the conditions in Purgatory.[7] Peopled only with traces, memories and images, however, the text offers few indications as to the social identity of the narrator afflicted by this civil commission, afflicted, indeed, to the point of incivility. Resources of narrative appear rather, as the blurb for *Lessness* suggests, in states of disorder.

The situation of these texts is briefly summarized in the phrase 'imagination dead imagine', the title of one of the prose pieces and the opening words of *All Strange Away*. The phrase offers a negative loop of language, strung out once more from the possibility of imagining the death of imagination. The force of 'imagine' offers either an exclamation of disbelief; or an imperative to imagine again whose source seems unnamable; or a lament for imagination's death in a rhetorical question: imagination is dead, can you imagine it? The prose moves on from such minimal conditions, turning back on its scant resources to find new imperatives and exclamations of disbelief. *Ping* concludes:

> Light heat all known all white heart breath no sound. Head haught eyes white fixed front old ping last murmur one second perhaps not alone eye unlustrous black and white half closed long lashes imploring ping silence ping over.[8]

This is perhaps Beckett's most uncompromisingly lifeless and unpeopled mode. Little but the bones of syntax remain to articulate a destructured world of imagined figures. The agency which holds the head 'haught' seems not to be haughty. It is described as if the head does not hold itself high, but is held aloft by some other force. The name 'ping' might name a trace character, echoing the estranged and abbreviated casts of names in Beckett's other works. More simply, 'ping' might indicate the carriage return of a typewriter. Character and writing resist each other in the non-identity of a name which seems to name and unname the unspeakable. Amid the unspeakable, however, it is still possible to make out the image of a head held high against the surrounding white noise.

The image of a human figure's last ditch resistance to the forces commanding submission could be traced in Beckett's plays from the figure of Lucky in *Waiting for Godot* to the figure of the Protagonist in *Catastrophe*.[9] This image recurs in the late prose, but *Ping* affords one of its least recognizably human incarnations. In the phrase 'perhaps not alone', 'perhaps' reflexively corrects any tenuous impression of a known totality of isolation. The semantic ambiguity of the agency which directs the lashes suggests that even eyelashes may command a reflex action rather than implore. The lash of the eye whips seeing, and here reading, into further restless motion. Silence is then an effect both of the end of this restless movement of words and of the cessation of seeing and reading. Breathless writing is brought into awkward proximity with the speech it purports to represent, even if writing has become almost mindless. The imagined death of imagination struggles on to investigate imagination's conditions, an investigation which is Beckett's most challenging mode of aesthetic dissidence.

Beckett's reference to the refuge last attempted in *Ping* is, then, no simple recommendation to pursue. It is hard to imagine an eager consumer charmed by such an introduction. Beckett's blurb begins to operate as a negative allegory of the inflated shop talk of book promotion. Two important principles emerge. On the one hand, these short pieces presuppose each other and ask for careful reading of Beckett's work as a consciously developed oeuvre. On the other hand, the relation between refuge and refugee is offered, amid categories of ruin, as a formal parameter within which to explore these texts. Seeking refuge, these texts are at home in the homelessness of language. The word 'refuge', for example, does not appear in *Ping*, and it requires some imagination to see how *Ping* could be read as though it were an attempt to construct a refuge. But it is just such an imagination the writing asks for. The reader, like the writing, winds first in one disorder, then in another, becoming a refugee in search of refuge from wilderness and mindlessness.

Beckett's prose can be read, accordingly, as a search for refuge in an imagined space of writing, writing which tries to resist its own violence and negativity to protect a head held aloft in writing. These texts could then be read as testaments of the imagination in flight from unspecified dreads and griefs. What are the motives and conditions of the refugee status of the imagination? What is the imagination in flight from? *Lessness* takes up the theme of refuge in its opening line: 'Ruins true refuge long last towards which so many false time out of mind.'[10] Sense can be made by supplying words, as if the sentence were a stenographically abbreviated version of a badly dictated longer sentence. But reconstructions involve a reader in hope for a refuge in meaning which the sentence itself appears to forsake. Beckett's dissidence challenges readers who are used to writing which is on better speaking terms with the resources of fiction.

A common critical response to such demands is to see these texts as enacting a mode of reflexivity which subverts the formal presuppositions of fiction. Many readers see these texts as offering not a reduction to absurdity, but the reduction to boredom of the pleasures of the text. Two modernist problems emerge. The first is the problem of purposeless tedium. The determination to subvert conventions of meaning can produce an overdetermined repetition of the determination to do so. Semantic potential is then not free but imprisoned within the oscillation of determinate and indeterminate possibilities, while possible meanings cannot be reconciled with the conventions which make such meanings possible. Ideologically, this is often misconstrued as an experiment in obscurity rather than the articulation of imagination's difficulties. The second problem is the way radical compressions of language prevent the sustained articulation of a longer work. Without further semantic counterpoint, the tensions necessary to sustain attention wilt into weary acquiescence. Social categories of experience implicit within the dominant use of prose as an instrument of rational communication overdetermine any use of prose as an aesthetic medium. In a longer prose work the negation of the conventions of prose narrative threatens to become a 'habit' which suggests not mindlessness, but a new kind of omniscient narrator.[11] Over and above the specific negations of form there appears to be a new kind of indifferent organizer whose organization afflicts the totality. In effect, the text implies a narrator who functions as a bureaucrat of indeterminacy.

This new kind of narrator reflects a crisis of form analogous to a wider political crisis shaping formal laws of representation and expressive freedoms within such laws. On the one hand, limitless choice mirrors the illusion of free choice within consumerist society. On the other hand, an overarching bureaucratic indeterminacy mirrors social awareness of the systematic organization of life in terms of work, of social content in terms of economic forms. The ethos of work for work's sake, with needs and feelings subordinated to economic action, has been understood in the light of Max Weber as the Protestant work ethic. Max Weber suggests that Protestant ethics are one of the preconditions for the development of the spirit of capitalism. The spirit of capitalism is then an unintended consequence of aspects of Protestantism whose affects can still be discerned long after the demise of Protestantism as an active system of belief. Weber also suggests that the processes of rationalization involved in modern bureaucracy separate means from ends, forms from contents. A further unintended consequence of Protestant ethics, then, is the combination of a vocation for work within a merely formal understanding of the reasons for work. In this light, the effect of bureaucratic indeterminacy in Beckett's disintegrating narrators might be compared with the effects of a Protestant work ethic applied to language so as to produce a contentless formalism. Beckett's work could be read as an investigation into the ethics of imagination within capitalism so as to illuminate the legacy of religious and existential questions within Beckett's writing compulsions. The difficulty, then, would be to distinguish the dissident asceticism of Protestantism from the qualities of asceticism and protest in Beckett's dissidence. This begins to suggest deeper structures in the compulsion of Beckett's texts to go on, to continue working without belief in the values sustaining the work in progress. But perhaps it is just such reconciliations of work and value which are unimaginable in contemporary society.

Beckett was familiar with analogous problems of literary form in Gertrude Stein's work and in James Joyce's *Finnegans Wake*. Such texts work the imagination to an early bed, if not to death. Beckett's shorter prose texts represent his failure to find a way beyond his own acute diagnosis of fiction and imagination in *How It Is* (1964). *How It Is* speaks of others who 'have sought refuge in a desert place to be alone at last and vent their sorrows unheard' and describes 'progress properly so called' as 'ruins in prospect'.[12] Against the mud of murmurs, *How It Is* asks: 'if it is still possible at this late hour to conceive of other worlds.' This other world is quickly qualified by a characteristically Beckettian inversion, as a world which is: 'as just as ours but less exquisitely organized'.[13] The negative freedom of imagination suggests the incapacity of a representation of contemporary reality, of 'how it is', to offer fictions of freedom. The struggle is to conceive of other worlds without collapsing imagination into a fiction which flees reality. The tension between 'is' and 'ought' is maintained in a tension between the facts and values of 'how it is'. But merely formal freedom prevents a more determinate imagination of absent political realities, realities whose stress is nevertheless felt. Conventions of prose fiction are not merely subverted: the dissident imagination articulates its resistance to the constraining ideological forms of narrative. *How It Is* negates the remaining vestiges of the narrator as a fictional subject of narration. In *The Lost Ones* and *Nohow On*, however, narrator and narration are reintegrated, reanimating otherwise unreconciled experiences of ruin, restlessness and refuge.

Beckett's penultimate text, *Stirrings Still* (1988), provides a succinct retrospective of the development of his oeuvre. 'Still' can be read as an imperative (stirrings be still); a description (stirrings that are bestilled); an exclaimed lament (still more stirrings); or a rhetorical question of disbelief (can there be stirrings still?). The text lives up to its title in a play of stirrings and stillness, whose simpler surface is more reconciled than the prose-scape of *How It Is* or *Lessness*. *Stirrings Still* begins with sentences of beguiling simplicity: 'One night as he sat at his table head on hands he saw himself rise and go. One night or day. For when his own light went out he was not left in the dark.'[14] The third person male character immediately splits into a character seen to rise and go. The quality of sight seems at first directly perceived, as if the narrator simply reports from an external viewpoint. But reflection suggests that the conventions of realism do not allow self-perception to be so literal. The viewpoint is internal to the character and cannot be visible in a literal sense. The sight involved, then, is imagined seeing, either an imagined memory of rising and going; a projected vision of rising and going; or a prospect of some future action. The apparent indifference of 'One night *or* day' works as a corrective to the contradiction between the moment of narration and the imagined time of the narrator. This reworks the narrative paradox performed at the end of *Molloy*: 'Then I went back into the house and wrote, It is midnight. The rain is beating on the window. It was not midnight. It was not raining.'[15] But in *Stirrings Still* this earlier mode of denial has modulated into a more implicit negativity of narrative. Negativity is nevertheless at work in the statement that when his own light went out he was not left in the dark. The possessive of 'his table' seems simple, but the description of a light as 'his *own* light' is rather less perspicuous. If without this light he was not left in the dark, the sentence negates the initial coordinations of sense. The 'light' is imagined or metaphorical. The focus perhaps needs to be on what it means to be left, left without his own light but not alone, and illuminated accordingly by some other light, such as that cast by the narrator's fickle choice of 'night' as the text's first light. Imagined light begins to refract the expression 'rise and go', perhaps to imagine 'life's light', a soul rising and leaving the body, a flight of fancy, or a movement of imagined after-life.

The calm but less than omniscient narrator of *Stirrings Still* goes through a series of disappearances and reappearances which lead the narrative into: 'Another place in the place where he sat at his table head on hands. The same place and table as when Darly for example died and left him' (*Ss*, 115–16). This table, like the character, splits into another table in the same place, a table associated with the proper name Darly, who is described 'for example', as if merely one among unspecified others. Overlapping temporal associations split the presence of identity into imagined times, with grief as a motive force in this movement of selves: 'And patience till the one true end to time and grief and second self his own' (*Ss,* 120). Remains of reason are brought to bear on this grief and its perplexity, but provide no help. This recognition leads to a simply stated disarray: 'Bringing to bear on all this his remains of reason he sought help in the thought that his memory of indoors was perhaps at fault and found it of none' (*Ss* 122). At the text's end grief remains, even if the movement from self to second self has been reduced to hopes of an end: 'the hubbub in his mind so-called till nothing left from deep within but only ever fainter oh to end. Time and grief and self so-called. Oh all to end' (*Ss* 128).

In *Stirrings Still* past and future are denied and affirmed within an envelope of grief which refuses the consolations of mind and self so-called. Using a critical vocabulary suggested by Gillian Rose, *Stirrings Still* offers a fiction of aberrated rather than inaugurated mourning.[16] Aberrated mourning, suggests Rose, is mourning which remains incomplete, unable to relinquish the devastations of grief by working through the contradictory emotions aroused by bereavement. Inaugurated mourning, by contrast, accepts the working through of grief as a negotiation which can return to the laws of the everyday, by finding forms for grief which can be reconciled within the laws of ethical life. In *Stirrings Still* the fiction of grief involves a mourning whose affectivity resists becoming subject to formal laws of identification and recognition. The narrative nevertheless threatens to turn mourning into a literary form. The loss of the ability to know and be known, to look and have one's gaze returned, even by conjuring up lost love, falters and leaves the form in an aporia of misrecognition. The possibility of recognition is presented sceptically but the attempt is made to imagine a refuge from this aporia. Tarrying with the imperative of 'imagination dead imagine' this aporia is coordinated, however negatively, by presuppositions about the formal reconciliations of narrative intelligibility. Narrative intelligibility involves the way sense can be made of the narrative forms of *Stirrings Still* by applying conventions of narrative interpretation even if the relevance of such conventions is called into question. Although called into question, *Stirrings Still* acknowledges the attempt to formalise the work of grief in the imagination of death. At the same time, however, *Stirrings Still* continues to stir and refuses to allow the labour of new recognitions to reconcile fiction and the grief-stricken imagination.

Even within this brief and apparently autonomous text there are references which reverberate through Beckett's oeuvre. 'Darly' can be referred back to the Dr Arthur Darley Beckett met while working at the Irish Red Cross Hospital in Saint-Lô on the Normandy coast. Darley died in 1948 and Beckett wrote a memorial poem for him.[17] The reference to Darly as one among others who have died can then also be referred back to a text Beckett wrote for Irish radio about the hospital at Saint-Lô. Broadcast in 1946, 'The Capital of the Ruins' corrects Irish criticisms of French attitudes to 'the Irish bringing gifts' in the construction of an Irish Hospital in French soil. Beckett concludes by hoping that some of the Irish in Saint-Lô:

> will come home realising that they got at least as good as they gave, that they got indeed what they could hardly give, a vision and sense of a time-honoured conception of humanity in ruins, and perhaps even an inkling of the terms in which our condition is to be thought again. These will have been in France.[18]

This suggests social and political analogues for the exploration of humanity in ruins and the need of a refuge for refugees in Beckett's subsequent prose fictions.

Beckett's most articulate diagnosis of the problems of imaginative refuge in fictional worlds is *The Lost Ones*. *The Lost Ones* is narrated from a position which is external to the enclosed world described and which has no place within the terms of the fiction. The Kafkaesque tone of a semi-detached narrator afflicted by a grave form of bureaucratic positivism contrasts what is narrated and the manner in which it is narrated. The original French title of *The Lost Ones* is *Le Dépeupleur*, and might also be translated as 'the depopulator' or 'the depeopler'. This term for a singularly inhuman agent is lost in translation, but the action of thinning out the social world can be imagined as that of the inhuman agency of the narrator and of narration as such. The narrative voice appropriates the point of view from which representation can be observed with apparent passivity, describing the ruins of progress which have produced an imagined world of lost ones. The narrator's matter-of-factness seems dead to the horror described, a deadness which undermines the narrator's pseudo-objectivity. The narrative opens:

> Abode where lost bodies roam each searching for its lost one. Vast enough for search to be in vain. Narrow enough for flight to be in vain. Inside a flattened cylinder fifty metres round and sixteen high for the sake of harmony.[19]

With Swiftian savagery, all here is sacrificed for the sake of a harmony which warrants comparison with the clinical engineering of a gas chamber. The ironic tone works against both the narrator and the narrated.

This imagined world oscillates between unreconciled restlessness and moments of dead stillness. However comic, the narrator's semi-detached tone offers scant solace for a reader seeking to enjoy an analogous comic detachment. The narrator even denies the existence or authority of the perspective which enables the narrator to narrate. Unlike the comedy of purgatory in Dante's *Divine Comedy*, there is no way out leading to heaven. The comedy of *The Lost Ones* leads only to a description of the pointlessness of the sectarian squabbles between different conceptions of salvation. The game of snakes and ladders in *The Lost Ones* is harsh even on the sedentary semi-sages who affect indifference to the ladders of possible salvation, but whose vanity is 'morbidly susceptible to the least want of consideration'.[20] Irony is also turned against readers tempted by the comforts of cool analysis:

> And the thinking being coldly intent on all these data and evidences could scarcely escape at the close of his analysis the mistaken conclusion that instead of speaking of the vanquished with the slight taint of pathos attaching to the term it would be more correct to speak of the blind and leave it at that.[21]

The imagination would indeed be dead if the description of this imagined world could be left at that so blindly. Amid a series of beautifully warped estrangements from the prose postures of conventional description, the text rips apart the fabric of its own articulations to suggest both the poverty of imagination in this imagined purgatory, and the inadequacy of the terms in which other possible worlds might still be imagined. The concluding section pauses to remark drily that the persistence of motion suggests that all is not yet quite for the best in this world. A final image of a bowed head concludes the narrative's dissident challenge to fictions of imagined submission, a challenge which returns reflection to the agencies of depopulation and loss.

The achievement of *The Lost Ones* also generates an impasse in the development of Beckett's subsequent prose fiction. This helps to explain the shift in tone and narrative structure evident in *Company, Ill Seen Ill Said* and *Worstward Ho*. Beckett's critique of the search for a fictional refuge is brought to a reflexive conclusion in *The Lost Ones*. What emerges is the instability of the narrative tone which allows an ironic distance between narrator and narration. If the imperative of 'imagination dead imagine' reveals a peculiarly dead narrative voice, it also becomes clear that the attempt to re-articulate the experience of the refugee has been sacrificed to the fiction of the imagined refuge.

Beckett's recognition that he has exhausted this mode finds its first

faltering steps in a series of plays and very short texts which articulate
a sense of lost home, lost family environment and lost loved ones. This
sense of loss appears at first to domesticate Beckett's restless processes
of narration into something more like autobiographical fiction. It is as
if, despite his early criticism of Proust, Beckett returns to a Proustian
mode of narrative reflection using images generated not by imagination but by associative memory. But the impression of autobiography
reveals a further level of the desire for narrative solace, a desire which
these narratives rework into fables of the imagination. The source of
the voice that narrates memories becomes in *Company* a disbelieving
form of companionship. Memory is subjected to the corrective sense of
imagination's failure to rest in peace developed by his earlier works.
Company opens with the words: 'A voice comes to one in the dark.
Imagine' (*No*, 5). This 'one' is quickly qualified and shifted into the
position of a third person male character who cannot be integrated
into a first-person narrator or narrative subject. *Company* also re-
deploys the affirmation and denial of past and future in the fictional
oscillation between remembered time and the time in which times are
remembered:

> To one on his back in the dark a voice tells of a past. With occasional
> allusion to a present and more rarely to a future as for example, You
> will end as you now are. And in another dark or in the same another
> devising it all for company. Quick leave him. (*No*, 5)

Faced with minimal conditions with which to imagine voices for company, a narrative voice urges 'quick leave him', as if urging the writing
itself to break from the structure devised for company. The text moves
on quickly, redescribing the third person as a cankerous other. The
reflexive but estranged narrator of *The Lost Ones* presented a relatively stable mode of narration and dramatic irony. In *Company*, however, the text continually fables with its narrative voice, a process of
play defined by the conclusion of *Company*:

> With every inane word a little nearer to the last. And how the fable too.
> The fable of one with you in the dark. The fable of one fabling of one
> with you in the dark. And how better in the end labour lost and silence.
> And you as you always were. Alone. (*No*, 51–2)

Conventional functions of narrative development appear, but the flow
of questions, imperatives, assertions, denials, corrections and repetitions does not resolve into a stable narrative voice. Rather, the veri-
similitude of memory is fabled from 'nought anew' through a desire
for 'the unthinkable last of all. Unnamable. Last Person. I' (*No*, 19).

This narrative combines reflexivity with a more temperate negativity than the resistance to habitual identity in Beckett's earlier narrations of the narrator.

Company recapitulates scenes and images which recur throughout Beckett's oeuvre. The text seems to work to fuse Beckett's memories with narrative categories of experience involving gender, family, adolescent sexuality, mourning, the loss of childhood and above all a lost sense of what it is to be at home in the world. The text encapsulates its wonder and disbelief in the exclamation: 'Home!' Among the predominant images is that of a child walking with a parent, usually the father, an image with biographical echoes which also suggests comparison with Virgil walking with Dante through the journey of *The Divine Comedy*. The more significant question posed by remembrance in *Company* is the way the text refers to places from the Ireland of Beckett's childhood. Perhaps the most poetically apt is 'Croker's Acres'. Aesthetic decisions mediate the aches of the croaker. The text looks back not in anger but in disbelief, refusing to succumb to its own spurious fictions of authenticity and heritage. *Company* requires careful reading if the shifting narrative turns of imagination are to be given the aesthetic freedom not to disassociate disbelief, memory and imagination. The more reconciled and temperate tone combines imagined stories with a dissenting comic detachment which remains restless. As such, the text articulates a dissident urge to imagine company not as a public limited company, but as the struggle with the imagination of unlimited companies. The work of *Company* earns the ambiguities of its title.

A dissidence of disbelief is stated with more severity by the title *Ill Seen Ill Said* (1982), first written and published as *Mal vu mal dit* (1981). The 'plot' of the title moves from seeing to saying, from imagined seeing to the representation of imagined visions in language. If the principal characters of this fiction are sight and language, each betrays the other: both are 'ill'. The problem of imagined vision, discussed above with reference to *Stirrings Still*, is announced by the opening words of *Ill Seen Ill Said*: 'From where she lies she sees Venus rise. On. From where she lies when the skies are clear she sees Venus rise followed by the sun. Then she rails at the source of all life. On' (*No*, 57). To imagine the possibility of seeing Venus through clear skies is to imagine these minimal units of narrative as fictions. The seeing involved, however, is not a process of phenomenological description, but the movement through language of the imagination's betrayal of the evidence of the senses, evidence transformed by the art of 'lies'. And here the familiar troubled identity of the narrator – 'you must go on, I can't go on, I'll go on' – has crystallized into the simply stated imaginative imperative of a one-word sentence: 'On.' The narrative goes on to describe the situation of the place where 'she lies' as being 'At the inexistent centre of a formless place' (*No*, 58). If the narrative is to be believed, the situation of this lying imagination is without existence or form, groundless. And the plot, to say the least, is difficult to map. The 'she' who is narrated might be compared with the image of a woman in a rocking-chair in Beckett's play *Rockaby*. In *Ill Seen Ill Said*, however, she does not rock, but is described as adopting 'the rigid Memnon pose' (*No*, 78). This can be read as an allusion to the statue of Amenhotep III at Thebes in Egypt, thought by the Greeks to be of Memnon and believed to give out a musical sound at sunrise in salutation of the dawn. This 'pose' is distinct from the way she lies at the beginning of the text, but allows us to make some sense of moments in the narrative which refer to land, sea, light and the whispering music of celestial winds.

The problem, however, of imagining a reconciliation between narrator and narration is sustained in *Ill Seen Ill Said*. Various vignettes and narrative sketches might explain the overall narrative, but the plot's suspense is never resolved. Numerous apparently illuminating details are offered, but each dissents from the fiction of illumination. Details of description are suffused with doubts, desires and griefs. Descriptions emote rather than narrate: 'Riveted to some detail of the desert the eye fills with tears. Imagination at wit's end spreads its sad wings. Gone she hears one night the sea as if afar' (*No*, 65). Focusing on the details of such passages reveals Beckett's subtle transformations of familiar idioms and dead metaphors. Rather than being riveted 'by' some detail, the imagination is riveted 'to' its details, and yet seeks to escape this iron grip of vision in tears whose waters irrigate the parched desert of fact. Conventional idiom refers to 'wits' end', where the wits are plural. The wit here is singular. It takes flight from land's end in imaginations of sound, moving from the sight of the desert to the sounds of a sea of troubles. The imagination moves quickly and denies its need of a source of light: 'Having no need of light to see the eye makes haste' (*No*, 69). Later the text tells itself: 'Hear from here the howls of laughter of the damned' (*No*, 92). This imaginative struggle against the literal force of description can be traced in the following passage, which begins by commenting on its own description of a face:

> Livid pallor. Not a wrinkle. How serene it seems this ancient mask. Worthy those worn by certain newly dead. True the light leaves to be desired. The lids occult the longed-for eyes. Time will tell them washen blue. Where tears perhaps not for nothing. Unimaginable tears of old. (*No*, 70–1)

The ancient face is the art of a death mask. The quality of the unimaginable aspect of the grieving eye speaks in the brevity with which Beckett rings changes of syntax and semantics. 'True the light leaves to be desired' leaves much to the imagination, as if abbreviating idiomatic expressions such as 'leaves little to be desired'. And this gentle railing against the light echoes the opening words directed at the sun as the source of life. Other passages explicitly comment on the difficulty of making description and imagination into a truth which coheres: 'Already all confusion. Things and imaginings. As of always. Confusion amounting to nothing. Despite precautions. If only she could be pure figment. Unalloyed' (*No*, 67). But the desire for pure figments of the imagination confuses reality with desire:

> Such the confusion now between the real and – how say its contrary?
> No matter. That old tandem. Such now the confusion between them
> once so twain. And such the farrago from eye to mind. For it to make
> what sad sense of it may. No matter now. Such equal liars both. Real
> and – how ill say its contrary? The counter-poison. (*No*, 82)

'Counter-poison' translates the French expression 'contre-poison'. Imagination is not the antidote to reality but the bitter pill which negates the real. No truth ensues from a tandem of equally confused liars. Saying the contrary is to say 'ill', to 'ill say', the movement from eye to mind which is 'ill seen' and 'ill said'. Against the insistence to go 'on', *Ill Seen Ill Said* is interrupted, or at least checked, by a range of one-word injunctions. These include: 'Careful', 'Enough', 'Away', 'Ah' and the inversion of 'On' into 'No'. These one-word sentences qualify the quality of narrative development, dissenting from the illusions of unreflective progress, but without the stasis of paradoxical contradiction suggested by 'I'll go on, I can't go on'. Perhaps the most interesting of such injunctions in *Ill Seen Ill Said* is the recurrent sentence: 'Gently gently.' The doubling of the word moves 'gently' from adverb to descriptive injunction, as if the imagination tells itself to take things gently. The text's final words provide the most surprising of such ambiguous injunctions: 'Know happiness' (*No*, 97). This unexpected conclusion enjoins a reconciliation between the motive forces of imagination and the desire to know the limits of the imagination. Such a conclusion refuses to succumb to the lie of literal-minded description or the solace of flights of fancy. The imagination may be ill, but if it persists with the labour of dissidence the good life can be imagined as the end of fiction.

A fatal pun nevertheless joins 'know' and 'no' in *Nohow On*. The subtle music of *Ill Seen Ill Said* is rudely broken up in *Worstward Ho*.

The occasional brief word sentences which punctuate *Ill Seen Ill Said* become the rule in *Worstward Ho*, and the ambiguity of such brief commands, laments and exclamations becomes a more monotonous incantation of inarticulacy:

> Say a body. Where none. No mind. Where none. That at least. A place. Where none. For the body. To be in. Move in. Out of. Back into. No. No out. No back. Only in. Stay in. On in. Still. (*No*, 101)

The text cannot muster enough wind to let the imagination pass the cordon of insistent denial and negative law. If passages in *Ill Seen Ill Said* risk allowing the space of writing to imagine a poetics of dissidence, *Worstward Ho* appears to be determined not to fall for any tincture of imaginative sentiment. *Worstward Ho* could be read as a hymn to the imagination's labour of negativity, but the restless movement of denial is unhappy and sick, and threatened by the tedium of a purposelessness which cannot sustain the text. The oscillations are overdetermined and too rapid to allow formal negativity to determine its own content:

> First the body. No. First the place. No. First both. Now either. Now the other. Sick of the either try the other. Sick of it back sick of the either. So on. Somehow on. Till sick of both. Throw up and go. Where neither. Till sick of there. Throw up and back. (*No*, 128)

What in *Ill Seen Ill Said* might have been 'ill' is here 'sick'.

Beckett's willingness to throw up his hands in such helpless formalism might be taken as evidence of the ruthless integrity of his oeuvre, a willingness to transgress conventions of taste in order to imagine again from nought anew. *Worstward Ho* offers some of the most violently fractured versions of characteristic themes, expressions and images, but the sustaining narrative tensions have collapsed and crumbled into bare skull and language bones: 'Skull better worse. What left of skull. Of soft. Worst why of all of all. So skull not go. What left of skull not go. Into it still the hole. Into what left of soft' (*No*, 128). This formal abbreviation does not achieve a negativity of dissidence which articulates protest against its conditions, but an all too insistent series of merely formal negations. The formal negations which make the dissidence of *Worstward Ho* intelligible provide an aesthetic which approaches the conditions of a contentless imperative. The writing continually stops and starts, but it goes on in a way which suggests that the imperative to work for the sake of work triumphs over the play of the imagination. Indicative verbs become commands. The struggle for recognition between the commander and the commanded becomes a contentless agency of denial. The imperatives of social convention are denied, but the social imperatives which prompt this denial are not recognizable. As with *Ill Seen Ill Ill Said* this agency of denial sustains a refusal to rest in peace with the available conditions of mourning, whether such mourning is merely imagined or bound to its worst words. And yet in *Worstward Ho* this agency cannot quite resolve its restless refusal to think through its misrecognitions. Rather, misrecognition is purely restated as an imperative of the labour of telling and of being told. The contradiction between mourning and the labour of narration cannot speak of the griefs to which this restlessness bears witness.

While Beckett is a singular and ideologically unusual witness of such contradictions, the mourning of dissident form in *Worstward Ho* succumbs to the law of its forms. *The Lost Ones* and *Ill Seen Ill Said* are two of the finest if least known or knowable dissident fictions of contemporary writing. *Worstward Ho*, however, indicates the limits of Beckett's dissident imagination. Beckett's final prose piece, 'what is the word' (1990), suggests that the 'folly for to need to seem to glimpse . . .'[22] has turned the ends of fiction to pure folly. But Beckett's achievement is to have produced an oeuvre whose imaginative dissidence refuses to be reconciled with existing society and refuses to be reduced to its own folly. His writing turns this refusal against itself and against the comforts of its aesthetic illusions. The denial of explicit social or political commitments in his writing nevertheless offers an imaginative resistance to the prevailing fictions of contemporary society. Recognition of the dissident loop of 'imagination dead imagine' in Beckett's work cannot rest in peace with this resistance, but struggles for refuge from formal negativity in the dissident imagination.

Notes

1 S. Beckett, *The Beckett Trilogy* (London: Pan, 1979), p. 382.
2 S. Beckett, *Nohow On* (London: Calder, 1989), p. 128. The parts of *Nohow On* were first published as *Company* (1980), *Ill Seen Ill Said* (1982) and *Worstward Ho* (1983). References hereafter included in the main text with the abbreviation 'No' followed by page number.
3 S. Beckett, *Texts for Nothing, Collected Shorter Prose, 1945–1980* (London: Calder, 1984), pp. 109–10. First published in *Nouvelles et textes pour rien* (1955); and in English in *No's Knife* (1967).
4 Beckett, *Texts for Nothing*, p. 115.
5 Quoted in James Knowlson, *Damned to Fame* (London: Bloomsbury, 1996), p. 564. According to Steven Connor, the manuscript of Beckett's blurb 'is to be found among the drafts for Beckett's translation of *Sans* in the Yale University library', *Samuel Beckett: Repetition, Theory and Text*

(Oxford: Basil Blackwell, 1988), p. 216 n. 21.

6 These texts are collected in *Collected Shorter Prose. The Lost Ones* was first published in French, as *Le Dépeupleur* (1970) and in English in 1972.

7 A. Alvarez, *Beckett* (London: Collins, 1973), p. 128. Quoted in Connor, *Samuel Beckett*, p. 105.

8 *Ping, Collected Shorter Prose*, p.151.

9 See S. Beckett, *The Complete Dramatic Works* (London: Faber and Faber, 1986).

10 *Lessness, Collected Shorter Prose*, p. 153.

11 For his comments on 'habit' see S. Beckett, *Proust* (London: Chatto & Windus, 1931), repr. in S. Beckett, *Proust* and *Three Dialogues* (1965).

12 S. Beckett, *How It Is* (London: Calder, 1964), p. 24. First published in French as *Comment c'est* (1961).

13 Ibid., p. 156.

14 S. Beckett, *Stirrings Still*, in *As the Story Was Told* (London: Calder, 1990), p. 113. References included hereafter in the main text as '*Ss* ' and page number.

15 *The Beckett Trilogy*, p. 162.

16 See Gillian Rose, *Mourning Becomes the Law* (Cambridge: Cambridge University Press, 1996).

17 S. Beckett, 'Mort de A.D.', in *Collected Poems, 1930–1978* (London: Calder, 1984), p. 56.

18 S. Beckett, 'The Capital of the Ruins' in *As the Story Was Told*, p. 27–8.

19 S. Beckett, *The Lost Ones*, in *Collected Shorter Prose* , p. 159.

20 Ibid., p. 166.

21 Ibid., p. 170.

22 'what is the word', in *As the Story Was Told*, p. 134.

6 The Mutations of William Burroughs

Geoff Ward

Born in 1914, William Burroughs had already reached the elderly side of middle age by the year from which this collection takes its starting-point. Although the early 1970s would see the publication of some of his most significant work, the writer began the decade at a low ebb. Only ten years had passed between the publication of *The Naked Lunch* and the completion of *The Wild Boys*, but the seismic cultural changes wrought by the counter-culture which ironically he had helped create left Burroughs temporarily stranded. The time of the Beat Movement had now passed, and the phase in which he would be celebrated as the most influential novelist of the second half of the twentieth century had not yet arrived. Touchstones were crumbling: Jack Kerouac, whose hipster narrative of disaffected romanticism *On the Road* had brought the Beats to prominence and who had donated the title of Burroughs's most famous novel, died from drink in October 1969. Burroughs heard the news in London where he had been installed in a flat in Duke Street, St James's since 1966, off heroin but decidedly on alcohol, alternately living alone in un-Hoovered dust and with a succession of 'Dilly boys', as the hustlers of Piccadilly Circus were known. Post-Stonewall only in a technical sense, these arrangements would follow a traditional pattern of dependence and recrimination, beginning with seven-course meals and orgies of cleaning but ending with theft and sometimes violence. Only, it seems, in the utopian eruptions of *The Wild Boys* and *Port of Saints*, where the Dilly boys mutate into figments of dream-poetry while wreaking armed revenge on mainstream society, could sex ever be uncomplicated.

Patterns of guilt and of flight marked the writer's relationship with his family, and were not merely active in, but by his own account responsible for, the books. Almost a year to the day after Kerouac's demise, Burroughs's mother Laura died in a St Louis nursing home after years of mental decline and major operations, throughout which her writer-son had singally failed to visit, confining his good wishes to cards sent for Mother's Day. Such mistakes too monstrous for remorse, to adopt a phrase used by Burroughs's (basically friendly) biographer Ted Morgan, were replicated in the writer's lifelong neglect of his son Billy, who died in his thirties in 1981. Author of two appropriately hyperactive novels of amphetamine addiction, *Speed* and *Kentucky Ham*, Billy had wanted to live like Burroughs but died like Kerouac, following the unusual achievement of developing cirrhosis twice, first in his own and then in his transplanted liver. Burroughs Junior was quite literally a born junkie as a result of his mother's habits, sustained throughout pregnancy. Herself the central figure in Burroughs's most monstrous mistake of all, Joan Vollmer was shot and killed by the writer in Mexico City in 1951 in a drunken 'William Tell' stunt. This defining incident resonates throughout Burroughs's entire writing career, and in the Preface to *Queer*, which predates *The Naked Lunch* in its time of composition but which the author refused to release until the 1980s, he states unequivocally that 'I would never have become a writer but for Joan's death . . . I have had no choice except to write my way out' (p.18). Paradoxically the image of the novelist firing the fatal shot would become – even more than the stereotype of the heroin-injecting addict – the image dominating public perception of Burroughs's work during the final years, partly because of his own increased openness about the incident, an emphasis reinforced by the two biographies to have appeared so far, and because of David Cronenberg's 1992 film, entitled *Naked Lunch* but in truth an oneiric rendition of Morgan's biography, and one that focuses on the shooting.

The writer's own fortunes were to change with his return to the United States in 1974. Living off the Bowery in a converted but windowless YMCA locker-room known as the Bunker, Burroughs was feted by Andy Warhol and the Manhattan glitterati, while rock stars such as David Bowie and Patti Smith who had followed the Velvet Underground in adapting Burroughs's self-conscious decadence for vinyl purposes, came to pay homage. Where the writer once had collaborators like Brion Gysin, he now had an entourage. Victor Bockris and other minders would invite Mick Jagger or some such luminary to dine in the Bunker, together with photographers, and these spontaneous festivities are retrieved in *With William Burroughs: A Report from the Bunker* (1981) and elsewhere. The writer's remoteness and solipsism began to appeal to a curiously wide audience. Blessed with what was (to say the least) a memorable speaking voice, and radiating via his banker's suits and parchment visage a suppression of presence so ghostly as to become its own powerful identity, Burroughs was able to develop his talents as a touring performer. Decades of self-abuse had kept him spry, and between 1974 and 1984 he gave 150 readings in America and Europe, netting around $75,000. Indeed, I remember presenting him with £700 of this, gathered in a biscuit tin in Liverpool in 1982 on the 'Final Academy' tour. It was evident from that night as from the next reading at Manchester's Hacienda and others that his audience was now drawn largely from the post-punk club-goers, who would have come to his work via the name-checks in Bowie and Laurie Anderson. Like *Trainspotting* author Irvine Welsh in the 1990s, Burroughs had become the writer for those who do not normally read. Nevertheless, the novels of the 1980s were his most successful commercially (though not artistically), and where the initial print-run of *The Wild Boys* by Grove Press in 1971 amounted to 5,619 copies, *Cities of the Red Night* (1981) would sell four times that in the American hardback edition alone. As a result of this Indian Summer, Burroughs's final two decades saw the appearance not only of new books but of much reprinted, revised or rediscovered work. The vast array of photographs, films and recordings as well as texts forced attention on to the political, as well as his own personal past, and as the numbers of his biological peers who continued to occupy the planet dwindled, Burroughs became one of the last living witnesses to the paranoia and repression characterizing earlier decades in the twentieth century that the nostalgia industries hungered to idealize.

Of course to those intent on denigrating his achievements, Burroughs could always be nailed as a one-book writer. This happened to all the Beats, perhaps with justice in the case of Allen Ginsberg and *Howl*, less so with Kerouac and not at all with Burroughs. It is true that *On the Road* and *The Naked Lunch* would always carry special resonance for a particular generation determined to escape the orthodoxy of enforced consumerism-plus-austerity in a particular phase of the Cold War. Burroughs may also have fallen victim to something that began as mutual support in a dark time, but that turned into self-publicizing; the Beats refer continually to their own earlier selves and to each other in their writings. This helped to promote the group in life, and to mythologize it both at the time and thereafter. In Burroughs's case such overt self-referentiality is so habitual as to carry through to the individual phrase, so that 'silver spots boiled in front of his eyes' or 'a distant hand lifted' or 'No glot . . . Clom fliday' (originally, a response to the attempted purchase of opium in a Chinese laundry) are repeated like favourite riffs in texts forty years apart. One of his most affecting pieces, *Cobble Stone Gardens* (1976) reworks material from the first draft of *The Naked Lunch*. Such deliberate circularity makes it impossible to discuss Burroughs after 1970 in separation from what went before. Yet he is not a one-book writer in either the weak sense, or indeed the amplified sense in which Frank O'Hara or for that matter Emily Dickinson were constantly adding to one vast work which death alone would bring to publication.

He may, however, have been if not a one-book then a four-phase writer, with certain features tending to recur in each phase. The first phase produced *Junky*, *Queer* and the various sketches collected later in the overlapping anthologies *Early Routines* (1982) and *Interzone* (1989). The second, crucial phase began in the mid-1950s following the death of Joan, with Burroughs installed in the Hotel Muniriya in Tangier, free of addiction, using one wall of his room as a shooting gallery in moments of high excitement, and typing out the thousand pages that would form the basis of *The Naked Lunch* (1959), *The Soft Machine* (1961, 1966, 1968), *The Ticket That Exploded* (1962, 1967) and *Nova Express* (1964). The middle two books exist in different drafts, but whereas the final version of *Ticket* is basically an expansion of the Olympia Press original, the first and last *Soft Machines* are radically different. Burroughs's revisions and ordering of the tetralogy established a pattern of mood and approach that would be repeated in the succeeding phases of his writing. A first novel explores new themes in a dramatic and partly satirical mode: *The Wild Boys* (1971) and *Cities of the Red Night* (1981). A second novel resembles the first thematically, as *Soft Machine* partners *Naked Lunch*, but is written in a more poetic and elegiac form that also carries autobiographical resonance: *Port of Saints* (1973, 1980), the most obsessional and yet the most lyrical of the books, and *The Place of Dead Roads* (1983). The final volumes in each phase set up a critical distance from what is now thoroughly reworked material, and comprise speculations which are primarily didactic and theoretical: *The Third Mind* (1978), a collaboration with Brion Gysin concerning cut-ups, fold-ins, Mayan codices and other enthusiasms, and finally his weakest book but his last full-length work, *The Western Lands* (1987). Each phase also generated various brief, satellite texts some of which were gathered eventually under such titles as *Exterminator!* (1973; subtitled, disingenuously, 'a novel'), *Ah Pook is Here* (1974) and, probably the most rewarding, *The Burroughs File* (1984). The author's sunset years as a Kansas homesteader produced a last flurry of diaries, short stories and dream-journals, out of which *Tornado Alley* (1989) comes nearest to kicking up a storm, and *The Cat Inside* (1986, 1992) ought in fairness to have been drowned at birth.

While first-time readers might well think this map rather finicky,

Burroughs addicts are wont to complain that, even given the variants, the 'wrong' drafts have been published. The writer relied heavily on outside advice concerning the final organization of his material. Where early advisers such as Allen Ginsberg were benign and constructive, commercial and other pressures exerted a dangerous effect in the post-1970s phases. One of the biographies comes close to alleging that *Cities of the Red Night* was authored in part by friends, such as his secretary James Grauerholz, and Steven Lowe, who turned out novels for a Mafia-controlled porn sweatshop for a living but who wrote material for Burroughs on the eighteenth century, on piracy and other topics that receive extended treatment in the novel. (The book is also indebted to *A Touch of Danger*, a thriller by James Jones.) We also know that the extant version of *Place of Dead Roads* (the best thing from the 1980s, and definitely written by Burroughs) is the action-centred fifth draft, only published in preference to the more poetic sixth version after a fight. Those who heard any of the Final Academy readings in the UK, done straight after the completion of the novel, will recall lengthy chunks involving the gay English aesthete Denton Welch – a displaced self-portrait, clearly – none of which survive in the published text. All of this will provide food for the non-final academicians now that the author's life has sadly ended. More important to register is the principle of revision, affecting the writings of William Burroughs from without and from within, in the best and in the weakest stretches. For him, fiction was mutation, and to write was, *ab initio*, an act of revision. He claimed no interest in literary theory beyond his own but, as Robin Lydenberg shows in her monograph *Word Cultures* (1987), the texts frequently echo the determinations of French post-structuralist discourse, as when Burroughs's intuitions regarding the primacy of written over spoken language in *The Job* (1970) match Jacques Derrida's pronouncements of the same period. The difference is that Burroughs thought writing was *dangerous*.

Like his literary hero Joseph Conrad, Burroughs lived with physical danger in the first half of his life, then wrote about it (but, unlike Conrad, carried on living with it) in the second. His first major novel was published when he was forty-five years old. Despite the emphasis placed by his graphic texts on anatomical process, he relished his nickname *el hombre invisible*, flitting through countries and occupations like a spirit possessing a new body before moving on. He studied literature at Harvard, medicine in Vienna, Buddhism in Colorado and Scientology in East Grinstead, taking something from everything and reviling all; stole from drunks in the subway and was arrested for firearms, drugs and other offences; worked as bartender, private detective, and (the only job he enjoyed) public exterminator; underwent psychoanalysis, shearing off a finger-joint in an access of self-hatred; a famous photograph shows him carrying a pith helmet in the jungle outside Macao, on finding the mysterious yage vine, said to confer telepathic powers on the user. (He discovered that only writing can do this.) Another St Louis collagist, T. S. Eliot, once wrote to Herbert Read that someday he would like to write an essay about a man who wasn't anything, anywhere. Poetically he already had, offering in *The Waste Land* a *tour de force* of compulsive pastiche signalling the ruin of integrity from both a social and a psychological perspective. Burroughs too used poetic techniques to give life to flickering pseudo-characters who are ultimately one more feature of collage, though it is a world-collage streaked with the tears of memory and regret. Both figures may be read as recording the vertigo that had been bequeathed by Whitman and Emerson to American writers less sanguine than themselves about the freedom to reinvent the self. But where Eliot tried to retreat from the twentieth century into ritual and conservatism, Burroughs stares down the authoritarianism in those concepts, giving Babel free speech. The question to be asked of his writing since 1970 is, where is the *hombre invisible* most firmly located? In the recordings and performances, with their sharply individual vocalizations; in the (perhaps) ghosted inscriptions of commercial success; or the more ghostly, stranded books such as *Port of Saints* that belong neither to the Beat Movement nor the reading circuit?

To answer the question is to broach matters of ontological as well as literary authenticity. The recalcitrance of William Burroughs in the face of legalities situates him as the outlaw, the stranger whose disaffiliation stands as an index of rocky integrity. The nearest thing to a 'character' in the early novels is the now-you-see-him-now-you-don't persona of the drug-fiend. The voice of 1970s novels such as *The Wild Boys* and *Port of Saints* is even more discorporated, has a remote past and a satirical voice but inhabits no body. The body in which it is interested is now all that it is not, projected as the desirable other; young, sexually eager, primitive, generally wordless, amnesiac and murderous without conscience. In late novels such as *Cities* or *Place of Dead Roads* this youthful figure is reinternalized as a novice pirate or (more successfully) a Western gunslinger, Kim Carsons. Yet all these personae are there in the prose and then gone like knots in water. The texts are based in the mutation of writing, and not in the nineteenth-century understanding of 'character' that continues to dominate fiction. This understanding was exploded by Burroughs in his most famous novel. One important factor in the overshadowing of his later books by *The Naked Lunch* is that it is in a profound sense a work of the avant-garde, challenging other fiction methodologically, and it is not

clear that anything written since has moved decisively beyond it. The
extent to which this is a question of the intrepidity of a particular text,
or evidence that the concept of a literary avant-garde died with William
Burroughs, has yet to be settled.

II

The methods and successes of the later fiction are bound up with questions of authenticity that were broached by even the earliest work.
Junkie (1953) was published by the new paperback firm of Ace Books,
through the good offices of an uncle of Carl Solomon, whom Ginsberg
had met in mental hospital and to whom *Howl* is dedicated. The cover
design, of a curvaceous young woman in red being physically pre-
vented from lighting a 'reefer' by a stern young male, sends out conflicting signals, as does the publisher's subtitle 'Confessions of an
Unredeemed Drug Addict' with its arch and De Quinceyan overtones.
Ace's editors were probably caught between the urge to make the Bo-
hemian world a selling-point and the need to add a moralizing overlay
at a time when talk of drug use was inseparable in the public mind from
serious criminality. Apart from the jazz world – essentially the black
man's territory – there were no 'subcultures' at this stage, only the underworld. Also, at this point in American publishing history, paper-
backs were a novelty bought from neighbourhood stores and stations
rather than bookshops, and the distinction between cloth and paper was
absolute; in 1953 a hardback novel would probably not be paperbacked,
even if its first run sold well. Consequently Burroughs was bypassing
any serious chance of a review by going with Ace and by writing about
junk. (Not that he had much choice; like all the major New York
houses approached by Ginsberg on his friend's behalf, Doubleday rejected the book, noting that 'the prose is not very good. This could
only work if it were written by someone like Winston Churchill', a
concept that grows stranger the more one pauses over it.) To add to
the confusion of intention, *Junkie* was bound up with a True Detective yarn, *Narcotic Agent* by Maurice Heilbrant, printed as it were
upside down with the back cover of Burroughs's text as its front cover.
For his *nom de plume*, Burroughs took his mother's maiden name,
calling himself William Lee.

I lay stress on these circumstances because what appear to have
been constraints laid on the first-time author are also features of psychology and self-presentation that Burroughs would replicate even at
a much later time, when he enjoyed far more control over his output.
Everything about the book conspires to queer the authenticity which

would appear to have been its *raison d'être*. *Junkie* is neither autobiography nor novel, neither a condemnation nor a defence of drugs,
by one who is and is not 'William Lee'. Even the title is blurred, as
some subsequent editions show a mutation of the -ie into -y. A crucial
element of the inauthentic runs to the roots of the prose, and is there
from the opening page. 'I was born in 1914 in a solid, three-story,
brick house in a large Midwestern city.' This is an overture that proposes the narrator as epitomizing reliability, as do the references to
the father's flourishing lumber business, the shiny black Lincoln and
the drives in the park on Sunday. Yet these details are exploded at the
end of page one, not so much by the statement that all this 'is now
gone forever' but by the sneer that enters into the tone:

> I could put down one of those nostalgic routines about the old German
> doctor who lived next door and the rats running around in the back
> yard and my pet toad that lived by the fish pond.
>   Actually my earliest memories are colored by a fear of nightmares. I
> was afraid to be alone, and afraid of the dark, and afraid to go to sleep
> because of dreams where a supernatural horror seemed always on the
> point of taking shape. I was afraid some day the dream would still be
> there when I woke up. I recall hearing a maid talk about opium and
> how smoking opium brings sweet dreams, and I said: 'I will smoke
> opium when I grow up.'
>   I was subject to hallucinations as a child. Once I woke up in the early
> morning light and saw little men playing in a block house I had made
> . . .
>   I went to a progressive school with the future solid citizens, the law-
> yers, doctors and businessmen of a large Midwest town. I was timid
> with the other children . . . One aggressive little Lesbian would pull my
> hair whenever she saw me. I would like to shove her face in right now,
> but she fell off her horse and broke her neck years ago. (pp. xi–xii)

Prompted by Ace Books to write a straightforward account of his criminal activities, Burroughs proved incapable of either sticking to or re-
linquishing the appropriate style. The laconic monotone, indebted
chiefly to Dashiell Hammett and so at ease with dead metaphor and
repetition, keeps sliding into romantic irony or poeticisms which, in-
trinsic to the style of the later books, transgress the limits of the confessional genre to which the text was supposed to stay loyal. The
hypnagogic visions and the acutely literary invocation of opium threaten
credibility, just as 'I could put down one of those nostalgic routines'
pulls the rug from under the realism proffered by the opening. The
cheerful viciousness of 'I would like to shove her face in right now'
certainly carries the ring of truth, but is completely inappropriate in

an account purporting to describe 'a safe, comfortable life that is now gone forever'. (It is of course pure Burroughs: he can safely be imagined putting a curse on the little girl's horse.) The net result is to throw absolutely everything into doubt. Ironically, the details of the narrative can generally be checked from other sources and are correct. It is not the events related but the persona that is inauthentic: yet this is exactly where the power of Burroughs's writing will ultimately lie.

Although this crucial factor is present in Burroughs's writing from the start, there is still a quantum leap in style between *Junkie* and *The Naked Lunch*. The first page of the latter is actually a rewrite of a page from the first book, in which an agent in a white trench coat stalks the narrator, who is carrying dope in a cigarette pack. After various feints and manoeuvres 'I vaulted the subway turnstile and shoved the cigarette package into the space at the side of a gum machine. I ran down one level and got a train up to the Square' (*Junkie*, p. 54). The terse sentences and even tone recall Hammett and ultimately Hemingway; delinquent in content, they are filial in style. Recast in *Naked Lunch*, the same incidents convey something far more complex:

> I can feel the heat closing in, feel them out there making their moves, setting up their devil doll stool pigeons, crooning over my spoon and dropper I throw away at Washington Square Station, vault a turnstile and two flights down the iron stairs, catch an uptown A train . . . And right on time this narcotics dick in a white trench coat (imagine tailing somebody in a white trench coat – trying to pass as a fag I guess) hit the platform . . .
> But the subway is moving.
> 'So long flatfoot!' I yell, giving the fruit his B production. (*The Naked Lunch*, p. 7)

What is metaphorical and what factual are jammed together without pointers or hierarchy, so that 'devil doll stool pigeons' and 'spoon and dropper' sound equally literal. This is a device used frequently in Surrealist poetry, but a radical departure for an American novelist. The scornful tone of dismissal sprayed at the agent's white trench coat locates it as a prop from a 'B production' like *The Big Sleep*, an excessively obvious conformity to type, and to code. Ironically it is the agent who is a literary signifier, where the narrator is *el hombre invisible*, there and then gone as the subway train starts to move. The signs that confer social authenticity are quite literally seen through by the junkie, a social ghost exercising all the ghost's privileges of haunting and provocation, and alive only in the writing.

Roughly speaking, the texts that work most powerfully are those where this flitting is given the freest rein, unhampered by the vestiges of characterization. Its alternating aspects in the later books, typified by these two gobbets from *Port of Saints*, tend to a carnivalesque riot which is familiar from the earlier books and a free-floating melancholia which is less so:

> They take refuge in a strip club...
>   Girl prances out . . . 'I've got that je n'sais quoi...'
> She flips her hand and a claw springs out.
> 'I'VE GOT THAT I DON'T KNOW WHAT...'
> Insect fangs break through her face.
> 'I'VE GOT THAT HUMMMBUBBLERGUBBLLLLLUGH...'
> The audience rushes for the exits as the horrible black stench of insect mutation fills the room. Police sirens . . . Audrey and the Dib running down alley as police cars block them off. Blank wall ahead . . . Audrey throws the last egg and the wall turns into a transparent membrane. They squeeze through as the cops rush up shooting. (pp. 39–40)

> Somewhere a long time ago the summer ended. Old pulp magazines on the white steps. Grimy pants stood clearly even the stains. Last time together last dust of hope out there in the blue flight of adolescence on road of the Stranger. Remember who the Stranger was breathing the writer's self-knowledge and God guilt? Remember who the Stranger was breathing leaves in red hair your smell of peanuts in his hand? An obscene word scrawled on the further shore long ago. Cold dust of the dead boy a last trip home across the gleaming sky empty fragments of lost words will you his last expedition. Long long how long in the lost town heard he was a caddy years later. (p. 138)

The insect episode recalls many moments of insurrection-through-mutation in Burroughs, including the transformation of the Complete All American Deanxietized Man into a giant centipede in *The Naked Lunch*. It invites us to welcome, because of the havoc it wreaks with normality, something that would be grotesquely repellent in another context, a device traditional to black comedy and to the horror film – genres which would merge increasingly during the writer's lifetime. The mutations of the second passage are obviously of a different order, but equally intent on denying individuality, even in the falling cadences and autumnal images that would announce something desperately 'personal' from the hands of another writer. Here the pronouns are interchangeable so that the text can say, like one of the voices in *The Wild Boys*, 'I am nobody I am everybody . . . I stay present I stay absent' (p. 140). Words like cold, empty, lost, long ago resound but say that both sexual bliss and regret at its passing, both estrangement and self-knowledge are viral energies that inhabit us for while, mutate and move on. 'And then you get the blue light explosion that blows the YOU and ME right out of your head' (p. 165).

'It all has to do with making a new person from a cutting', and both this phrase and the anally retentive machine that does the job appear recurrently in the 1970s books, a gay S&M fantasy that is also profoundly and objectionably misogynist, as Burroughs's writing often was. Wild boys only need other wild boys, and growing up is not on the agenda. There is, however, a more benign sense in which the texts ask for a 'new person' free of enslavement to nationhood and sectarianism, a 'biologic adaptive' like those in *Port of Saints* who have learned to breathe under water. 'You run into intolerable oily currents under these vile oily waters, a proliferating world of film sludge, plots, armies, invisible inaudible screaming for light and sound they fall away like grey shadows. Keep walking' (p. 101). The poetics of this fusion of stoicism and utopia will outlive Burroughs's political agenda, cranky to say the least. The books are peppered with sensible suggestions: 'So why not put the royal family in a Darlington semidetached on a middle-class income and let them prove themselves in a TV serial' (*Exterminator!*, p. 112). And the books of the 1980s do predict the Waco debacle and New Age cultic implosions with a startling prescience, though with an equally alarming uncertainty as to which side Burroughs would have supported. His puerile obsession with guns – particularly culpable in a man whose life was haunted by a lethal shooting – could fuel the case against, reportedly made by the English Surrealist Philip O'Connor, as given by Ted Morgan. 'In Burroughs there was an old-fashioned man, an authoritarian individualist, who tried to escape from his own narcissism through various out-of-the-body strategies' (Morgan, *Literary Outlaw*, p. 451). And yet he may have been an old-fashioned man in a more interesting and courageous sense, albeit one bound to the legacy of Romanticism whereby, viewing life as a choice between the darkness and the light, he went without hesitation into the dark.

The post-1970 period was not that in which early novels like *The Naked Lunch* were written, but it was the period in which they passed beyond their initial shock-value and became influential. Cyberpunk maestro William Gibson, Angela Carter, Kathy Acker, Iain Sinclair, Irvine Welsh and Alan Warner are among the novelists who have pushed further into territories first explored by Burroughs. Most writers of fiction have found the cut-ups – that is, the slicing and collaging of 'found' literary materials to generate new texts – hard going, but the influence on poets of the cut-ups and other aspects of Burroughs's work has been immense. The 'children of Albion' who emerged from the 1960s underground press in Britain, the Language group in the

United States, and the Canadian poet Christopher Dewdney are among those who have found new uses for Burroughs's early work. Film-makers including Cronenberg, Gus Van Sant, Nicholas Roeg, Conrad Rooks and Anthony Balch made varied use of Burroughs or his style, and the influence on rock music has been mentioned. Partly in consequence, the post-1970 period was also that in which the writer himself became famous. Despite these widening contexts, his most interesting work of the period was done or published in the early 1970s, when Burroughs was most cut-off and thrown back on the resources of an isolation that seemed likely to increase. It is only superficially a paradox that this novelist, who could stare down the horrors of the twentieth century and swallow them whole, spoke most powerfully of his times when his own place in them was lonely, beached. The century's dominant themes followed him wherever he went, and even his high school was commandeered as a production site for the atomic bomb. Yet it is the remoteness of his printed voice that speaks most intimately of the Cold War. A lauded novel by Don DeLillo, *Underworld* (1998) strives to cover exactly this terrain and yet fails, for all its impressiveness, by comparison with Burroughs's work of the early 1970s. DeLillo's novel is a *tour de force* of absorbency, indefatigable in its appetite for American detail, forever alleging the links and analogies rather than the differences between individuals, serial killings, mass destruction, garbage and baseball. Burroughs once noted that the paranoiac is simply the man in full possession of all the facts, but while *Underworld* has been praised for exactly this tendency towards compendious extremism, its range is finally disabled by its very failure to encounter resistance. The book resembles a Sears Roebuck catalogue of everything that has happened in the last fifty years, and is equally interested in and unfazed by each and any item; happy, ultimately. Texts by Burroughs such as *Port of Saints* and *Cobble Stone Gardens* may well come to seem more enduring documents of their time precisely because of their unhappy lacunae, their failure to join the dots or make a case, their picking at scabs and morbid isolation.

In this phase of Burroughs's work, *Cobble Stone Gardens* in particular is for all its brevity a masterpiece, defying paraphrase. Sometimes it works through lucidity: 'A welching Christ is taken down from the cross and removed in an ambulance' (p. 220). Sometimes its poetry recalls dream, quite literally the source of much of Burroughs's writing: 'Suddenly the Commandante looked up, his eyes shining in the dark office under dripping trees' (p. 219). How to account for a passage like the following, which echoes Surrealism vaguely, and sort-of anticipates the manoeuvres of Language poetry, while actually resisting contextualization?

The high school Christmas play . . . a chorus of retarded boys yellow hair blue eyes prance out naked their bodies glittering with points of light. They chant in unison.

'Hello there. Looka me.'

The Death Chakra in the back of each neck lights up incandescent blue.

'The faculty was beautiful.' Some were. Some aren't.

'Hello there. Looka me. The trustees were beautiful.' Absenteeism crude and rampant. They had taken to living on a slope of aristocracy.

'Hello there. Looka me. The students were beautiful.' Most of them are. They strip off their clothes and light up like Christmas trees, chanting 'Hello there. Looka me. The students are beautiful.'

We drank Fundador in the waterfront bar. (p. 216)

As I type, the curriculum is filling like a rush-hour compartment with post-colonial fictions allegedly challenging our assumptions about gender, race, class, border, identity. Some do. Most don't. The accompanying primers diagnose a crisis in representation, though the faculty seem happy about it and a conference is planned. Who will win the next Booker Prize? Hello there, looka me. Professionalism crude and rampant. As J. G. Ballard noted in an obituary notice for The *Guardian* (4 August 1997), now that William Burroughs has gone, all that we are left with are the career novelists.

References

Significant reference is made in the chapter to the following editions of books by William Burroughs:

Queer (London: Picador, 1985).
Junky (alt. *Junkie*) (Harmondsworth: Penguin, 1977).
The Naked Lunch (Paris: Olympia Press, 1959).
The Wild Boys: A Book of the Dead (London: Calder and Boyars, 1972).
Exterminator! (London: Calder and Boyars, 1974).
Port of Saints (Berkeley: Blue Wind Press, 1980).
Cobble Stone Gardens is reprinted in *The Burroughs File* (San Francisco: City Lights Books, 1984).

Much of the biographical information in the chapter is drawn from Ted Morgan, *Literary Outlaw: The Life and Times of William S. Burroughs* (London: Pimlico, 1988).

7 1973 The End of History: Cultural Change According to Muriel Spark

Rod Mengham

Muriel Spark's novel *The Takeover* (1976) is one of the earliest as well as one of the most wide-ranging and systematic articulations of the idea that European culture in its postmodern phase is in the process of crossing a threshold that marks the 'end of history'. This book certainly identifies a moment of crisis in the recent past which represents something like a breakdown in the narrative of history; or rather, it suggests that the terms of that narrative have been utterly transformed, that conditions of knowledge at the time of composition in 1973–4 are wholly new, reflections of certain kinds of profound change. The text argues by implication for the necessity of rethinking relationships within the social contract, and that rethinking is approximated in formal terms by the way in which the text itself is organized.

The novel, coming from Spark's middle period, is the most intellectually ambitious of her works, although a plot summary would make it seem relatively narrow in focus, relatively superficial in its treatment of affluent middle-class and bourgeois-bohemian mores. Its range of character types matches that of a basic template laid down for every novel by Spark in the last twenty years, up to and including the most recent, *Reality and Dreams* (1996). The story elements concern the owners and occupiers of three houses near Lake Nemi in Italy. At the start of the narrative, both readers and characters assume that the owner of all three houses is the fabulously wealthy Maggie Radcliffe, but her claim to the properties is of a wholly material nature, and is progressively challenged in various ways.

The first house is occupied by a playwright, Hubert Mallindaine, together with his assistant, Pauline Thin, and various male 'secretaries'. Although Hubert used to be Maggie's chief adviser, his influence over her has waned considerably by the time the novel starts. In fact, their relations have deteriorated so far that Maggie has decided to evict Hubert. Her third husband Berto, an Italian nobleman, keeps up the pressure behind Maggie's determination to carry her threat into effect. Hubert fights back by laying spiritual claim to the territory of Nemi; he founds a new religious movement based on the cult of Diana, numbering the goddess among his ancestors. At the same time, he averts financial ruin by secretly arranging to replace with copies the paintings and furnishings of the house he occupies.

Maggie's second house is tenanted by her son, Michael, his American wife, Mary, and their manservant, Lauro, who acts as a go-between for various characters in all three houses. A decisive turning-point in the plot is reached when Lauro marries Betty, whose family give the couple a wedding present of some land, which turns out to be the very land on which Maggie's three houses have been built – illegally, as it now appears.

In the third house are found Dr Emilio Bernardini, an international business lawyer, his son Pietro, a would-be film director, his daughter Letizia, an Italian nationalist student, and the children's so-called tutor, Nancy Cowan, who ends up in bed with Emilio. It is Emilio who plays havoc, unintentionally, with Maggie's fortune by introducing her to the investment adviser Coco de Renault, who proves to be a confidence trickster on an epic scale.

The playfulness, even whimsicality, with which the characters' interactions are portrayed contrasts strongly with the dramatic emphasis, sometimes over-emphasis, on the cultural context of the events narrated. There is a very firm insistence throughout the text on the historical conditions that determine the structure of the narrative. There is a series of allusions to Watergate, to the 'American government scandals of which everyone's latent anarchism drank deep that summer'. In *The Abbess of Crewe* (1974), Spark had provided a full-blown allegory of the Watergate affair, but in *The Takeover* Watergate becomes simply the most concrete reference in a series of crucial allusions to the surreptitious power of political intelligence, and to a newly realized political reality of institutionalized perjury and deception. There are also numerous references to war in the Middle East, accompanying statements of belief that 'Things would never be the same again' – most obviously, because of the war's effect on the world-wide price of oil. The single most important social fact the text appears to depend on is 'the deterioration of money in general', and the central, fundamental significance of this transmutation in Western society is indicated in a passage that occurs halfway through the novel:

It was not in their minds at the time that this last quarter of the year they had entered, that of 1973, was in fact the beginning of something new in their world; a change in the meaning of property and money. They all understood these were changing in value, and they talked from time to time of recession and inflation, of losses on the stock-market, failure in business, bargains in real-estate; they habitually bandied the phrases of the newspaper economists and unquestioningly used the news-paper writers' figures of speech. They talked of hedges against inflation, as if mathematics could contain actual air and some row of hawthorn could stop an army of numbers from marching over it. They spoke of the mood of the stock-market, the health of the economy as if these were living creatures with moods and blood. And thus they personal-ized and demonologized the abstractions of their lives, believing them to be fundamentally real, indeed changeless. But it did not occur to one of those spirited and in various ways intelligent people round Berto's table that a complete mutation of our means of nourishment had al-ready come into being where the concept of money and property were concerned, a complete mutation not merely to be defined as a collapse of the capitalist system, or a global recession, but such a sea-change in the nature of reality as could not have been envisaged by Karl Marx or Sigmund Freud. Such a mutation that what were assets were to be liabilities and no armed guards could be found and fed sufficient to guard those armed guards who failed to protect the properties they guarded, whether hoarded in banks or built on confined territories, whether they were priceless works of art, or merely hieroglyphics regis-tered in the computers. (pp. 107–8)[1]

Despite the authoritative effect of this passage, it does not really have much analytic value. Unlike the characters, who are almost naively unknowing, the narratorial point of view is not innocent of future developments. What it does succeed at is registering the difficulty of grasping the nature of the 'sea-change' it refers to. First of all, it regis-ters the sheer *scale* of the problem, and then it identifies, as the single most influential factor in the overall change, a 'change in the meaning of property and money'. It invites reflection on the relative and sym-bolic nature of the value of property and money. The novel provides a subsequent little disquisition on this topic which is fixed historically in a passage which treats of events a year later:

It was the autumn of 1974 and Maggie had not succeeded in turning Hubert out of her villa, partly because she had been distracted through-out that year by little thumps of suspicion within her mind at roughly six-week intervals concerning the manipulation of her fortune, with all its ramifications from Switzerland to the Dutch Antilles and the Bahamas, from the distilleries of Canada through New York to the

chain-storedom of California, and from the military bases of Green-
land's icy mountains to the hotel business of India's coral strand.
Brilliant Monsieur de Renault was now the overlord of Maggie's network. Mysterious and intangible, money of Maggie's sort was able to
take lightning trips round the world without ever packing its bags or
booking its seat on a plane. Indeed, money of any sort is, in reality,
unspendable and unwasteable; it can only pass hands wisely or unwisely,
or else by means of violence, and, colourless, odourless and tasteless, it
is a token for the exchange of colours, smells and savours, for food and
shelter and clothing and for representations of beauty, however beauty
may be defined by the person who buys it. Only in appearance does
money multiply itself; in reality it multiplies the human race, so that
even money lavished on funerals is not wasted, neither directly nor indirectly, since it nourishes the undertaker's children as the body fert-
ilizes the earth. (p. 118)

What is behind this line of thought in the narrative is essentially the
observation that money functions no longer as a means of enabling
the subject to consume a material object that satisfies a rational need,
but is primarily a means of enabling the subject to place herself or
himself within a communication structure in which those exchanges
which ensure the reproduction of the system are first and foremost
symbolic ones.

In general terms, the text hinges on the belief that what it bears
witness to is the death of an old dispensation, or the extinction of an
old social contract, and its supersession by a different order of reality.
One political reflection of this exhaustion of an old social contract is
the evidence of the Italian election results of 1975, when 51 per cent of
the vote went to a Christian Democrat-led coalition, as against 49 per
cent to a Communist-led coalition. One of the novel's characters, Berto,
assumes that 'Italy had turned half communist overnight', but the results are more likely to represent a negative vote against the old social
contract, rather than a positive vote for a new one.

However, the contractual basis of society that is most extensively
examined in the novel is that of the law. The book is full of legal
arrangements and, indeed, of lawyers. One of them, Massimo de Vita,
is a communist sympathizer, 'having sentimental sympathies towards
the political left wing'. He turns upside down the usual position of the
lawyer whose disinterestedness is demonstrated in his taking up the
case of a client irrespective of personal convictions about the client's
moral condition. Massimo rather evinces his belief in the immorality,
or moral instability, of the law by taking up the cases of two clients in
conflict with each other, and exploiting the interests of one to the advantage of the other. This is far from being the only situation in which

the meaninglessness of the law is argued for. Perhaps the most striking complications arise from the constant struggles of the characters over the ownership of the three houses. The laws of property end up appearing nonsensical when it is revealed that the characters' dispute is about houses which do not legally exist. Maggie has been tricked by a counterfeit lawyer who has negotiated the sale of some land belonging to an individual he has absolutely no professional relationship with. As a result, the houses Maggie has had built on the land 'do not exist', which means that she can neither charge rent for them, nor evict tenants from them. This provokes Hubert, the tenant to be evicted, to remark that 'Italian law is very exciting. Positively mystical. I approve strongly of Italian law.'

The argument of the book, if it can be said to have one, consists in its setting up a forum in which mutually exclusive definitions of property, ownership and possession fight it out among themselves. The narrative is constantly pursuing situations in which the characters' sense of what is privately theirs is being tested and questioned. Textual competition between several definitions of 'property' works to shake it free from any stable relationship with morality. Maggie's legal entitlement to her three houses becomes illegal overnight. This is the most dramatic example of the shifting nature of the rights and wrongs of ownership, but the book is full of variations on a situation in which the difference between legal possession and illegal appropriation is blurred. Numerous spectacular robberies are committed: there is the theft of Maggie's jewels, the plundering of Berto's Palladian villa, the prospective burgling of Hubert's villa, the ransacking of Mary's bank. However, the outraged victims of these crimes are themselves guilty of smuggling into the country in the first place the art-objects that are subsequently stolen from them. They are equally guilty of tax-evasion and, some of them, even capable of resorting to terrorist measures in order to redress the balance of their depleted fortunes. The behaviour of Maggie in particular illustrates Hubert's thesis delivered in one of his little sermons after the foundation of his religious movement: ' "The concepts of property and material possession are the direct causes of such concepts as perjury, lying, deception and fraud." ' Hubert does not enunciate this from a position of moral superiority, of course, since he is lying and deceiving when he tries to oppose what is initially thought of as Maggie's 'material possession' of the villa with what he claims is his spiritual ownership of it. He bases his 'mystical and spiritual' entitlement to Nemi on his genealogical descent from the goddess Diana, whose temple is now tellingly overgrown and filled with rubbish. Just as Maggie's legal claim turns out to be empty, so Hubert's spiritual claim is also a fake. Then there is a third claim, lodged by Letizia, a moral claim that the land ought to belong to an Italian, since it is part of 'our national patrimony'.

There are paradoxes involved in all three claims, but Hubert's contention with regard to 'spiritual ownership' is perhaps the most richly ambiguous. The dubious relationship between the concepts of 'spirituality' and 'ownership' is inherent in the multifaceted nature of the word 'possession', whose overtones of control by an evil spirit are fully exploited by the book. Psychological possession is at the basis of all Hubert's relationships with others, and particularly with Maggie; his Svengali-like hold on her, already loosened by the start of the narrative, is only the most blatant example of the hypnotic powers exercised in so many of the book's relationships. Maggie, in recalling her dependence on Hubert's advice, explains in the plainest terms how '"It's really hypnotic when you get in someone's clutches."' Hypnosis is aligned not only with the private psychological battles of the characters, but also with the manipulation of power on the largest scale: on the scale, for example, of the 'American government scandals' that Hubert is reported to be 'hypnotized' by.

Being hypnotized, being possessed, losing control of oneself is a recurrent anxiety for the characters. Self-awareness seems to hinge on an awareness of either taking over someone else or of being taken over (and this sheds a strong light on one aspect of the novel's title). Once the necessity for takeover is no longer current (when, for example, there is no financial incentive to take someone over), the abandoned victim is given the appearance of having been entirely emptied of life or motivation, and functions only by means of nervous reaction to the withdrawal of control. One obvious instance is that of Kurt, Hubert's 'secretary', who ends up losing all control over his own body, speaking as if operated by a ventriloquist.

The double-edged character of the various 'spiritual' takeover bids depicted in the novel is inherent in the world-wide religious phenomenon that Spark treats as highly symptomatic of the conditions of knowledge in which the old social contracts have become meaningless. The period of the mid-1970s is defined vividly by the growth of fundamentalism, by the development of a Charismatic Renewal movement found not only in Christianity but also in other religions. Charismatic Renewal is read as a reaction against the exhaustion of the old dispensation, as a return to the spirit as opposed to the letter of the law, at a time when the letter of the law has become so meaningless. And yet the various returns to the spirit depicted in the book are revealed sooner or later as pretexts for power-seeking, for the extension of psychological or political control by other means.

Hubert bases his new church on the worship of Diana, but hopes to recruit followers from the Catholic movement, acting on the assumption voiced by a Jesuit priest, Father Gerard, that Catholicism is susceptible to this kind of renovation: '"underneath it there is a large area of pagan remainder to be explored. And absorbed into Christianity. A very rich seam."' Hubert envisages reversing this absorption process, while Father Gerard's interest in pagan ecology reinforces the link between spirituality and territoriality in the idea of the holy place: the shrine or sanctuary, which mixes inextricably the notions of spiritual and material occupancy. This ecological fundamentalism is paralleled in political terms by a folk-consciousness in the nationalism of a character like Letizia.

The replacing of the old dispensation with the new actually involves the renovation of something much older, but it is a renovation that is compromised and corrupted by an investment in power, control and possession. This is suggested by the repeated use of a language of paradox, as in the announcement of 'the new world which was arising out of the ashes of the old, *avid* for *immaterialism*' (my emphases): a contradiction of motives is implied by the almost oxymoronic combination of elements. The mythological strand in the book is there chiefly to bring out the extent to which charismatic renewal represents the provision of a spiritual pretext in order to accomplish what are really very pragmatic aims. The cult of Diana provides the most appropriate illustration of this equivocation. Its history reflects a spectacular transformation of its original meaning. The goddess Diana, whose symbol is the moon, was originally associated with chastity, but by the time of Paul the Apostle's attempt to convert the Ephesians, she had become linked with fertility, and represented by statues with multiple egg-shaped breasts. According to Acts 19, Paul was unable to preach at Ephesus, because he could not make himself heard above the shouts of 'Great is Diana!' The clamour was raised by the makers of statues of Diana – whom Spark refers to succinctly as the 'silversmiths lobby' – craftsmen whose livelihood would have been destroyed in the event of Christianity supplanting Diana's cult. The ambivalent basis of this particular religious tradition is virtually symbolized by the present-day state of Diana's temple at Nemi, whose niches are re-named 'the Devil's Grottoes' and filled with rubbish. The devaluation of the spiritual is one of the most powerful emphases of the book. Dispersed throughout the text are numerous unobtrusive misuses of religious and ethical terms. In conversation with Emilio, Maggie demonstrates a certain amount of know-how about his paintings, 'thus establishing with him the higher market-place *communion* that exists between rich and rich' (my emphasis). Pauline, when she is faced with the sexual indifference of Hubert, who has homosexual preferences, states her intention of 'converting' him to women. Her eventual defiance of him is of course anticipated in the apostolic first syllable of her name. And on her first visit to Rome with one of the chairs that Hubert intends to have faked, Pauline provides the occasion for a whole series of linguistic misapplications: the chair, which is said to be covered with 'penitential' sackcloth, is pointedly 'unshrouded', while Pauline has trouble in finding an oddly denominated 'legitimate' parking place. Quite simply, words which carry a certain amount of conceptual freight are used in contexts which do not allow them their full weight.

This degradation of the language of values is habitually exposed by the writing, which is clearly attempting to force the reader to put up some resistance to it, as in the following instance: 'Where is the poetry of my life? Hubert thought. He retained an inkling that the poetry was still there and would return. Wordsworth defined poetry as "emotion recollected in tranquillity". Hubert took a tranquillizer, quite a mild one called Mitigil, and knew he would feel better in about ten minutes.' This is trivial and throwaway, but it forces on the reader an awareness of a paradoxical use of language that is habitual among the characters of this book, and with regard to which there is shown to be a dangerously increasing lack of awareness. For example, no psychological tension whatever is registered in the indirect account of Maggie's '*access* of financial *morality*' (my emphases), as if morality were something characteristically sporadic, impulsive: something definitively momentary in one's experience.

The devaluation of language is concerted with the devaluation of money, and with a general devaluation in a situation where nothing has value apart from its face-value. As Hubert proclaims, ' "If you imagine that appearances may belie the reality, then you are wrong. Appearances are *reality*." ' Hubert himself goes a long way towards helping to create the circumstances in which this becomes possible, by arranging for the manufacture of phoney antiques, and for the copying of paintings by Gauguin and Constable (he has plans also for canvases by Sickert, Corot and Turner, even though the last-named turns out to be a fake already). Hubert, of course, also fakes himself, as Priest and descendant of Diana. And he is not the only one to fall into this category. Coco de Renault, who is introduced as a 'short man with very black dyed-looking hair and a taut, very cosmetically-surgeoned face' turns out to have changed his appearance twice before by plastic surgery. The novel is thickly populated by parallel cases, such as that of the lawyer who cheated Maggie over the sale of the land, or that of the 'false Catholic prelate' who sets up as a rival to Hubert at Nemi. Not only are counterfeits put into circulation, usurping the value of originals, but the originals themselves are often disowned, or submitted to the pretence that they are in fact fakes, in order to prevent their being stolen or kidnapped. This would apply not only to Maggie's jewels, but also eventually to Maggie herself, who adopts various disguises in order to avoid capture.

The society portrayed in the book is one that has forfeited any secure or stable means of evaluation. Once it has lost the distinction between the licit and the illicit, it cannot establish any basis for a critique of its own conditions. And this withdrawal of critical consciousness is observable on a truly global scale. The businessmen and lawyers who are the professional manipulators of this public reality belong to a trend towards an international and ever-expanding scale of operations – or of 'takeovers'. Emilio is a business lawyer 'occupied between Rome, Milan and Zurich', while Coco de Renault's schemes span continents. His network is significantly decentred; he disbands Maggie's headquarters, so that she loses all control and even any idea of what is happening to her fortune, and is completely unable to track him down. The characters become subject to conditions which are immanent and universal and which have become mystified. The various 'takeovers' seem to act almost of their own accord, subject to laws of their own and beyond the reach or recall of any individual.

Feelings of individual powerlessness, of being 'taken over', are extended beyond the complications of intense personal relationships to characterize a general condition of being remotely controlled or monitored. Maggie's personal Svengali, Hubert, is also described as being her 'central information agent' in a sequence of words whose initial letters seem to redefine him as an example of an ubiquitous process or system of surveillance and intelligence-gathering. The Charismatic Renewal movement is conspicuously international and Hubert proposes to galvanize his own followers with what is variously referred to as an 'international synod', a 'world congress' and a 'global convergence'. This giddy expansion and contraction of scale in spatial terms, whereby the individual's private experience is immediately set in an universal context in a way that is overpowering, excludes any intermediate social context in which individual acts of acceptance or rejection of the conditions of knowledge could be made to seem effectual. And this is paralleled by a similar incongruity of scales in temporal terms. The narrative dates methodically the successive occurrences, but the temporal scope of the events is made perplexing and unmeasurable: ' "Eras pass," thought Hubert, "They pass every day." ' The inability to measure the scale of events and to attribute with any confidence meaning or value to them is reckoned to issue from the breakdown in the narrative of history, from the abandonment, as it were, of the narrative contract.

The breakdown of the narrative entails a loss of coordinates, produces an inability to map one's position: to explain it, account for it, identify its causes and foresee its effects. The individual's relation to history becomes a case of hypnosis, of capitulation to the irresistible, of imprisonment within a circular pattern; history, it begins to be assumed, is something that repeats itself so that one is simply taken over by the role one is given to play. Hubert, Maggie, Coco and Lauro all re-enact an episode of 'fictional' history, a preordained mythological narrative which mystifies their historically specific, concrete situation. This myth is the myth of the Golden Bough, as elaborated by Frazer, which Spark has perhaps chosen with an eye to literary history, in order to stress the manipulative role that art can play with regard to the assigning of historical meaning and value. Spark quotes at length Frazer's 'celebrated account of the priesthood of Diana' and its 'tragedy'.

> In the sacred grove there grew a certain tree round which at any time of the day, and probably far into the night, a grim figure might be seen to prowl. In his hand he carried a drawn sword, and he kept peering warily about him as if at every instant he expected to be set upon by an enemy. He was a priest and a murderer; and the man for whom he looked was sooner or later to murder him and hold the priesthood in his stead. Such was the rule of the sanctuary. A candidate for the priesthood could only succeed to office by slaying the priest, and having slain him, he retained office till he was himself slain by a stronger or craftier.
>
> The post which he held by this precarious tenure carried with it the title of king; but surely no crowned head ever lay uneasier, or was visited by more evil dreams, than his. For year in year out, in summer and winter, in fair weather and in foul, he had to keep his lonely watch, and whenever he snatched a troubled slumber it was at the peril of his life. The least relaxation of his vigilance, the smallest abatement of his strength of limb or skill of fence, put him in jeopardy; grey hairs might seal his death-warrant . . . Within the sanctuary at Nemi grew a certain tree of which no branch might be broken. Only a runaway slave was allowed to break off, if he could, one of its boughs. Success in the attempt entitled him to fight the priest in single combat, and if he slew him he reigned in his stead with the title of King of the Wood (*Rex Nemorensis*). According to the public opinion of the ancients the fateful branch was that Golden Bough which, at the Sibyl's bidding, Aeneas plucked before he essayed the perilous journey to the world of the dead. . . . This rule of succession by the sword was observed down to imperial times; for amongst his other freaks Caligula, thinking that the priest of Nemi had held office too long, hired a more stalwart ruffian to slay him; and a Greek traveller, who visited Italy in the age of the Antonines, remarks that down to his time the priesthood was still the prize of victory in a single combat.[2]

There are obvious resonances of this scenario in Spark's novel. The priests are represented by Hubert and Coco, the runaway slave by Lauro, and Diana by Maggie. Maggie actually refers to herself as Diana, and at the end of the book is associated with the moon and identified as a kind of huntress. What the text suggests is that to adopt the circular view of history that this promotes involves a form of derangement: in *The Takeover*, it is a perspective ultimately derived from Hubert's dotty aunts, two figures with unsettlingly crude haircuts, who walk around hand-in-hand, lighting bonfires and offering up unlikely prayers. In the world of *The Takeover*, a world of automatic responses and helplessness, the characters are found trying to initiate some kind of control over their lives through writing. The text is punctuated by a series of different kinds of documents: lists of coins, lists of guests, archives, legal papers, letters and Maggie's various 'plans'. These textual projects are all failed attempts by the characters to account for the difficulties they find themselves in; they are prototypes, as it were, for the design of the novel *The Takeover*, whose writing is orientated by the necessity to try to 'plot' the events it covers.

In a sense, *The Takeover* is a text which attempts to establish its control over material that does not fit comfortably into the scale of a novel. And this lack of fit is seemingly underlined by a series of formal contradictions. On the one hand, the text can enjoy moments of confidence, of firm prolepsis, when the sequence of events seems to be manageable; but on the other hand there are also moments of disorientation, of insecurity about the meaning and value of the events, and the scale of their significance. Trivial occurrences can be given an aspect of unlikely historical grandeur, as if to compensate for a lack of sure knowledge on the part of the narrator, while at other times there are frank admissions of narratorial bewilderment, or even casual indifference: 'On her return to the house, after her careful shower and before going down to dinner, Mary had sat for a long while in her room, with her head in her hands, *thinking God knows what*' (my emphases).

There is a fundamental lack of balance in this uncertainty about the status of the narrative and the authority of the narrator, who begins to look something like Diana's high priest, losing her or his grip and casting about desperately for narrative expedients. It is as if the narrator is in a position to be usurped, ready to become the victim of a 'takeover' and be succeeded, logically speaking, by a reader who has been made to recognize that the old narrative contract no longer obtains. The text works to arouse suspicion of the narrator and to instigate a certain degree of psychological detachment and independent intellectual resourcefulness on the part of the reader. It operates as a troubling narrative, embodied in a text intended to make the reader reflect on the troubles afflicting the narrative of history. These include conspiracy theories, fundamentalist religious movements, the increasingly international scope of financial transactions in late capitalism, a change in the meaning of property and money, the increasingly powerful role of the media through which models of subjectivity are imposed, the covert nature of many governmental operations, the degradation of the language of values, the undermining of the concepts of authenticity and originality (particularly in art), and the mythologizing of history. The importance of *The Takeover* lies in its construction of a plot and practice of writing that relates all of these things and which offers a new fictional paradigm for their combined effect, in what is nothing less than 'a sea-change in the nature of reality'.

Notes

1 Page references throughout are to the paperback edition: Muriel Spark, *The Takeover* (London: Granada, 1985).
2 Sir James Frazer, *The Golden Bough: A Study in Magic and Religion*, 3rd edn (London: Macmillan, 1911), vol. 1, pp. 8–11.

8 Oswald our Contemporary: Don DeLillo's *Libra*

N. H. Reeve

To parody a famous question: where were you when you first read a book, or saw a film or TV programme, about the assassination of John F. Kennedy? For those old enough to remember 1963, the famous question itself can evoke both pathos and a certain satisfaction, as if the real motive for asking it were the desire for a shared history, for a collective experience which momentarily eclipsed the fragmented, privatized, consumerist banalities of contemporary existence. Being able to answer would be at some level a token of belonging, an affirmation that the space one occupied once took on the extra significance of interfusion with a whole world turned suddenly the same way. The memory would not only vibrate with the thrill of great events, but would open again its precious glimpse, in the midst of tragedy, of a redemptive social bond. At the same time, as Fredric Jameson has pointed out, what one may really be remembering is not so much the grief or trauma but the impact on consciousness of the global news media, unleashing their full forces for the first time; television in particular taking possession of the events and subjecting them to the repertoire of ubiquity, package, instant replay and reconstruction which now is taken for granted, but which constituted at the time an unbalancing lurch into a new way of receiving images and information.[1]

The parody of the famous question is intended to indicate the degree to which the assassination, in narrative and imagery, has permeated contemporary culture, and the depth of its implication in the arguments and practices of the 'postmodern' condition: indeed, as Art Simon implies in *Dangerous Knowledge: The JFK Assassination in Art and Film* (1995), the failure of the official investigation by the Warren Commission to provide a convincing and coherent narrative, one which could stabilize the meaning of what had happened, may well have been one of the most powerful accelerators of the aesthetic and epistemological crises of the contemporary West. So many of the characteristics most frequently assigned to postmodernism are gathered in to the assassination and its aftermath; the resistance to narrative closure, for example, since each attempt to pin the story down merely opens a fresh chapter; the incredulity towards totalizing explanations or 'metanarratives', in Lyotard's term, since the authority and legitimacy of explanation itself is put into question along with the motives of those offering one; a raft of what might really be called 'undecidable' questions (how many gunmen? how many shots? was Kennedy hit from behind or from the front? was there a conspiracy? was there a cover-up?), and the variety of reaction generated by them. There were paranoid theories on the one hand, each claiming to offer the authentic narrative which rival accounts had either failed to produce or had deliberately suppressed; and on the other hand, there was a faith, underpinning each competing theory, in certain fundamental forms of evidence which permit access to a Truth beneath the wearying play of signification. The Zapruder film of the motorcade, or the shape and size of bullet marks on the President's corpse, or the photograph of Oswald holding the alleged murder weapon, have all been appealed to in turn, as if they were unimpeachable guarantees which could protect the world from the chaos of arbitrariness.

As each theory is challenged by a fresh one, with its different interrogations of the same forms of evidence, each of these guarantees turns out to be as open to interpretation as everything else; previously accepted sources of meaning are compromised, 'facts' which are supposed to tell a single story start to release multiple stories, and each injection of doubt sets up its reflex of nostalgic rage for the pure and the uncontaminated – one of the defining features of American ideology from the beginning. It is the same kind of rage which, as is suggested in Don DeLillo's novel *Libra*,[2] motivated the conspirators against Kennedy in the first place, and which now infects those who attempt to trace them. Nicholas Branch, the character in *Libra* who is employed by the CIA to compile a secret history of the assassination, complains, as he struggles through the morass of data and testimony, that 'he wants a thing to be what it is' (p. 79); while his comment on the famous Zapruder film, that it shows 'the powerful moment of death' with 'the surrounding blurs, patches and shadows' (p. 441), is in a way a comment on the whole condition of discourse established by the event, a condition in which death alone seems able to stand out amidst a swirl of contestables.

What kind of contribution does *Libra* make to these debates?

DeLillo's previous novel, *White Noise*,[3] had presented a powerfully satirical account of a postmodern America whose inhabitants, uncertain of their identities in a bewildering world of information overload, attempt to gain some illusory sense of empowerment by fitting themselves and their life-histories into pre-formed narratives and scenarios, either of their own design or borrowed from the general culture, narratives of steady progress and clear outcome. The characters in *White Noise* act in so many ways like plotters and conspirators. They change their appearances, or adapt their behaviour, to suit the images they wish to project and hide behind; or else they try to fend off disaster by anticipating and rehearsing for it, imagining its contours, so that the contingencies of reality can be neutralized or discounted in advance. Meanwhile, chemicals released in an environmental accident nearby start to seep insidiously into the body, producing a toxic reality which evades all efforts to shape and control it, a 'nebulous mass' inside the characters aggravating the paranoia from which they already suffer. *White Noise* examines the postmodern condition without ever presuming that the place from which it is examined is somehow free from its effects; even when the narrator, Jack Gladney, draws back in confused revulsion from his attempt to murder his supposed sexual rival, and tries to act humanely instead, his change of behaviour is open to the doubt that, rather than representing a true moral recovery, it might simply have been borrowed from another, equally thrilling scenario: 'It hadn't occurred to me that a man's attempts to redeem himself might prolong the elation he felt when he committed the crime he now sought to make up for' (*White Noise*, p. 315). *Libra* traces a good deal of this world of evasion, doubt and self-processing back to the figure of Lee Harvey Oswald, a figure who seems half-wittingly to have set postmodernity circulating around him.

The story of America's response to Oswald's presumed involvement in the assassination is essentially the story of a shift, from early efforts to secure him within certain historically specific narratives (as a former defector with a grudge, as a pro-Castro secret agent, as the fall-guy for a particular plot), to a new set of more generalized psychological narratives, depicting him as a symptom of a deep national malaise; a morbid narcissism, an Oedipal anxiety, a fatherless man who kills the symbolic Father. Oswald was frequently constructed as Kennedy's antitype, the 'villainy' of the one perversely matching and endorsing the 'virtue' of the other. Oswald sets difficulties both for those who want to read him as exemplary and those who see him as a one-off. He lied and manipulated; he laid false trails about himself; he had unpredictable spurts of decency, affection and viciousness; his delusions of grandeur left him bored and alienated; his impulsiveness seemed calculated and his calculations seemed impulsive; in a somehow touch-ingly suggestive way he had to empty his rubbish into other people's bins because he could not afford one of his own.

Libra not only has things to say about this continuing need on Amer-ica's part to explain or protect itself from so elusive a phenomenon; it also appeared, whether by accident or design (!), at a special moment in the history of that need, the twenty-fifth anniversary year, just when fresh attention would have been expected, and from a writer who had after long obscurity recently established himself as an authoritative commentator. With such appurtenances *Libra* seemed to be interven-ing almost in the manner of a magisterial summing-up, that which, as one publisher's blurb announced, 'the shaken American psyche has been awaiting'. But the novel knows that magisterial summing-up remains exactly what the 'postmodernist' aspects of the case resist. Questions moreover inevitably arise as to how and to what extent the summaries offered by the novel to the history it works with could be distinguished from those offered by the paranoia which the novel sets out to confront. To write a novel about so slippery a subject as Oswald is not quite to challenge or subvert an authorized version of history, in the manner of numerous postmodern novels which the critic Linda Hutcheon has called 'historiographic metafictions'.[4] Such novels, her examples of which include Salman Rushdie's *Shame*, Graham Swift's *Waterland,* or J. M. Coetzee's *Foe*, do not use 'history' and 'fiction' to mean 'truth' and 'falsehood', but expose them to be alternative, paral-lel signifying systems, each with its own set of codes and conventions to produce meaning, and neither privileged over the other. But, as we have seen, the assassination-story not only has never had an author-ized version that was not put under such challenge from the begin-ning, but has itself already done more than any postmodern novel to undermine the supposed authority of historical accounts and objec-tive overviews. What might be called the 'Oswald case' arrives already implicated in contemporary fictional practices. *Libra* tries to distil from it, in the manner of a more traditional humanist novel, certain recur-rent patterns and processes – to assist in clarifying things that con-sciousness finds hard to tolerate in their obscurity; while at the same time, writing from within postmodernism, to suggest how the sheer extent of these recurrences shows the Oswald case successfully repro-ducing itself, like a rogue cell, and infiltrating everywhere the world of its posterity.

To summarize briefly: there are three interwoven narratives in *Libra*: scenes from Oswald's life; scenes from the lives of those who, like his mother Marguerite, or Nicholas Branch, are trying to understand him afterwards; and scenes from the life of the conspiracy towards which the novel imagines him being drawn. The conspiracy is hatched by a group of former CIA agents nursing grievances about the Bay of Pigs fiasco in Cuba in 1961, when Kennedy pulled back at the last minute from fully supporting a CIA-backed attempt by Cuban exiles to invade the island and overthrow Castro. Win Everett, the leader of this disaffected group, plans to set up a 'failed' assassination attempt on the President which can be traced back to Castro supporters: a deliberate miss which can be made to look like a narrow escape, rousing American public opinion in outrage against Castro and forcing Kennedy to sanction a proper invasion. The brilliant perfection of this plot will have a cleansing effect on a sullied world. But to Everett's dismay and terror everything grows rapidly beyond his control.

Firstly, the most vengeful of the conspirators, T. J. Mackey, semi-secretly takes the plot over in order to kill Kennedy rather than miss him. Secondly, Oswald appears on the scene: Oswald, who seems to be the exact double of the mock-up 'assassin', the traceable fall-guy Everett had been creating on paper – an embittered loner with a gun and a biography full of incriminating pro-Communist details. Oswald matches the desired profile so precisely as to induce 'a sensation of the eeriest panic' in Everett, 'a glimpse of the fiction he'd been devising . . . living prematurely in the world' (p. 179). A man-made 'Oswald' would have offered everything the conspiracy needed; a real one stirs up all the paranoid sense of impotence in these ageing CIA veterans which the conspiracy was designed to overcome. Have we really stumbled on this man fortuitously, or is he a spy, an informer, a plant from some parallel conspiracy to ours? How could he exist before we imagined him? Can we trust him to do what we require, or will he wander off on his own, or betray us? As the forces Everett has unleashed spiral away from him, and the confusions build to their tragic climax, Oswald, rather like the toxic chemicals in *White Noise,* increasingly seems to infect with a creeping disorder everything he touches; none of the plots can turn out properly once he is involved. Even Mackey, the legendarily ruthless military expert, who had planned to have Oswald silenced immediately after the assassination, is forced to watch him being noisily arrested instead. As Kirilenko, the KGB agent who interrogated Oswald when he defected to Russia, had mused, 'Unknowing, partly knowing, knowing but not saying, the boy had a quality of trailing chaos behind him, causing disasters without seeing them happen, making riddles of his life and possibly fools of us all' (p. 194).

Most of *Libra*'s narrative of Oswald's life stays close to what can be biographically verified, but Kirilenko's reflections occur during an episode which DeLillo has clearly invented, and which precisely for that reason may best gather together his work's concerns with pattern and resemblance: Oswald has been brought secretly to Moscow by the KGB to witness the interrogation of Powers, the pilot of the U-2 spy plane famously shot down over the Urals in 1960. The idea of Oswald's having such clandestine importance in one of the crucial episodes of the Cold War is imaginatively compelling almost because the truth was so different. The evidence assembled in Norman Mailer's biographical study *Oswald's Tale* (1995) suggests that Oswald was in fact terrified at first of the possible repercussions of the U-2 incident on himself, as an American living in Minsk, and secondly both relieved and rather annoyed when nothing ensued – annoyed because it confirmed his *lack* of importance to the world he had expected to create a sensation in by defecting. The Oswald of *Libra* may be fantasizing the whole thing – the text just allows us to think so – as compensation for the Soviets' failure to take him seriously. After all, Oswald clearly believed he was destined for greatness; that his experience of both communist and capitalist systems gave him unique political insight; and that the neglect and humiliation he had suffered in his youth resembled those in the classic life-narratives of the future Leader – be it Hitler, Lenin, or Trotsky – on which he modelled himself. Now circumstances arise when the KGB have need of him – and on two counts: that he knows about the U-2 from his time as a Marine radar operator and can cross-check Powers's claims about it, and that he is an American, able to read the 'telltale inflections' (p. 194), the codes of specifically American demeanour in Powers which a Russian interrogator might miss. Oswald is called upon to act as a rather contradictory mixture of lie-detector and semiological critic – contradictory, since for the latter meanings operate only within the local cultural systems that produce them, while the former looks to the nervous system of the body, for example, to yield up universal and final meanings, visible to all and transcending cultural differences. Oswald thus finds himself placed, with comic precision, on a cusp between traditional and postmodernist ways of assessing someone else's discourse – and he cannot perform reliably in either capacity; Kirilenko realizes that Oswald's recollections of the U-2 are untrustworthy, while the comments Oswald makes on Powers's 'American' bearing seem deliberately composed for self-referential effect: ' "A hardworking, sincere, honest fellow . . . being crushed by the pressure exerted from opposite directions. That makes him typical, I guess." ' (p. 198)

Oswald seems to have chanced upon a figure who replicates in the flesh many of his fantasies of himself. He identifies with Powers on a number of levels. For a brief time the pilot had touched an apex of mastery; all the apparatus of American military might had risen to this point, beyond range of radar tracking, where his plane's spy cameras could penetrate secret places that would never know he had seen them. *Libra* began with the young Oswald riding the New York subway: 'He stood at the front of the first car, hands flat against the glass. The view down the tracks was a form of power. It was a secret and a power. The beams picked out secret things' (p. 13). These systems of power are supportive, protective, embracing; they insulate the self from the outside world, turn others into objects or targets. All the conspirators in the novel experience comparable sensations, whether the insulating power involves CIA euphemism (Everest always refers to Kennedy by his code-name, 'Lancer', in an effort to pre-empt humane inhibitions), or the superstitious rapture of David Ferrie's belief in destiny, or a film-scenario to imitate (as when the hitman Wayne Elko thinks of himself as one of the Seven Samurai, living by an elite warrior code and volunteering to protect an ignorant and ungrateful public; he fails in fact to shoot Oswald in the cinema when he was supposed to, because he was waiting to synchronize the shot with the swell and tension of the film they were both watching).

At the same time, these secrecies enable someone like Oswald to manipulate the forms that protect him, to work from a private agenda hidden inside the anonymity of his official role; his relish on the dark subway was not just for the metallic shriek of power but for his sense of the other passengers' ignorance of his thoughts and motives among them. He identifies with Powers's loyalty to himself in a crisis, his refusal to take his poison pill on being captured: 'You were right, good for you, disobey' (p. 196). Powers has stepped outside the plot he was cast in, talked when he was supposed to be silent, refused to subordinate himself to anyone else's scheme. Oswald sees nothing abject about Powers, no sense that his collapse from awesome control into weakness and exposure offers a chastening reminder of human frailty; he sees rather how the whole sequence has given birth to a celebrity, celebrity which is a new and even more powerful hiding place for the self:

> It occurred to Oswald that everyone called the prisoner by his full name . . . Once you did something notorious, they tagged you with an extra name, a middle name that was ordinarily never used . . . Francis Gary Powers. In just these few days, the name had taken on a resonance . . . It already sounded historic. (p. 198)

Kirilenko had designed the juxtaposition of Powers and Oswald in an attempt to establish authenticity, but Oswald comes away with an enhanced sense of how readily the self could seize opportunities to be reconstructed and repositioned (he subsequently adopts Kirilenko's own name, Alek, to use as one of his numerous aliases).

There are other patterns and replications at work in this scene. The narrative contours of the U-2 story anticipate those of the assassination: the dark, glittering, powerful thing is mysteriously shot down, the shattered wreckage is put on display, read and reread into conflicting theories. Had the plane been flying beyond radar range or not? Was it hit by a missile fired at it or caught in the chance explosion of one nearby? Was it not hit at all, but brought down by mechanical failure? Was it sabotaged by the CIA, or a secret group within the CIA, to scupper the upcoming disarmament talks? Everett's conspiracy reproduces the same sequence: it begins in secrecy, in perfection of design, recording and controlling the behaviour of a world unaware of its presence; it frays at the edges, and then collapses altogether, in confusion, accident, sudden weakness. And in each case the same unstable afterlife that Oswald intuited, the glow of celebrity and mystique, blurs the traditional moral messages lodged in the pattern, messages of a tragic or a fortunate, humanizing fall, mankind rescued from its dreams of perfect dominance by the very muddle and uncertainty those dreams sought to eradicate – the moral recovery which *White Noise* questioned without completely abandoning, and which is not all that far away from the closing theme of, say, Rex Warner's *The Aerodrome* (1941), a novel about the attractions of fascism, in which a climactic plane crash, a fall to earth, symbolizes the triumph of the contingent and the ordinary over the inhuman purity of mechanized airborne systems. Powers's fall to earth attracts some of the most softly cadenced writing in a novel inevitably suspicious of imaginative decoration:

> He comes floating down out of the endless pale, struck simultaneously by the beauty of the earth and a need to ask forgiveness . . . People come into view, farm hands, children racing toward the spot where the wind will set him down . . . He is near enough to hear them calling, the words bounced and steered and elongated by the contours of the land . . . this privileged vision of the earth is an inducement to truth. He wants to tell the truth. He wants to live another kind of life, outside secrecy and guilt and the pull of grave events. (p. 116)

This urge to confess, to break out of the capsule, links Powers with Everett, who, as he felt the force of the chaos he had unleashed, began to yearn for the chance to *take* a lie-detector test, to make contact again even at his own expense with something absolute that could confer absolution, the purity that for all paranoiacs lies on the other side of secrecy:

It would be a deliverance in a way to be confronted, polygraphed, forced to tell the truth. He believed in the truth . . . His body would . . . yield up its unprotected data . . . There was something intimate about the polygraph . . . Devices make us pliant. We want to please them. The machine was his only hope of deliverance after what he'd done . . . They would nod and understand. A forgiveness would come to their eyes. (pp. 361-3)

But Oswald has no such moral yearning, even one like this with the self-serving accents of childhood regression. He is always looking to loop ahead from the crisis of present experience to the future package into which it can be fitted, the new self that will have emerged from it. On the ship back from Russia to the US he prepared and memorized two separate accounts of himself, to be used according to whether he received a hostile or a friendly welcome. Whenever he gives up control for a moment, or seems to abandon himself to fate, there is always a sense of a semi-deliberate collapse into helplessness, half-authentic and half-tactical: even his suicide attempt in Russia seems neither quite real nor quite attention-seeking – ' "Did you feel, in all seriousness, you were dying?" – "I wanted to let someone else decide. It was out of my hands"' (pp. 157–8). Perhaps many suicide attempts have this exploratory air to them, but Oswald also supplies a commentary on his for his diary: *'somewhere, a violin plays, as I watch my life whirl away'* (p. 152). (Mailer's study suggests that Oswald's diary entries deliberately falsified – or misremembered? – the time of day of these events, to give them a more composed, sunset quality.[5]) All the time Oswald is having his life he is also planning a future narrative of it, from which his current insecurities of feeling, and the real presences of the other participants, have been smoothed out: as a boy meeting Ferrie for the first time, 'he experienced what was happening and at the same moment, although slightly apart, recounted it all . . . relishing his own broad manner of description even as the moment was unfolding in the present' (p. 45); or, losing his virginity in Japan, 'he was partly outside the scene. He had sex with her and monitored the scene, waiting for the pleasure to grip him . . . He thought about what was happening rather than saw it, although he saw it too' (pp. 74–5).

Powers's vision of spring and welcome, as he floats gently down, gives the earth a traditional gender-identity, a maternal lap where rest and emotional relief seem most natural. Conspiracy, secrecy, control are exclusively male preoccupations in *Libra*, but all the players in the assassination drama feel somewhere behind them a kind of feminized, domestic bedrock, a world of pragmatism and acceptance at odds with their ambitions. In conversations like the following, between Jack Ruby, the man who eventually shoots Oswald (probably on Mafia orders), and one of the strippers at his club, the woman's shorthand prompts are answered by the man's evasive self-dramatizing:

> 'You never married, Jack, but how come.'
> 'I'm a sloven in my heart.'
> 'Personal-appearance-wise, you dress and groom.'
> 'In my heart, Brenda. There's a chaos that's enormous.' (p. 253)

When Brenda says to him, 'You're always off somewhere in your mind. Carrying on your own conversation. You don't listen to people,' she could be complaining against any of the men in the novel; the humble beginnings, perhaps, of a feminist assault on the paranoid and ego-centric mind-set. But the idea of women occupying a separate territory, salutary and life-affirming, in touch with elemental truths that men pass over, could of course as easily derive from that mind-set as under-mine it. Win Everett, for example, projects onto his wife the idealized innocent openness he wishes for himself, and by locating innocence in a space he cannot enter, makes his own impurity seem not willed but tragic and inevitable: 'He said her name and watched her eyes come open to that deep wondering of hers, that trust she placed in the ordinary mysteries. She was in the world as he could never be. She meant the world' (p. 76).

Everett's plot emerged in large part from his sense of emasculation, from having been shunted sideways by the CIA to a teaching post at an all-female university and a late-arriving family life which he finds at once pleasing and threatening. His co-conspirators are similarly fret-ting indoors, seeking to revive former male-bonding glories, the days when missions ran like clockwork: Banister, one of the FBI team who shot the 'public enemy' John Dillinger; Parmenter, a veteran of the textbook Guatemala invasion. Oswald himself, joining the Marines straight from school because his brother did, feels more than any of them the unmanning force of his dependency on women, not least since an engagement, like his, in permanent self-invention, is in one sense a denial of the mother, a denial that has to be a form of homage. When he married his Russian wife Marina, he told her his mother was dead; when he separates temporarily from his wife he pretends he doesn't have one: 'He didn't explain about Marina and how much he missed her and needed her and how it made him angry, knowing this, trying to fight this off, another sneaking awareness he could not fight off' (p. 271).

There is a good deal of old-soldiers' rage in these various men against the vagueness and imprecision of peacetime emotions and the 'feminine' world, a world they need to imagine as the goal of their activities, but whose values are so different from theirs as to justify their desire to escape it. Everett is aware, as Powers had been, that there could yet be an alternative, domesticated role for him, 'outside secrecy and guilt and the pull of grave events' (p. 116), but his very awareness takes the form of another scenario, impeding the full absorption in the moment which his wife seems able to have: 'He went down the steps to help Mary Frances take the groceries inside. He gripped the heavy bags. A wind sprang from the east, an idea of rain, sudden, pervading the air. He saw himself go inside, a fellow on a quiet street doing ordinary things, unafraid of being watched' (p. 51). Eventually Everett's terrors consume his household, to the point where his daughter starts to use her dolls as fetishes and to suspect that her parents are not really hers; the father destroys the child's trustfulness that might have saved him.

Libra seems ambivalent about the sentiments attached to these ideas. There is a trace here of another historically specific, late-1980s, post-stockmarket-slide American subtext, of the bad father who neglects love and family for the sake of corrosive ambition (although in the Hollywood versions he usually sees his mistake in time); another psychological structure put round the assassination story, the benchmark for all blighted hopes. It is as if the doubt and unease embedded in that story has made it impossible to say whether there really could be any protected spaces which its condition has not reached, spaces where, as is said of Mary Frances Everett, 'happiness lived minute by minute in the things she saw and heard' (p. 135), where one could live at ease with contingency and the unplanned moment: the writing rather remorselessly suggests how much the idea of such spaces is itself a product of the paranoia they are supposed to resist.

There is one graphic illustration of the space of private feeling being violently invaded by the postmodern world: Beryl Parmenter, whose husband, unbeknown to her, was one of the conspirators, watches the TV coverage of Jack Ruby shooting Oswald. She identifies with Ruby's need for vengeance, for 'some measure of recompense' (p. 446) for Kennedy's murder; she, too, had wanted Oswald erased. But as TV repeats and repeats the event, a strange immortality comes to be conferred, upon Oswald, upon the men around him, and upon her own sense of silent complicity in his murder; what should have been final dissolves into endless replication:

Why do they keep running it, over and over? Will it make Oswald go away forever if they show it a thousand times? . . . This footage only deepened and prolonged the horror . . . After some hours the horror became mechanical . . . a process that drained life from the men in the picture, sealed them in the frame. They began to seem timeless to her, identically dead. (pp. 446-7)

She had been in the habit of sending newspaper clippings to her friends, carefully prising out with her scissors these orderly, manageable messages which 'all said something about the way she felt . . . these are the things that tell us how we live' (p. 261). But now TV brings an unmanageable chaos of noise and threat into her room, insisting that she confront it: 'These men were in her house with their hats and guns . . . They'd located her, forced her to look, and it was not at all like the news items she clipped and mailed to friends. She felt this violence spilling in, over and over' (p. 446). Most unmanageable of all is the sense that Oswald has somehow insinuated himself into her consciousness the instant before he dies, that he has jumped across the gap between our space and his, blurring again the spontaneous with the calculated, experience with narration:

> Something in Oswald's face, a glance at the camera before he was shot, that put him here in the audience . . . a way of telling us that he knows who we are and how we feel, that he has brought our perceptions and interpretations into his sense of the crime. Something in the look, some sly intelligence . . . tells us that he is outside the moment, watching with the rest of us . . . He is commenting on the documentary footage even as it is being shot. Then he himself is shot, and shot, and shot, and the look becomes another kind of knowledge. But he has made us part of his dying. (p. 447)

He dies watching himself on TV, an image of Powers running through his head: 'the white nightmare of noon, high in the sky over Russia . . . He is a stranger, in a mask, falling' (p. 440). For Beryl, it is as though Oswald has fulfilled the mission of the spy plane, to reach with 'sly intelligence' into the most intimate and protected corners and to smear them with a ghostly suspicion that nothing thereafter can ever be quite clean: 'She wanted to crawl out of the room. But something held her there. It was probably Oswald' (p. 447).

Beryl is suffering what Jameson suggested we half-remember, the first overpowering of events by television, whose replays and re-enactments seem to mock the deep analysis they claim to offer and instead drain meaning out. Her desire for narrative, to give shape to the rush of things, is answered by repetition without progress: the tantalizing sense on the one hand that one more showing might reveal some previously unnoticed, clinching significance, and on the other that the cumulative showings are turning the event more and more into a performance, robotic and self-conscious. The most painful articulations of human distress seem baffled by the forms they cannot avoid adopting; Marguerite, Oswald's mother, testifying before the Warren Commission, offers monologues of shambolic protest against the official versions and packages in which her son's life is being sealed, but can herself only present him through the grid of another, equally reductive package, in which the American government betrays the American ethos, the secret state conspires against the brave, humble, pioneer spirit:

> I have struggled to raise my boys on mingy sums of money . . . There are stories inside stories, judge . . . TV gave the cue and Lee was shot . . . I intend to research this case and present my findings . . . I have lived in many places but never filthy dirty, never without the personal loving touch . . . I am smiling, judge, as the accused mother who must read the falsehoods they are writing about my boy . . . The point is how far back have they been using him? He used to climb the tops of roofs with binoculars, looking at the stars, and they sent him to Russia on a mission. Lee Harvey Oswald is more than meets the eye. (pp. 450–1)

Her chaotic narratives, with their obsessive pursuit of yet more overlooked detail in which a clear truth might be hiding, can only mimic all the other narratives which they seek to challenge.

If this then-new cultural condition is now dominant, if the individual voice is barely representable in a world of simulacra, if its scattered scraps of feeling cannot be reconnected without a violent and damaging reduction, then in DeLillo's view the outlook for the novel form is bleak. In *Mao II* (1991), the novel after *Libra*, it is resignedly suggested that 'the novel used to feed our search for meaning . . . but [now] we turn to the news, which provides an unremitting mood of catastrophe. This is where we find emotional experience not available elsewhere'.[6] *White Noise* had dealt with much the same idea, but with a satirical jauntiness which is now completely absent. The central figure in *Mao II* is a novelist, Bill Gray, trying like a Salinger or a Pynchon to hide from media intrusion, trying to preserve the private voice and resist the celebrity-status which Oswald so desired and ultimately, half-designedly achieved, the conversion of the identity into an image for others to feast on, imitate or speculate about. All Gray finds is that his reclusiveness, his attempt to protest against the permeations of celebrity-culture, has itself been commodified by that culture, turned into a spectacle of 'authenticity' in whose construction he has unwittingly collaborated. Gray's subsequent career is an increasingly exhausted and futile effort to keep one step ahead of 'the language of being noticed, the only language the West understands' (p. 157), the condition in which actions, like so many of Oswald's, seem to include or anticipate the ways they will be looked at, and thus rob each look of its chance to be a real engagement.

Mao II is full of idealized nostalgia for the novel as a kind of model democracy, a form that could bring out the humanity stifled everywhere else. To write a novel, Gray argues, is not to reproduce the paranoia of plotting, but to protect oneself from it: 'the experience of my own consciousness tells me how autocracy fails, how total control wrecks the spirit, how my characters deny my efforts to own them completely, how I need internal dissent, self-argument, how the world squashes me the minute I think it's mine' (p. 159). But these flourishes sound rather hollow in their context, of the utter marginalization of the liberal vision; and the appeal they make is uncomfortably close to that addressed in *Libra* to the imaginary, feminized places for the male ego to convalesce in, places offering that ego only an already discounted challenge. For Nicholas Branch, in *Libra,* there was another kind of 'novel', the text of the Warren Commission Report itself, 'the megaton novel James Joyce would have written if he'd moved to Iowa City and lived to be a hundred' (p. 181). The Report is full of fragments of human story, weird juxtaposings of disparate matter, documents, testimonies, miscellaneous data, disjointed pieces of existence which mock their collators' reasons for including them. They cannot provide evidence of anything, or be gathered towards a conclusion, least of all about the assassination to whose story they have been forced to belong. Branch sits in his room full of files as a mirror image of Everett from across the other side of the black hole of the assassination, trying to assemble a cut-and-paste 'Oswald' which will shear off whatever is superfluous and uncontrollable, and experiencing similar panic spurts to those Everett suffered, the fear of being manipulated by those who pass the information on to him, of being caught in something rippling out endlessly. But the Report has things in it which seem to point towards a state beyond the anxiety to connect or to extract meaning. As Branch stares at a photograph captioned *'Curtain rods found on shelf in garage of Ruth Paine',* he feels 'there is a loneliness, a strange desolation trapped here' (p. 182); a sense perhaps like that given off by some of Edward Hopper's paintings, scenes and objects which appear to cry out for a narrative to enfold them and take their solitude away, while simultaneously stopping each narrative dead in its tracks, and maintaining the distance of the viewer from the world, which neither retreats nor comes any closer. Such suspended things, 'arguing nothing, clarifying nothing' (p. 183), are not tokens of an unquenchable human spirit, nor fantasy-projections of a desire for refuge. If they intimate something real, it would be 'real' in the Lacanian use of the word, to mean that which defies representation, that which cannot be contained by the narratives set round it – like death, or, like Oswald, always just beyond the brink of the accessible.

Almost all DeLillo's writing has been in some sense about the assassination, the 'seven seconds that broke the back of the American century' (*Libra*, p. 181): an impulsion that perhaps only became fully clear with *Libra*'s attempt to exorcize it. His ten novels, from *Americana* (1971) onwards, find various ways of exploring what Win Everett calls 'the deathward-tending logic of a plot' (*Libra*, p. 363); they shape themselves towards murder, terrorism, power-fantasy, the distortions induced by media images, some overwhelming catastrophe that eludes definition. They satirize characters who attempt to cross the brink of the 'real', exposing the desperate narcissism of those who, caught in the stupor of late-capitalist culture, try to contrive encounters with something beyond the limit, something that can make them feel alive, whether it be inflicting pain on themselves or others, experiencing some previously unimaginable pornographic thrill, or risking death for the sake of a few seconds of local fame. But the angrier the satire, the more it seems to involve a displacement of the novels' own frustrated nostalgia for unmediated experience, the nostalgia that works its way through all these contrivings. DeLillo's writing, always gripped and always defeated by the event to which it constantly returns, shares in much of what it scrutinizes: the desire in so many Kennedy stories to return behind the assassination, to an imaginary time that was not broken-backed, to a continuity between self and world that was not fatally disrupted by media interventions. And to sense the pull of that desire is part, perhaps, of what it means to feel, like Beryl Parmenter, that Oswald has turned everyone into one of his accomplices, even those who now search their minds to remember where they were when he did what he did.

Notes

1 Frederic Jameson, *Postmodernism, or, The Cultural Logic of Late Capitalism* (London, 1991), p. 355.
2 Don DeLillo, *Libra* (New York, 1988).
3 Don DeLillo, *White Noise* (New York, 1984).
4 Linda Hutcheon, *A Poetics of Postmodernism* (London, 1988), pp. 105–23.
5 Norman Mailer, *Oswald's Tale* (New York, 1995), pp. 51–2.
6 Don DeLillo, *Mao II* (New York, 1991), p. 72.

9 Graham Swift and the Mourning After

Adrian Poole

I make no apology for the light joke in my title. 'The chastening bonds of bereavement' would make a respectably sombre alternative – it is a phrase that occurs in a fine early tale of Swift's called 'The Watch' (*LS*, p. 105)* – but there it is wreathed in a smile that deprecates its own pomposity, and this disappears out of context. Jocularity is a vital element in Swift's writing, and the joking he shares with characters and readers is more than a distraction from pity and terror. His fiction brims with good reasons for grief, with bereavements, abortions, suicides, wars, wounds, violence and madness. Why should we be grateful? Because, I suggest, of the things he does with the idea and practice of mourning. He creates complex fables of bereavement in which mourning takes forms that are spirited, heartening and sociable.

This is why joking is so important to his writing, not the jokes in themselves so much as their making. Think of Jack Dodds in his hospital bed in *Last Orders*, cracking the one about a pretty nurse who literally just takes the piss. This is better than a lot of the jokes the blokes make in the novel, many of which just depend on wry dry rhymes such as 'beef and grief'. This everyday jokiness is part of what binds the men to each other. Jack's dying jest will be one more little thing by which to remember him, not because it is a particularly good joke but because he makes it when he does.

Swift is good with bad jokes. On the route to Margate with Jack's ashes in a box, his mates stop at a pub in Rochester and Vince loudly orders grub from the barmaid, gesturing to the three older men and Jack's remains at a table: 'Three old codgers to look after, and one extra who ain't eating' (*LO*, p. 110). The joke is mildly aggressive. It is a way for Vince to declare his distance from the four other men, who are all of an age, even if one of them ain't ever going to eat again, and hence Vince's greater interest, surely, to the young barmaid who can tell he is a bit of a card even if she doesn't get the joke (which is just as well). It is an instance of failed or thwarted sociability, if you like, in that it gets Vince nowhere with the barmaid.

Or consider one last example, where the needs served by a 'bad' joke are more demanding, and the risks taken more perilous. Near the end of *Waterland*, after the horrific abortion scene in Martha Clay's hut, Tom Crick tells us how he tipped 'what the future's made of' out of a pail into the Ouse: 'A red spittle, floating, frothing, slowly sinking. Borne on the slow Ouse currents. Borne downstream. Borne all the way (but for the Ouse eels . . .) to the Wash. Where it all comes out' (*W*, p. 274). It is at once shocking and soothing at such a moment to be recalled to such a brave banality, that 'it all comes out in the wash'. Daring jests need perfect timing. The abortion has seemed such a monstrous, exceptional happening, yet, as Tom retells it, we hear at just this moment the first stirrings of relief. The event begins to recede, smiled gingerly into a long perspective, from which it will become in time – ever after – one of those things.

There is a smack of Hamlet in Tom's parenthetical allusion to the Ouse eels, as there is in the schoolboy jacket he describes as 'inky black'. The first-person narrator of *Ever After* tries hard to imagine himself as Hamlet, but fears he may really be only Polonius. Hamlet is certainly a good patron to have in mind when we are thinking about the relations between mourning, telling stories and making jokes.

The conventional wisdom about mourning to be gleaned from the psychologists might be summarized as follows.[1] Mourning is what happens when we lose something to which we are strongly attached, and so cannot instantly believe that it or she or he or they are gone for ever. The lost object persists in the fortress of imagination, besieged by the knowledge that death is real and irreparable. The work of mourning is to negotiate a truce or pact between knowledge and imagination, whereby each respects the rights of the other. Knowledge will permit imagination to preserve the lost object in memory, while imagination accepts that the lost object will not escape the asylum of memory and return *for* real, but will live there more or less happily proportioned and distanced *from* the real. This is the approved official version, described in various psychological narratives of benign progression, through phases of numbness, denial and anger, gradual acceptance to final closure. The pathological version – sometimes known as melancholia, after Freud, in distinction from good mourning – represents an arrested, thwarted, or incomplete process, in which the mourner remains stuck in numbness or denial, or reverts to it. In bad mourning memories just go on happening. It would be comforting to believe that a clear distinction could always be made between the stories of good and bad mourning. Perhaps it is not always easy to tell them apart, nor to know for sure when the story is over. Perhaps there is always some mourning after.

There is also a whole social and cultural dimension to mourning, such as Esther Schor stresses when she complains that 'we persist in regarding mourning through Freudian lenses, which magnify the exquisite pain of bereavement while obscuring the calm commerce of condolence'.[2] This position is helpful when we come to think about the relations between mourning and telling stories: namely that mourning is a social action, involving plural, indeterminate elements and agents, as regards both the mourner and what is mourned. Neither figure is singular, nor isolable from its ground. Every time that someone dies, more is lost than a singular person; every death affects more than a singular mourner. Mourning is a condition and an action that we suffer alone and share together.

This suggests a special kinship with telling stories, or rather with the modern form of story-telling in which the sense of solitude and community is most mysteriously mixed. Novels reproduce the conditions of modern mourning in the West in ways that distinguish them from other forms of story-telling. Theatre, film, television and newsprint gather more closely together in time their tellers and listeners and viewers. They do not permit or promote the special kind of gregarious solitude created by novels. They require spectacle, revelation, limelight. Writers may well crave such attention for themselves and their work. In an address made in 1987 Swift reflects on the significance, to an English writer like himself, of inhibition and exhibition, and he concedes that 'all writers are show-offs. We all want the attention of an audience, even if it is a silent and invisible one.' But he goes on promptly to insist that it is just this distance and darkness that mark off the art of the writer. The writer's is 'not a performing art', for all the contemporary pressures to the contrary, but 'an art consummated in that unseen, unheard but incomparable chemistry that occurs between the reader and the page'.[3] So we read, as we mourn, together and alone.

A lot of mourning is certainly done by characters within Swift's fiction, but I also want to suggest that mourning is concerned with the novel's own action, the forms of its telling. The first thing one notices about all Swift's writing is the immense emphasis he puts on the act of telling itself, on what he calls, in that same 1987 address, 'the bond of imaginative *need* that ties a narrative to its narrator'. Of his eleven collected short stories, all but one employ a first-person narrator (the exception is the title story itself, 'Learning to Swim'). In all the six novels so far, first-person narrators dominate, even when the voice moves between first and third persons, as it does to fine effect in *The Sweet Shop Owner* and *Waterland*, or when the number of first-person voices proliferates, as in *Out of this World* and *Last Orders*. All these tellers are in urgent search of listeners, interpreters, understanders. Sometimes they have specific figures in mind. Willy Chapman and Harry Beech, for example, address themselves specifically to their estranged, angry daughters in *The Sweet Shop Owner* and *Out of this World* respectively; Sophie Beech begins by addressing her analyst Dr Klein and ends, more auspiciously, by addressing her children. Tom Crick tells stories to his intrigued schoolchildren in *Waterland*. All the first-person narrators are talking to themselves, but also stretching out, with varying degrees of faith and hope, for the charity of a listener to confess to and confide in. *Last Orders* represents the most formally complicated experiment so far, with its multiple tellers all talking to themselves but also in some magical way to each other, while together they wait for the ideal listener who will never quite arrive, and for whom the reader must therefore stand in.

All Swift's characters tell stories as well as being in them, and all of them are in mourning. The great majority are males, and ageing males at that, though they all recollect their younger selves. They are mainly guilty, damaged, vulnerable, diffident figures of manhood – 'forlorn', to use an epithet that recurs in the early writing: Willy Chapman (*SSO*), Prentis (*Sh*), the doctor-narrator of the tale 'The Hypochondriac' (*LS*), Tom Crick (*W*), Harry Beech (*OOTW*), Bill Unwin (*EA*), Ray 'Lucky' Johnson (*LO*). They have all lost *something*, and they all feel some guilt about it, and the tales they tell are partly confessional, in search of an absolution that depends on neither the priest nor the therapist. What is it that they have lost? For what do they need forgiveness? Willy Chapman recalls asking his wife what the matter is with her father. She says she thinks he wants to be forgiven. '"Forgiven? What for?" "That's hard to say"' (*SSO*, p. 72). But hard to say as it may be, a preliminary and partial answer might be that all these men mourn an idea of their own manhood as sons and husbands and fathers, and want to be forgiven for failing it, or failing to find something better.

We get the simplest version of this story in *Shuttlecock* from its first-person narrator Prentis. The name suggests 'apprentice' (Tom Crick describes himself at one point as 'an apprentice spy': *W*, p. 212). Prentis idealizes his father, a war-hero who has broken down and withdrawn into silence, and has now – at the time of the telling – spent two years in a mental hospital. Prentis also has a surrogate father-figure towards whom he entertains all the ambivalent feelings of envy, hatred and admiration that he does not direct at his own father. This is Quinn, his boss at work. Both fathers seem to hide a secret story, partly embodied in a text or texts. In his real father's case this is a published memoir of his wartime exploits as a spy in France (the title of which is *Shuttlecock*); in Quinn's case, a set of incomplete files, on which Prentis has been set to work. (The two will turn out to be connected.) Prentis is particularly intrigued by his father's story of capture, torture and escape, shortly before the end of the war. And he is drawn to those moments in the text when his father seems to suffer a rare moment of indecision before slipping away 'into the realms of action and iron nerves; into the silence of a man on a hospital bench. That one moment of reflection, of perplexity. What was it like, Dad? What was it like to be brave and strong?' (*Sh*, p. 63). He gets the answers from Quinn and the other sheaf of texts. Or rather Quinn helps him to rephrase the questions, by opening up the strong possibility that his father was not a hero after all but a mere human being who broke down under torture and sent three fellow agents to their deaths. The father's memoir may well therefore be a lie, but it is also perhaps an oblique confession, through the vivid story it tells of flight and pursuit, and its final image of a small animal hunted to its lair. Prentis had thought that Quinn and his father both 'knew', and that only he was in the dark, the dupe, the victim, the helpless little creature. The idea of 'little creatures' recurs throughout Swift's writings. In this novel there is an important hamster, while elsewhere we find 'Hoffmeier's Antelope' in the tale of that name (*LS*), butterflies in *Ever After*, the resourceful eels in *Waterland*. At the very end of *Last Orders* Ray scoops and scoops 'like some small animal scratching out its burrow' (*LO*, p. 294).

Quinn makes a crucial confession about the origin of his artificial foot. It is a scene that will be repeated in *Out of this World*, to which I shall return, when Robert Beech recreates for his son Harry the moment in the First World War when he lost an arm and won the VC. Quinn tells Prentis that he behaved with a singular absence of heroism when he ran away from the enemy and stepped in panic on the face of a dying fellow soldier, only seconds later to have his foot blown off. He confesses that he cannot entirely rid himself of the superstition that the loss of his foot was a punishment for stepping on the man's face, but he knows it *is* a superstition. He has learned both to forgive himself and to live with his guilt. Or to put it in the terms in which I am interested, he has learned both to stop mourning for something and also to carry on. This is the wisdom his story tries to pass on to Prentis, that Prentis should say goodbye to the doubly oppressive idea, not only of his father's heroic and superhuman strength, but also of his father's repellent and creaturely weakness. Prentis is now armed with the question he could slay his father with: 'Did you betray your comrades?' But he chooses to give up the Oedipal showdown and live in uncertainty, neither to slay his father nor to be slain by him. So Quinn and Prentis together burn the crucial evidence that could prove the father's guilt or innocence. This funeral rite frees Prentis from a whole idea of what it means to be a father and son and sends him back to his long-suffering wife and his own growing sons a new man.

It is a strong little fable, but with no disrespect one can say that it is the least ambitious of the six novels so far, because the central figure is given so little grounding in the past, apart from the hamster he once tormented, and his father's memoir. The confrontation is for Swift an unusually singular one, between the son and the (double) father. In all the other novels, the men need to mourn not only an idea of what it means to be a son and father, but a whole world in which those ideas of manhood were formed. This explains the recurrent importance of war in Swift's work, and the historically specific, and specifically English, milieu of the Second World War and its immediate aftermath. Swift is providing much more than studies in the psychology of personal loss, bereavement and mourning, persuasive and moving as that is. What attracts readers at a deeper level is their recognition of imagined models of shared reality, something more than the personal possession – and loss – of an individual psyche or consciousness. The two biggest successes in his work so far are *Waterland* and *Last Orders*, because they create their own collective memory out of all the things the characters have in common or exchange between them – the locales, the landscapes, the genes, the machines, the sexual needs, the money, the jobs, the news, the jokes, the gossip, the songs. This shared reality is not of their own making but they all have a hand in it. And when it falls apart, and they fall into their solitudes, it is the lost sense of what they seemed to share together, for better and worse, that asks to be mourned.

Each of the novels establishes its own habitat, to use a term from natural history that complies with Swift's sense of human being as an animal occupation of space. But certain features recur from one to another, including a strong interest in kinship, its shifting patterns and vacancies; in wars and asylums; in the traffic between visual memories, mental images and photographs; in accidents, chances, exact dates and times; in the act of narration itself.

Kinship in Swift is above all a matter of patterns and structures, both genetic and fictive. Of course there are all sorts of classic psychological conflict and desire, Oedipal and other, seen and told mainly though not exclusively through the eyes and tongues of precarious males. There are sons troubled by fathers (Prentis in *Shuttlecock,* Harry Beech in

Out of this World, Vince Dodds in *Last Orders*), sons troubled by mothers (Tom Crick in *Waterland*, Bill Unwin in *Ever After*), fathers troubled by daughters (Willy Chapman in *The Sweet Shop Owner*, Harry Beech again in *Out of this World*, a whole quartet of them in *Last Orders* – Jack, Ray, Lenny and Vince). But these troubles are never seen in isolation from their family history (*Shuttlecock* being a partial exception). Willy Chapman's remorse and his daughter Dorry's rage, for example, which fill the foreground of *The Sweet Shop Owner*, the day of its telling, get their body from the slowly gathered stories of earlier damage, especially to the wife and mother Irene, who demands at any price the peace that her very name means. The combats Swift deals in are not single ones. The way they are interwoven and overlaid subordinates them to a larger sense of the extended patterns of kinship out of which they arise, into which they subside. This is most obviously true of *Waterland*, with its lengthy historical retrospect, and of *Last Orders*, with the local density of its Bermondsey tribe. To put it simply, whatever forces individuals towards and away from each other, to sexual unions, to violence, to escape, is less important in the lives of the central characters than the patterns of kinship that hold them together. There is more to be said about the characters who *do* escape or try to, especially the daughters, but this is not a story Swift usually tries to pursue. Sophie Beech is a major exception, and the most problematic main character he has tried to find a voice for.

These patterns are neither solid nor stable nor certainly knowable. But nor are they simply fictions. In the short story 'Chemistry', the boy-narrator gets a sudden nightmare vision of the endlessness of the physical world:

> It seemed to me that Grandfather's face before me was only a cross section from some infinite stick of rock, from which, at the right point, Mother's face and mine might also be cut. I thought: every face is like this. I had a sudden giddying feeling that there is no end to anything. I wanted to be told simple, precise facts. (*LS*, p. 127)

But simple, precise facts are hard to come by (though exact dates and times are precious in Swift for just this reason). What you need, perhaps all you have, is the power to keep telling stories and distinguish between them. In *Ever After* Bill Unwin's father may after all have been a train-driver he never knew rather than a diplomat who killed himself. He has modelled himself on the latter, and when his mother remarries he identifies with the dead man, through a self-conscious reference to Hamlet: 'This had been my father's position. I stood in his vacant place. And out of this ghostly identification I began to summon a father I had never really known: noble, virtuous, wronged' (*EA*, p. 63). Swift is especially interested in such 'fictive kinship', in the real needs it serves and effects it may have. In this novel, the central figure finds some solace in the ghostly identification he makes with his distant Victorian kinsman, Matthew Pearce. This is a real act of the imagination, in deliberate contrast to the feverish fictions about playing Hamlet. Swift regularly thinks of his figures as 'playing roles'. Sometimes this marks a character's sense of inner estrangement and helplessness, as if he or she were just a toy or puppet or even a skittle, helplessly waiting its doom (these are key metaphors in *The Sweet Shop Owner*). But at other times it marks a more spirited sense of choice and agency and conscious adoption. Thus Bill remembers his beloved wife Ruth – a real actress: 'There was this space that was always hers, just hers; this magic mobile space' (*EA*, p. 118).

Where the strong patterns and vacancies of kinship are concerned, the idea of adoption is indeed a critical one for Swift, in a sense beyond the restricted one in which we normally use the word, to refer to the legal adoption of a child such as Vince in *Last Orders*. Swift's people are constantly choosing each other and being chosen, to play roles, to fill vacancies, to make up a pattern. And it is this impossible dream of the full gathered family, a whole kith and kin, without absences, without strangers, that is at least one of the things that Swift's fictional worlds mourn for.

They also mourn for war or, to be more exact, the two world wars. *Out of this World* extends its perspective beyond the others to take in not only the death-camps and Nuremberg trials, but Vietnam, the Greek Civil War and the Falklands (the novel is headed with the date 'April 1982'). One may wonder if, for its high ambitions, the novel develops formal strategies sufficiently strong to deal with so much bad matter – by comparison with *Waterland* and *Last Orders*. All Swift's fictions move between a remembering present and remembered pasts, but they return again and again to the years of the Second World War. In *Waterland* the story that Tom Crick painfully recovers bit by bit, from the retrospect of 1980, belongs to the decade 1937–47. This is marked, both at the time and in retrospect, by the experience and knowledge of war – the American air-bases in Norfolk, the bombing of Dresden. In *Last Orders* four of the five leading men have fought in the Second World War. Big Jack Dodds and little Lucky Johnson meet in Egypt and see the war out together, while Lenny 'Gunner' Tate is serving elsewhere in the North African desert and Vic the undertaker is on the North Seas. The fifth, Vince Dodds, is orphaned by a bomb during the Blitz, and himself later enlists and serves in Aden. The Second World War is the last great *collective* ending the English have known, the last 'end of the world' within living memory. To adopt the contradiction extorted from Bill Unwin by the grief of his personal bereavement: 'It's not the end of the world. It is the end of the world' (*EA*, p. 120).

Behind these narratable memories of what Henry James called the 'visitable past', there looms the more distant Great War, more awesome and monumental precisely because it is more of a matter of images than of stories. As Harry Beech says in *Out of this World*:

> Everyone has their picture of the Great War. Somewhere in the picture is a horrific collision of the antiquated and the modern. A cavalry charge into the teeth of machine-guns. It was not the first or last, if it was the biggest of such collisions, but only the terrible prototype, perhaps, of further collisions that would go on happening, in even more polarized and grotesque forms. As when the latest in military science flattens overnight the fabric of ancient cities or consumes in balls of sticky fire the thatch and daub of a South-east Asian village. (*OOTW*, p. 196)

Collisions of the antiquated and the modern which go on happening: this is real and collective matter for mourning, one way of imagining modern tragedy. The only way to deal with the 'pictures' is to carry on telling the stories, sharing them out and finding listeners to believe them, mourning alone and together. As for the threat of apocalyptic fixation – something beyond the horrors of repetition – this too demands good mourning, all the more needfully.[4]

Swift is much concerned with the forms taken by modern memory, the means by which it is created and sustained, by 'images' and 'stories'. The camera can rip visual images out of time, out of history, out of this world, to create artificial memories that belong to no one and everyone – like stories. These 'pictures', as Harry Beech calls them, are something we cannot do without now, for better and worse, as objects of memory and imagination and fantasy. The whole idea of modern fiction is inconceivable without them, as it is inconceivable without the power of film to shuffle such images into new kinds of temporal sequence.

Swift's fiction is full of cameras and photographs and films, literal and metaphoric. As for instance when Willy Chapman recalls the death of his friend Smithy the barber: 'November the sixteenth, 1969. The figures on the pavement who had stopped to look moved on and the traffic in the High Street seemed to resume a halted progress like a film jerking back into life' (*SSO*, p. 165). Or when the doctor-narrator of 'The Hypochondriac' thinks of the happiness he thought he once felt when he looked at his much younger wife: 'only sometimes would I tell myself, these visions are like photographs whose real subject you do not touch' (*LS*, p. 69). There are lots of real photographs too. There's a fine scene in *The Sweet Shop Owner* at a family gathering during the war when photographs are called for, and Willy finds himself in charge of the camera, out of the picture, amid all sorts of awkwardness and hostility. He winces as he takes the last shot of his brothers-in-law, the Harrison boys in their naval uniform, for one of whom this will indeed prove to be a final pose: 'The moment captured: gallant figures locked in the view-finder' (*SSO*, p. 74). In *Last Orders* Ray and Vince both cherish photos of the parental figures who play a vivid role in their own inner lives. Vince begs a photo of his adoptive father Jack, laughing in the Egyptian desert, not like a soldier at all, more 'like a kid on a beach' (*LO*, p. 137). Ray's feelings for Jack's wife Amy – but also for Jack – are inflamed by the first sight he gets of her from the photo Jack shows him when they are on service in Egypt: 'I looked, and I thought, I want one of those. I want one like that' (*LO*, p. 89). The reader can't tell whether he means 'I want a woman like that' or 'I want a photograph like that'. He may well mean both.

Out of this World is the fiction that deals most explicitly, perhaps too explicitly, with this whole theme. It represents, through its central figure Harry Beech, an intelligent, restless meditation on the relations between technology and psychology, what all these prosthetic organs can make of our souls. The photographic image seems so precious for its defiance of time and even mortality, yet this is why it is just so dangerous, so deceptive, so liable to nourish in the bereaved a fixation with the past. Hence the need for stories that will animate these images; it is not a matter of erasing them but of giving them standing and position within the flow of lived, of living experience.

There is a particular scene, delayed to near the end of the narration, that marks a critical stage in Harry Beech's relations with his father. Harry has been a highly successful photo-journalist, a modern-day witness to some of the world's blackest spots. (The nearest thing to a real-life equivalent might be Don McCullin, whose own experience and reflections on it bear some comparison with Harry's.[5]) Like Prentis in *Shuttlecock*, Harry has a war-hero for a father (but from World War I). He has suffered badly from his father's desire for a son to follow in his footsteps and to take over the family arms business. It is not clear to the reader exactly what Robert Beech did to become a war-hero, but we suspect that it has something to do with his artificial arm (he makes the 'bad joke' himself about being an arms-dealer). Late on in the novel Harry gets round to the memory of his father's lost arm, or rather the occasion in 1969 when his father at long last tells him the real story of what happened in the trenches back in 1918 or, to be precise, on the morning of 30 March. The date matters, as dates do in Swift, because Harry was born three days earlier on 27

March and his mother died giving birth to him. Harry has known for a long time – and so have we, because he shares this knowledge with us early on – that his father has always blamed him for his mother's death, or rather, as Harry woundedly puts it, his father 'chose' to blame him. The relations between the two men have never recovered from this catastrophic beginning, until this moment in 1969 when the father tells the story. What happened, it seems, was that an enemy grenade landed close by him in the trenches, but even closer to his commanding officer, who was lying unconscious. He ran and picked it up but as he turned to throw it clear it exploded. He lost his arm but saved his CO's life, a heroic act which won him the VC. Thus the official interpretation of this moment, its caption or memorial, an 'act of heroism'. Heroism? stupidity? conditioned reflexes? or something else? Now Harry discovers for the first time that on 30 March his father had just heard the news of his wife's death – he had never supposed the news could have reached him so swiftly. Nobody can know what went through his father's mind in those life-and-death seconds when he picked up and held the grenade – for how long? – before throwing it, soon enough to save his own life and the CO's, too late to escape unscathed. Not even his father himself. That is all Harry knows, and we know, and his father knows, that his father knew that his wife had just died. But the difference it makes to Harry is all the difference, for it unlocks his father's heroic image and returns him to story, to mortality, to frailty – the frailty of a man who did not know what he was doing and might have wanted to die.

Out of this World is the grimmest of Swift's novels in the images of violence and destruction it invokes. But it is also the most wilfully optimistic about the possibilities of healing, reparation and revival for the damaged male figure. Not that one begrudges Harry the reunion with his estranged daughter Sophie that lies just beyond the novel's reach. Willy Chapman waits in pain and in vain for Dorry to return. Ray Johnson imagines seeing once more the daughter in Australia who left home twenty-five years ago. But only for Harry does the dream of the daughter's return seem bound to come true. More gratuitous is the miracle Harry enjoys when he advertises in the local paper and falls in love with a dream-woman forty years younger. As he wryly jests: 'Vacancy filled' (*OOTW*, p. 79). Luck and accident and chance are vital themes of Swift's writing and there is no reason why they should always be bad. But in *Last Orders* Ray's great gamble grows out of the plot and setting and all we know of the characters. Justice is done, or adjustment at least, and that is a little miracle, but it is just for a moment, and it is only moments from the end before Ray undoes the *in*justice he was going to commit in holding on to the money that belongs to Vince. This is complicated, but the point of comparison with *Out of this World* is that Harry Beech's dream-girl grows out of no such complexity – she comes out of the blue. In fact the novel uses the idea of colour quite explicitly, especially towards the end when Harry re-enters in memory his father's old world of which the dominant colour is brown, 'the colour of things lost' (*OOTW*, p. 204). It is possible to feel a certain disappointment, not only in *Out of this World* but also in *Ever After*, at the relative thinness of the novels' fictional presents by comparison with the deep, rich sense of their pasts. One can see Swift making a conscious decision, in the aftermath of *Waterland's* success, to move away from the dense and shifting medium out of which the main figures of the earlier novel emerged, a medium made out of solids and liquids, water and land, out of images and stories, memories, guilts and curiosities that they shared and exchanged with each other. But in doing so, he created a father and daughter who don't have enough to look back to together, whose wounds consequently need emergency treatment from strangers, from out of this world – that is, Sophie's psychoanalyst and Harry's dream-girl, unusually conventional figures.

'I see him now, I see him still', says the narrating Tom Crick, near the end of *Waterland* (p. 283). No need for photographs in this novel, so directly do the images of childhood and adolescence incise themselves into his memory. Like his mother's death: 'And though indeed, it only happened once, it's gone on happening, the way unique and momentous things do, for ever and ever, as long as there's a memory for them to happen in' (*W*, pp. 237–8). Or the terrible event in Martha Clay's cottage: 'But then we've already stepped into a different world. The one where things come to a stop; the one where the past will go on happening' (*W*, p. 263). The intensity of these memories requires the formalities of Tom's narration, its extraordinarily elaborate shifts of time and place and perspective, from the present of the telling in Greenwich in 1980, back to the events of the decade begun with his mother's death in January 1937 and concluded with his father's ten years later; then further back to the family history of the Cricks and Atkinsons, but especially the Atkinsons, and the culminating incestuous union between his grandfather Ernest and his mother Helen; then beyond and outside these personal and family histories, to the French Revolution, and the reproductive mysteries of the eel. In one sense a large part of Tom's story-telling is a means of delaying the crucial confessions about his own involvement in the events of the summer of 1943, and the consequent madness to which Mary succumbs over thirty-six years later: a means of deploying his guilt.

When young Mary tells him she is pregnant he throws a tantrum.

'Now why can't everything happen by accident? No history. No guilt, no blame. Just accidents. Accidents' (W, p. 228). But it doesn't; there is; they are not. In another sense his digressions are a means to the understanding of these traumatic truths, and a laying of memory to rest. It is as if Tom has to find a way of believing the thing Quinn told Prentis about guilt, though he too had to tell a story, that you cannot avoid it but you can be forgiven. And your best chance of finding forgiveness is to tell stories, as true as you can make them, that others will listen to and perhaps believe in. Hence Tom's attraction to the intelligent, unhappy young schoolboy called Price.

Yet Tom remains the most desolate of Swift's main narrators, the one most in need of the reader's kinship if he is ever to complete his own mourning. What he has to mourn entails not just the several deaths, of his mother and father (but especially his mother), and of the two unfinished creatures who are swept out to sea, the aborted embryo and the matured moron, his half-brother Dick; but somehow, in a way that Tom can never explain but only narrate, all the relations between these bereavements, and their consequence years later in Mary's madness, what he finally, helplessly calls 'the whole story'.

It is no accident that the two novels that have commanded most popularity and critical acclaim so far have been the most formally elaborate. They both boast the most ingenious shifts in space and time, but added to this in *Last Orders* is the multiplication of voices. The only real precedent for this is in *Out of this World*, Swift's first experiment in plural narration, though one should mention the important passage in *The Sweet Shop Owner* when Irene's voice breaks through (ch. 7). In *Out of this World* the thirty-five (unnumbered) sections are shared almost equally between the two main figures, Harry and Sophie Beech, while two secondary figures are given one entrance each towards the end, Sophie's husband Joe (number 27), and Harry's (dead) wife Anna (number 29). The timing is vital. The fact that they speak when they do seems to assist the melting of the two principal figures towards each other.

But *Last Orders* takes this all much further by sharing out the telling between seven of the characters. There are seventy-five sections, again unnumbered, all of them narrated in the first person and headed either by the name of the speaker or by a place-name. There are seventeen of these latter, and they mark the route taken by the four male mourners, from Bermondsey (1) to Margate (75). Several of these mark the entrance to and exit from lengthy stoppages, at Chatham (27–35), Wick's Farm (37–43), Canterbury (47–59) and Margate itself (68–75). All chapters headed by place-names take place in the fictional present which marks the novel's most forward limit in time. This is finally identified late on as 2 April 1990 – even more precise than the 'April 1982' which heads *Out of this World*. All these seventeen are taken by Ray, the dead man's best mate; he is also given more chapters headed by his own name than any of the others and so gets to narrate just over half of the total (thirty-nine). The next most frequent voice is that of Vince, the dead man's adopted son (twelve). The other two old mates in the car, Lenny and Vic, get eight apiece, while there are two surprise entrants (or, to be pedantic, three), rather as in *Out of this World*. There is Mandy, Vince's wife, and – like the dead Anna – the dead man Jack who recalls his *own* father's voice: 'He said, "Jack boy, it's all down to wastage"' (*LO*, p. 285). This doubled ghost contributes a wonderfully eerie note, just at the penultimate moment (74). This is as beautifully timed a last-gasp distraction as the penultimate section of *Waterland*, 'About Phlegm'.

But there is one further voice in *Last Orders*, whose importance is out of all proportion to the frequency with which it is heard. It is that of Amy, Jack's widow, the mother of Vince and June, the lovable woman still desired by Ray and, less hopefully, by Lenny. Consider the mothers we have met before in Swift's fiction: Irene in *The Sweet Shop Owner*, Helen Atkinson in *Waterland* (and Sarah Atkinson before her and Mary Metcalf after her), Anna in *Out of this World* (and Harry's own mother, dead in childbirth), Bill Unwin's mother, Sylvia Rawlinson, in *Ever After*. Fragile, mortal, desirable, out of their minds, dead – though not always quite speechless. Perhaps one of the things for which Swift's men mourn is exactly the *voice* of the mother. Its most eroticized version is certainly to be found in Bill Unwin's memories of his mother's ringing soprano: 'out of this woman, so unscrupulous, so indolent, so heartless, my mother, would come a sound so sweet and miraculous, it was impossible not to yield' (*EA*, p. 32). But we rarely hear from the mother herself, and this is what makes the return of Amy's voice in *Last Orders* so welcome. She refuses to join the male mourners on their journey to Margate. She goes instead on a last journey of her own to the asylum where her daughter June has spent the fifty years of her death-in-life. Amy will say goodbye to the daughter she chose instead of her husband, or – as she thinks of it – the daughter her husband refused to choose with her. Amy only gets to tell six chapters, the first early on (6), but her voice re-enters just after the men leave Canterbury for the final stage of their journey, and she then has five in quick succession (61, 63, 66, 70, 72). The story she tells is one of a rage, frozen for all these years, at what happened to June, and what happened to her and Jack. But it is a rage that at long last now starts to melt, into a kind of forgiveness. In *Shuttlecock* it was a son who visited his speechless father in an asylum and at last freed himself. Here it is a mother who finally says goodbye to her daughter as she says goodbye to her husband (*LO*, p. 278). Like Dick in *Waterland*, June is an 'accident of birth', a living embodiment of damaged happiness, of the worst luck, something which can never be forgotten but only mourned ever after.

I have tried to suggest some of the ways in which loss and mourning figure within Swift's fiction. But what is the position of the reader? And why are the novels so exciting? The answers go together. At one level, the reader participates in the thrill of a quest, the gradual discovery of a buried story, the re-membering of its mutilated and dispersed fragments, until an apparently whole little body of knowledge has been composed. This corresponds to one part of the work of mourning, its active searching out of things to remember about the lost object. Memories and images and scenes and stories are gathered together to make a whole figure which can then be more or less lodged or banked in the memory. Hence the pleasure and satisfaction for the reader in tracing this progressive pattern of discovery. In *Waterland* this means the buried story of the deaths of that central decade from 1937 to 1947. In *Ever After* it is, quite explicitly, the story contained in Matthew Pearce's notebooks and last letter to his wife Elizabeth, of their marital happiness and then catastrophe. In *Last Orders* it is the story of Ray's double-dealings with the dead Jack and his wife Amy, above all his brief love-affair with the latter, and the great last gamble he undertakes for the former, as a kind of magical reparation.

But this is only half the story and half an answer to the question of what it is that is mourned, and the reader's role in it. There is a whole other side to the activity of mourning, its 'depressive' aspect, which clings to the fragments of memory and refuses to let go, which resists exactly their progressive collation and insists there is more to be mourned than an isolable figure. There is a residue that can never be recovered because that figure once filled a time and space from which it cannot be separated. Hence the double sense the reader gets at the end of *Waterland* and *Last Orders*, that we are left both with a knowable pattern, an action completed, a coherence achieved, and with everything that such knowledge and completion and coherence must omit and can never recover, all the memories, desires and stories. Hence the strange double sense of cheerfulness and desolation.

There is also a sense in which Swift's novels could be said to mourn some of their own literary antecedents. This is more than a matter of specific debts, interesting as these may be to trace and important as it certainly is to make more intelligent sense of them than simply, for instance, to accuse Swift of borrowing 'inertly' from Faulkner.[6] Swift's stature and achievement are such that the questions to be asked are

larger than this. They are questions about the ways many novelists
from the nineteenth century onwards have found to mourn the lost
wholeness of a shattered world and to share this work with their readers. Swift's novels obviously look back, through all sorts of modernist
and postmodernist lenses, to some great nineteenth-century predecessors, from whom one would single out in particular George Eliot and
Thomas Hardy. His own two most ambitious novels, *Waterland* and
Last Orders, repeat some of their central ambitions: to create massive
vistas and perspectives against which human stories have to measure
themselves; to demonstrate the way nature and history collude in be-
queathing conditions that thwart human need and desire; to insist on
the continued responsibilities of choice in a world bereaved of collective faith and the rites that might sustain it. Their imaginary worlds
mourn for a real world in which terrible accidents happen that are not
all nor entirely accidents because human beings help to make them
happen.

But there are several ways in which Swift's fiction is bound to measure its own distance from such nineteenth-century predecessors. Where
they could still mourn the passing of certain religious, mythical and
metaphysical justifications for 'terrible accidents', Swift's fiction is
left to mourn the impossibility of such mourning. No good mourning
the impossibility of being another St Theresa, let alone railing against
the President of the Immortals. When Harry Beech remembers
Agamemnon's sacrifice of Iphigeneia it is not to give meaning to the
endless recurrence of war, nor to mourn its passing, but to mourn
the fact that humanity learns nothing from its own stories. And the
twentieth-century experience of war is the other, related thing that
separates Swift from an Eliot or a Hardy. The terrible accidents represented by the two world wars require kinds of explanation, about their
origins and consequences and thus their being something more than
just accidents, beyond the horizons of the nineteenth century. Hence
the need for forms of story-telling correspondingly more shattered and
more self-distrustful, within which there may survive a cautious but
obstinate little belief, in the need at least to go on telling stories.

When the four men in *Last Orders* go to pay their respects to the
war memorial at Chatham, Ray observes that it has 'a littling effect on
Vince' (*LO*, p. 134). There is a world of difference between being
littled and being belittled, just as there is between finding little hope in
someone and finding a little hope. Like George Eliot and Hardy, Swift
tries to put his figures in their place without putting them down, and
all the most auspicious figures and moments in his work are deliberately little. Like the lucky little man in *Last Orders*, who remembers
Amy saying to him once: 'Oh Ray, you're a lovely man, you're a lucky

man, you're a little ray of sunshine, you're a little ray of hope' (*LO* p. 284). There is plenty of blackness in Graham Swift, but if there is to be a morning after a dark night, then perhaps good mourning stories can help to bring it on.

Notes

Reference abbreviations

*Swift has published six novels and one collection of short stories so far. These are listed below with abbreviations used in the text and the date of first publication, followed by the editions referred to here in the text (the most widely available at the time of writing).

SSO	*The Sweet Shop Owner* (1980). Penguin Books, 1983.	
Sh	*Shuttlecock* (1981). Penguin Books, 1982.	
LS	*Learning to Swim & Other Stories* (1982). Picador, 1985.	
W	*Waterland* (1983). Picador, 1984.	
OOTW	*Out of this World* (1988). Viking, 1988.	
EA	*Ever After* (1992). Picador, 1992.	
LO	*Last Orders* (1996). Picador, 1996.	

1 I have in mind the following, for example: Sigmund Freud, 'Mourning and Melancholia' (1917), *Standard Edition of the Complete Psychological Works* (London, 1953–74), vol. 14; Melanie Klein, 'Mourning and its Relation to Manic Depressive States' (1940), in *Love, Guilt and Reparation and Other Papers, 1921–1946* (London, 1947); John Bowlby, *Loss: Sadness and Depression* [Attachment and Loss, vol. 3] (Harmondsworth, 1980); Julia Kristeva, *Black Sun: Depression and Melancholia*, trans. Leon S. Roudiez (New York, 1989).
2 Esther Schor, *Bearing the Dead: The British Culture of Mourning from the Enlightenment to Victoria* (Princeton, 1994). For other 'cultural' accounts of mourning, see for example Geoffrey Gorer, *Death, Grief and Mourning in Contemporary Britain* (London, 1965), and Jay Winter, *Sites of Memory, Sites of Mourning: The Great War in European Cultural History* (Cambridge, 1995).
3 'Throwing off our inhibitions', *The Times*, 5 March 1988 (adapted from an address to the 13th International Writers' Union in Lahti, Finland, June 1987). I am grateful to Sam Wallace for bringing this to my attention.
4 For a suggestive line of thought about the repression of mourning in postmodernist discourse, see Martin Jay, 'The Apocalyptic Imagination and the Inability to Mourn', in *Force Fields: Between Intellectual History and Cultural Critique* (London, 1993).
5 I am thinking here in particular of Don McCullin's autobiography (published several years after *Out of this World*), *Unreasonable Behaviour* (1990).

6 I refer to the little furore created by the curious decision of the *Independent on Sunday* to publicize some leaden observations by John Frow, to the effect that *Last Orders* is a 'direct and unacknowledged imitation' of William Faulkner's *As I Lay Dying* (9 March 1997), 'an inert borrowing' (16 March 1997). In the intervening week there was some malicious cackling in the highbrow British media, not only about Swift's alleged quasi-plagiarism but about the ignorance of Faulkner's classic displayed by the Booker Prize judges who had given him the award the previous autumn. However, the gossip was met with robust good sense by many intelligent observers, including Salman Rushdie in the *Guardian* (14 March 1997), and Kazuo Ishiguro in the *Independent on Sunday* (16 March 1997), as well as a puzzled Swift himself in *The Times* (10 March 1997), and again the *Independent on Sunday* (16 March 1997).

10 Mapping the Margins: Translation, Invasion and Celtic Islands in Brian Moore and John Fuller

Sophie Gilmartin

This essay is about islands in contemporary fiction. It comes of some thoughts I have had about England's self-representation in the nineteenth century, in an age of empire and the empire's geographical expansion. The English had long considered themselves a happy breed inhabiting the island which John of Gaunt describes in Shakespeare's *Richard II* as,

> This precious stone set in the silver sea
> Which serves it in the office of a wall,
> Or as a moat defensive to a house,
> Against the envy of less happier lands . . .[1]

Despite pushing her empire far beyond her sea-girt limits in the nineteenth century, the self-portrayal of England as a nation of happy islanders was an important part of her self-definition and recognition of who was English and who was the outsider. But at the same time that England saw herself as an island, she also saw herself as 'the British Isles'. Questions of assimilation versus difference came to the fore within Britain in the nineteenth century; these questions are figured forth in the disparity between England/Britain and between island/isles. Ireland, particularly, was troubling to England's sense of herself as a happy island. Culturally, linguistically and, as many thought, racially separate from England, Ireland was a rather big lump to swallow into the concept of a unified Britain. This essay is about the space of the insular as we view it,

or are trapped by it, in two novels, Brian Moore's *Catholics* (1972) and
John Fuller's *Flying to Nowhere* (1983). In their different ways both
these novels map the outer reaches of contemporary British and Irish
fiction – geographically at least – in what is still known as 'the British
Isles'.

Both novels are set on the remote fringes of Britain and Ireland, on
westernmost Celtic islands. Moore's novel takes place on the Irish
monastic island of Muck, off the Kerry coast of south-west Ireland;
Fuller's on a Welsh monastic island which is never named, but which
is modelled on the island of Bardsey, off the Lleyn peninsula in North
Wales.

Brian Moore's novel is set in a slightly futuristic period and begins
when a young American priest is sent from Rome to the island monastery. He comes with orders from Rome and the powers of the 'World
Ecumenical Council' to investigate and quell the religious practices of
the priests at Muck; these Irish monks have quietly kept the Latin
Mass, private confessions and other pre-Vatican II practices for years,
but by the opening of the novel news has spread and hundreds of
pilgrims are streaming to the Irish coast from all over the world to
hear the Latin liturgy. World television crews are covering the enormous popularity of the Latin Mass said by the monks from Muck, and
Rome sees the persistence of pre-Vatican II rituals as insubordination
which must be stopped.

John Fuller's novel is set in a time which is probably the sixteenth
century. Its plot is similar in some ways to Brian Moore's, in that an
outside investigator arrives on a remote Celtic monastic island with
ecclesiastical powers from a mainland centre of Church authority to
look into possibly heretical practices. But the investigation becomes
more of a murder mystery (similar at first to Umberto Eco's *The Name
of the Rose*) as the investigator seeks to discover why there are no
longer any pilgrims visiting the island's holy well of St Lleuddad, and
why many of those pilgrims who have visited the well in the past seem
to have disappeared.

Before retreating to these Celtic islands, however, I open some of
the following thoughts on insularity by moving to the Mediterranean
with a more recent island-novel by a British author, *Knowledge of
Angels* by Jill Paton Walsh, published in 1994 and shortlisted for the
Booker Prize. The novel takes place, as she puts it, 'on an island somewhat like Mallorca, but not Mallorca, at a time somewhat like 1450,
but not 1450'.[2] She prefaces the novel with a direct address to the
reader, who is asked to map out the topography of the island from
a bird's eye view, or from the view of and with the 'knowledge of
angels'.

> Suppose you are contemplating an island. It is not any island known to
> you. You are looking at it from a great height – you see fig orchards,
> vineyards, almond orchards, and apricot orchards. There are little towns
> topping the gentle rises on the ample plain, the houses with their
> pan-tiled rooftops like so many tiny ploughed sloping fields clustered
> around the naves and towers of churches . . . [You] see the wooded cliffs
> of the shore, the beaches of bright sand, the principal city, ringed by
> walls and rising from its harbour. You see along the northern and west-
> ern shores the great mountains, the complex of ridges and green well-
> watered valleys . . . At this height your viewpoint is more like that of an
> angel than that of any islander. But after all, the position of a reader in a
> book is very like that occupied by angels in the world, when angels still
> had any credibility. Yours is, like theirs, a hovering, gravely attentive
> presence, observing everything, from whom nothing is concealed. (p. xi)

Paton Walsh then brings our view closer; we are to see a path and then
climbers on it, struggling to ascend. After the preface the opening of
chapter 1 relinquishes the address to readers and their view of the
whole island, and we swoop down to the land level of the shepherds
on the path. In Paton Walsh's novel the reader is figured as a 'hovering, gravely attentive presence'. The first mapping of the island's territory is watchful but passive. Our initiation into the novel is like the
entrance to the island, a flight over and a gradual unintrusive descent
to the particular, to the mountain, the path, the small physical details
of the island and its inhabitants.

But is it possible to enter the island/text so unobtrusively, with the
unemotional observation of a distant hovering angel? Or does the conjunction of the mapping out of a territory, and the entrance of an
outsider into the closed system of an island, inevitably trace out the
charts of the invader?

If one transfers the mapping of the territory and the text from this
fictionalized Mallorca to the Celtic islands, there is certainly to be
found a long tradition of mapping and topographical books produced
for the purposes of facilitating invasion. In his play *Translations*, for
instance, the Irish playwright Brian Friel describes a moment in nineteenth-century history when English surveyors were attempting to map
Irish territory and, in doing so, to replace the Gaelic place-names with
English. The translation of place-names was of course a form of linguistic invasion as well as enabling the English to establish a firmer
control over the invaded territory of Ireland. In Wales the linguistic
and political invasion is encapsulated in the very name of the nation:
'Wales' is derived from the ancient Germanic word *wealas* meaning
'foreigner' and was given by the invading Anglo-Saxons to the res-
ident Celts, making them foreigners in their own land. As readers, our

own translations and linguistic invasions of the Celtic island texts considered in this essay come from a long line of invaders of Celtic lands.

One medieval linguistic and political invader was Gerald of Wales,
or Giraldus Cambrensis, whose book *The History and Topography of
Ireland* was probably written in 1185, after he had journeyed in
Ireland as a member of one of the leading Norman families involved
in the invasion of the island. This book was dedicated as a gift and
precious tool for invasion to 'Henry II, Illustrious King of the English'.
Gerald of Wales is especially pertinent to a discussion of Moore's and
Fuller's novels. He was a medieval Welsh monk of Norman family
who understood both invasion and the monastic brotherhood. His
lifelong dream was to be Archbishop of Wales, and to be consecrated
without having to acknowledge the English authority represented by
Canterbury. As an ambitious Welsh monk he chafed at the problems
of centre versus periphery, wishing the Pope to acknowledge Wales as
a religious centre separate from England, and not as a remote outpost
on the periphery of the civilized world. These questions of centre and
periphery are central to Moore's and Fuller's island-novels.

So, for the invader, territorial mapping is crucial to an easy entrance
and holding of these Celtic islands. The wood, bog, lake and mountain of the Celtic landscape sustained native resistance as the Welsh
and Irish 'rebels' retreated or were pushed further and further towards
the remote margins of their lands, and to the islands off the coast.
Muck Abbey, in Moore's novel, is one of the few Irish abbeys which
has escaped sacking and burning, either from Henry VIII or from
Cromwell, because it is so difficult to reach. As the Abbot tells his
visitor from Rome, 'There are advantages to being remote.'[3]

Within Britain and Ireland, there is no further remoteness than
these Celtic islands. Pushed increasingly to the territorial margins by
successive invasions over the centuries, flying from the enemy whether
that enemy be the Viking invaders, the troops of Henry II, Henry VIII,
Elizabeth I or Cromwell, from these far islands there is nowhere else to
go. Invaders coming to them come to the last bastion, and the native
islanders wishing to resist the change or destruction effected by invasion have nowhere to fly to; on a remote island 'on the edge of the
Gothic world', as Moore writes, these islanders would truly be 'flying
to nowhere', as John Fuller emphasizes in the title of his novel.

These islands are in effect on the edge of an abyss, on the edge of an
unknown ocean in the time of Fuller's novel, and on the edge of an
unknown and disturbing modern world in Brian Moore's novel. The
storms and the tides make them difficult to reach and difficult to leave.
Displaced peoples, hunted west to the coastal margins of their territory, cannot return to the mainland. As Geoffrey and Tetty wait for

the boat that never comes to take them off the island at the conclusion of *Flying to Nowhere*, it seems as if the pilgrims who had come to this holy place, never to return, are mimicking the earlier route of the many pilgrims and of those in flight from the invaders who have come before. There is a feeling of claustrophobia on the island, that this place on the margins of the land and sea is the end of the line for pilgrim and refugee. As Fuller's narrator writes,

> The island had seen many arrivals since the days of its first settlement, but it did not let men go willingly. How much easier to be a pilgrim of the spirit than to be a pilgrim of the flesh . . . [Geoffrey and Tetty] knew that the longer they waited [for the boat] the more they would recognize the power of the dead to keep them from making a new life.[4]

Moore's American priest, visiting the island, feels 'the loneliness of islands, the sense of being shut in, here on a barren outcropping on the edge of Europe, surrounded by this desolation of ocean' (p. 87).

Unlike the gentle hovering over the island of Paton Walsh's angel-reader, access to the island in both Moore's and Fuller's novels is difficult and holds out the possibility of a violent and destructive forced entry. Perhaps exhibiting some trace of a historical understanding of the relationship between the remoteness of Muck island and the intact state of its island-monastery, the native islanders in Moore's novel do not allow James Kinsella, the American Catholic priest, an easy access. As far as they are concerned, Kinsella has come to destroy their Church, the traditional Church of the old rituals and the 'one true Church', as they see it. One of the monks on the island comments sarcastically to Kinsella, 'That's a grand outfit you're wearing. Dashing! You look like a soldier boy!' (p. 71). Appropriately this futuristic and perhaps final invader comes from the Vatican dressed in army fatigues and carrying a 'paramilitary dispatch case'. Influenced at Harvard by his study with a South American revolutionary priest, Kinsella sees himself as a type of soldier; if he has any faith, it is in what he believes to be the crucial marriage of holy orders and revolutionary theory. Kinsella's repeatedly thwarted efforts to get onto Muck island are a comic but potentially violent opening to the novel. The telephone communications between the mainland and Muck are erratic, a storm is coming up, and finally, when one of the island fishermen is sent out by the monks to fetch Kinsella from the mainland, the fisherman approaching the quay refuses to take Kinsella onto his boat. He is looking for a priest, but the man trying to force his way onto the boat looks like a soldier, and until now Muck island has managed wisely to keep soldiers

away. Kinsella tries to grab the side of the boat: 'Padraig, the boatman, let go of one oar, seized up a steel rowlock from beneath it
and, swift as a biting dog, struck the knuckles which held the curragh's
stern. With a gasp of pain, Kinsella drew his hand back' (p. 20).
Furious, frustrated, and certainly quite ridiculous at this point,
Kinsella gets to the nearest pub phone and hires a helicopter to take
him to Muck.

Unlike that 'hovering, grave presence' over the island in the preface
to Jill Paton Walsh's novel, this hovering craft is a violent and noisy
invader. It flies over Muck, its pilot mapping out the island terrain
below for Kinsella; there is the 'spine of the island', its four deserted
cottages, the road, the mountain pass, medieval castle and monastery.
Flying over the castle, the pilot informs Kinsella that the ruin is 'the
fort of Granuaile. . . very old. Grace O'Malley built it. . . Grace
O'Malley. The Sea Queen. Granuaile.' Kinsella learns from the pilot
both the mapping of the key points of the island and a translation of a
mythic place name. The helicopter pilot's place-naming and mapping
owe much to traditional Irish bardic cartography. In ancient Celtic
culture the landscape was 'studied, discussed and referenced: every place
had its legend and its own mythic identity. The Gaelic *Dindsenchas*,
the celebration of place names, was a feature of this poetic or mythic
topography.'[5] But with Kinsella's entrance to the island the conjunction of mapping and place-naming is less reminiscent of the traditional native *Dindsenchas*, and more clearly resembles that other
conjunction of mapping and the translation of place-names, the prel-
ude to invasion. There is the mapping preliminary to a military invasion,
but also the nature of this mapping which in itself is involved with
linguistic invasion, as it effects a renaming or translation of Gaelic mythic
place-names.

The language to be translated in Moore's novel, in the Vatican 'invasion' of Muck island, is Latin to English, rather than Gaelic to English. But linguistic difference and what it symbolizes is still central to
the novel, and is represented by an invasion from Rome which had its
precedent in earlier invasions of the Celtic territory. Indeed, Rome
had sent its envoys to Ireland before, in the early Celtic church, because in those days too the Irish monks were firmly adhering to their
own ancient rituals. The monks living in the Celtic margins in those
early times had been taken to task by the central authority in Rome
over questions of tonsure, the dating of Easter, and also some church
rites which seemed to be derived from pagan ritual. At the time of the
Moore novel's setting, the monks of Muck Abbey cling to the language which their order was taught to follow by Rome centuries before, and which they carefully preserved through the 'dark ages' of the

Church on the Continent. Now Rome has changed its mind about the language of the Church and, reminiscent of the military invaders, wants everything translated or renamed. Kinsella has come to translate the Mass, the prayers and all the rites which the Irish priests practised in Latin. A revolutionary, he also explains to them that Rome now regards the Mass as merely symbolic, and that what used to be its 'miracle' – the literal transformation of the bread and wine into the body and blood of Christ – is to be seen as figurative, symbolic. Miracles are out of favour with the new invaders from Rome and, like the old invaders from England, they must find a new language to name the same physical objects. These physical objects have very different mythical and spiritual values to the two cultures of the invader and the invaded. The Celtic topography and place-naming call an ancient castle ruin the home of the Sea Queen, and the Celtic monastery of Muck calls bread and wine flesh and blood. Literal and figurative language is part of an old battle, and miracles and myths, whether Christian or pagan, cling to the periphery. Also clinging to this periphery, clinging in a sense to the cliff edge of the abbey island, over the abyss of the western ocean, is the spiritual faith of its Abbot. The Abbot remembers a pilgrimage he took to Lourdes years ago when, horrified by the tawdry commercialism of the shrine, he experienced a crisis of faith and found himself unable to pray. At the time of the novel, the Abbot is still unable to pray, although he is the leader of the religious community on Muck. He has become in his own thoughts:

> A man wearing the habit of a religious, sitting in a building, staring at a table called an altar on which there is a box called a tabernacle and inside the tabernacle there is a chalice with a lid called a ciborium, and inside the ciborium are twelve round wafers of unleavened bread made by the Sisters of Knock Convent, Co. Mayo. That is all that is there. That is all that is in the tabernacle in this building which is said to be the house of God. And the man who sits facing the tabernacle is a man with the apt title of *prelatus nullius*, nobody's prelate, belonging to nobody . . . who, when he tries to pray enters null. (pp. 78–9)

The Abbot keeps his secret from the other monks on the island, his hidden horror of prayer which, when attempted, brings him to the brink of the abyss, and over the edge 'into null'. This short novel concludes with the departure of James Kinsella from the island. He leaves as he came twenty-four hours earlier, by helicopter, having been assured of the Abbot's agreement to conform to Vatican edicts. He leaves behind men who will never leave the island and who will struggle to keep their faith when its rituals and meanings have been so radically altered. The Abbot must convince the monks to follow the Church's dictates, but they are on the brink of revolution in their desperation to cling to the old order of their faith. On the point of failure to persuade and comfort the men, the Abbot sees that, to gain their confidence and to calm them, he must 'do something he has never done, give something he has never given in these, his years as their Abbot. What has kept him in fear since Lourdes, must now be faced. What he feared most to do must now be done. And if, in so doing it, I enter null and never return, amen. My time has come' (p. 100). To save their faith, the Abbot sacrifices his own by leading the monks in the words of prayer which for him are empty, null:

> He bent his head. 'Our Father, Who are in Heaven,' he said.
> His trembling increased. He entered null.
> He would never come back. In null.
>
> He heard them kneel. 'Our Father, Who art in Heaven.'
> Relieved their voices echoed his.
> 'Hallowed be Thy name', the Abbot said.
> 'Hallowed be Thy name'. (pp. 101–2)

These last words of the novel, 'Hallowed be Thy name', echo in the abyss, over a western ocean which is not listening because the island is the last place where, as far as its monks are concerned, the name *is* hallowed, even if it cannot be for its Abbot. For the island brotherhood the name is crucial, and over the centuries various linguistic invasions have named and renamed their gods, their sacred places, and finally their Christian God. Names have been tampered with, blasphemed against, translated and taken in vain. The monks' faith will suffer unless the Abbot sacrifices himself for them by entering null, an abyss of no faith, through uttering the words of prayer and naming a God in whom he cannot believe. Ironically his empty words reinstate the confidence in their fullness of meaning for the other monks.

Some poetic words which probably have been taken in vain and devalued by repetition are those of Donne's 'Devotions upon Emergent Occasions'. I repeat them here at the risk of devaluing them, because they throw into relief the irony and the paradox of the Abbot's sacrifice of himself for his island brotherhood:

> No man is an island entire of itself. Every man is a piece of the continent, a part of the main; if a clod be washed away by the sea, Europe is the less, as well as if a Promontory were, as well as if a Manor of thy friends or of thine own were; any man's death diminishes me, because I am involved in Mankind, And therefore never send to know for whom the bell tolls; it tolls for thee.

Because he is 'involved in mankind,' involved with the only humanity that he knows intimately – the island brotherhood – the Abbot sacrifices himself for them. But in that sacrifice he truly becomes an island unto himself. Literally and spiritually isolated, he enters the void alone.

Similar to Kinsella's violent entry to Muck island, Fuller's *Flying to Nowhere* opens with the violent imagery of Vane, the ecclesiastical investigator, gaining a troubled access to the Welsh monastic island. Vane has brought his high-blooded stallion with him on the ship, but when the boatman tells him that the horse will not be able to make the journey to shore on the small boat from the ship, he still insists. The stallion, destroying the small boat, is finally cut loose, and attempts to leap to the shore, only to break and cripple itself on the rocks. The slowly dying body of the horse lies on the beach for days until visited a last time by Vane's young servant, Geoffrey, who has been fond of the animal. When Geoffrey approaches the horse from a distance, it looks as if it is 'sitting at ease and looking down the shore':

> Geoffrey was seized with a sudden hope that he might, after all, not yet be dead, and had made his way down to the rocks where the beast had leapt and fallen. As he approached, he could hear above the lapping of the sea another, stranger, sound, like the wind in the tops of trees – only there was no wind. It came from the body of the horse which Geoffrey could now see was quite dead, for its haunches were already decomposed, leaving the spine arched like a flying buttress. Beneath it, heaped and massed within the collapsing bulk of the animal, was an army of maggots the volume of a broken sack of meal. He came closer and watched them with a sickened respect for this ferocious process of corruption. (pp. 60–1)

Fuller's novel is, like the horse's body, riddled with images of corruption, decay and death. The Abbot at the head of the island monastery is obsessed, on the other hand, with bringing corpses to life; he searches for the 'seat of the soul', in order to reverse the process of corruption. Here Fuller may have been thinking of stories told of a Celtic island in Gerald of Wales's twelfth-century work *The History and Topography of Ireland*, discussed earlier in relation to the theme of invasion. A passage which seems particularly relevant to Fuller's novel states:

> There is an island in the sea west of Connacht which is said to have been consecrated by Saint Brendan. In this island human corpses are not buried and do not putrefy, but are placed in the open and remain without corruption. Here men see with some wonder and recognize their grandfathers, great-grandfathers, great-great grandfathers and a long line of ancestors.[6]

The pilgrims of Fuller's novel come to the island's holy well for cures and to seek spiritual life, but eventually they meet with certain physical death and are consigned to the exploratory scalpel of the Abbot's dissecting chamber. Gerald of Wales's credulous writings about the 'miracles' on the Celtic islands, such as the one I have just quoted, are typical of Celtic Christianity, that Christianity which was grafted onto a pagan religion. The Celtic Church's holy places, wells and rocks were often originally sacred places of the pre-Christian beliefs. A letter in Fuller's novel from one of the pilgrims to his brother gives some indication that the Celtic rites are still occurring on the remote outposts of Celtic Christianity: 'they were truly pagans at Clynnof Fawr and not to be trusted for I was informed they did offer heifers to St. Beuno like a god of the old world and not a Christian saint' (p. 24).

With the failure of the island's holy well to produce miraculous cures, the Abbot seeks to perform his own 'miracles' by attempting to bring the pilgrims' decaying corpses back to life with the water from the well. This literal and figurative play with language is taken to extreme lengths in the novel. The Abbot takes flesh and blood and attempts to give it life, playing God on his little island. But Fuller's description of the decay and corruption of death is so graphic that the transubstantiation – the 'miracle of the Mass' – is blasphemed; the flesh and the blood become so far removed from the symbolic – so literally flesh and blood as to be subject to putrefaction – that the transubstantiation of the Mass is itself corrupted. It is no longer the transmutation of the bread and wine of life into the living flesh and blood of Christ, but a transformation into deathly flesh and blood. In a similar manner the 'water of life', that of the holy well, now leads to death.

In a novel of such graphic and realistic detail – the sensual description of fleshly death and decay, the almost modern scientific investigations of the Abbot who does not believe in spiritual miracles, but in the 'miracles' of science – the end comes as a suprise. We are unprepared for a miracle, but, as the Abbot slides about the wet floor of his dissecting room, the waters of the flooding holy well (dug out by the foreign investigator Vane) are coming into contact with the leather bindings and paper of his library's books. The books, rather than the corpses, begin to come to life; the leather bindings turn back into a herd of cows, the paper into the trees and roots from which it was derived. Fuller writes in the last paragraph of the novel:

Words were indeed more enduring than the body. Mrs. Ffedderbompau's letter had fallen from his fingers as he had battled with the foliage, and had lain for a few minutes in the warm well water. Now small shoots of reeds pushed up from the paper, and hair-like roots wiggled to seek the lodging of cracks in the stone. Gall and insect ichor trickled down the fronds, and from the bubbling seal came a sweet stench of wax and a buzzing murmur. The Abbot stooped in sudden love to this miniature landscape which spread like a riverbank by his feet. (pp. 104–5)

Literally, then, in this novel, the word becomes life. The final invasion of this remote Celtic outpost, of this Welsh island monastery, is the literal invasion by the text as the books spring forth vegetation which grows over all traces of human settlement.

The final miracle of Fuller's novel offers a prospective vision of an island overgrown and difficult to penetrate. The pages of the Abbot's books have been transformed into a miniature landscape which spreads like a river bank; language, the written words, have become landscape – a miniature topography mapped out at the Abbot's feet. If maps, placed in the hands of the colonizers, can serve as tools for invasion, then this transformation of language into landscape defeats the invader as books, maps and charts in the Abbot's library grow over the island, eventually perhaps to cover over human traces and known mapped territory.

In some ways Fuller's novel uses language to mirror the impenetrable island by placing untranslated Welsh in the midst of its English text. Because *Flying to Nowhere* begins by offering to the reader all the signs of a detective novel, the reader is not, like Jill Paton Walsh's angel-reader a 'hovering, gravely attentive presence', but is instead a searching colonizer of the text who maps out clues, and hunts down discrepancies which may lead to a solution to the mysteries of the novel. For the many readers who cannot read Welsh there must be a heightened sense of frustration and curiosity over the occasional phrases, scraps of poetry and riddles which are placed in the novel, often at times when they might seem to offer a clue to an unexplained mystery. For example, the strange and heretical ordination ritual of a novice monk is left a mystery to the reader at the end of chapter 19. We do not know why 'When they drew the curtains of the bed, they found the novice shaking in terror' (p. 93), and as a result a pressure is brought to bear upon the untranslated Welsh riddle which precedes this sentence. Its impenetrability for non-Welsh-speaking readers is tantalizing, and throws into relief how language and the problem of translation can repel the reader/invader in a similar way to the miraculously transformed text covering the island in a landscape impenetrable to the invader at the close of the novel. A return to a language which existed before the Anglo-Saxon invasions also emphasizes the island-text's resistance to linguistic invasion.

Fuller's *Flying to Nowhere* and Moore's *Catholics* are island stories which offer an alternative to what is often claimed to be the most familiar and potent island myth in Western literature, Defoe's *Robinson Crusoe*. James Joyce described the power of this novel in a lecture on Defoe:

> The true symbol of the British conquest is Robinson Crusoe, who, cast away on a desert island, in his pocket a knife and a pipe, becomes an architect, a carpenter, a knife grinder, an astronomer, a baker, a ship-wright, a potter, a saddler, a farmer, a tailor, an umbrella-maker, and a clergyman. He is the true prototype of the British colonist, as Friday . . . is the symbol of the subject races. The whole Anglo-Saxon spirit is in Crusoe . . . Whoever rereads this simple, moving book in the light of subsequent history cannot help but fall under its prophetic spell.[7]

Crusoe builds fences around the territory that he colonizes, makes lists of the number of cannibals he has shot, and counts his goats. Although he claims that his experiences on the island effect his spiritual conversion, his spirituality is very much allied to material substance – to what he owns, counts and maps out as his property. In the history of the novel genre, Defoe's *Robinson Crusoe* is a famous example of the early realist novel, and the realism partly relies upon an unquestioning confidence that material substance – goats, a slave, the island itself – will conform to the wishes and expectations of the English colonist.

Brian Moore's and John Fuller's island-novels address questions of spirit and substance with quite different results. Their islands do not conform to the Protestant 'Anglo-Saxon spirit' (as Joyce called it) of Crusoe's story, but to Celtic hagiography in which islands are places of miracles, and not of realism. On these Celtic islands, substance and spirit behave less predictably than on Crusoe's island; as on St Columba's island of Iona, in *Flying to Nowhere* the saint stamps on a rock which then gives forth a holy well of miraculous properties. The Abbot in Fuller's novel tries to find the seat of the soul through surgical dissection, but in the end the holy well performs a miracle which overwhelms and negates his material, scientific researches, and spirituality replaces rationality. The monks of Muck Abbey defy the edicts brought by the latest invader to their island; they refuse to accept the Church's new teaching that there is no transubstantiation – that the 'miracle of the Mass' is merely symbolic.

Fuller's novel deceptively begins as a detective novel, encouraging readers to name, categorize and collect substantial clues – to behave as if they were in a realist novel – and then ends with a miracle which defies the rational approach of the detective. Moore's novel closes with painful doubt and uncertainty about miracles because we do not know whether the Abbot's sacrifice means that he has rediscovered his faith, or whether he has entered the 'null' of disbelief. James Joyce wrote of *Crusoe* that it 'reveals, as perhaps no other book throughout the long history of English literature does, the wary and heroic instinct of the rational animal and the prophecy of the empire'. The island-story of the rational colonizer is resisted in Fuller's and Moore's Celtic island-stories, which deal not with certainties and substance, but with spirituality, miracles and doubt.

Perhaps to combat the power or the spell of Crusoe's colonized realm, post-colonial fiction has turned to the view of the island, not from the invasive, intrusive eye of the outsider, but from the viewpoint of the native islander who has been invaded; from the perspective, for example, of Bertha Mason as Mr Rochester comes to her West Indies island in Jean Rhys's *Wide Sargasso Sea*, or from a version of Crusoe's Friday in Coetzee's *Foe*.

Both Moore's and Fuller's tales of Celtic islands on the very margins of the Celtic fringe are in their turn full of the shadows of former texts which describe or facilitate invasion of these islands (such as Gerald of Wales's topography) or of stories of pre-invasion Celtic myths of islands. These island-stories ignore the 'prophetic spell', as Joyce described it, of that famous island myth told from the centre – the expansionist colonist story of Robinson Crusoe. Resistance to invasion, and especially linguistic invasion, is effected by concentrating on an alternative island mythology which comes from the periphery rather than the centre. The tiny Celtic monastic outposts in Moore's and Fuller's novels become metaphors for the resistance to that colonial trinity of textual, linguistic and political invasion. The stories told here are not of a single man on a desert island setting up a little kingdom, but of an island community clinging to its own mappings on the edge of the void.

Notes

1 Shakespeare, *Richard II*, II. i. 46–9.
2 Jill Paton Walsh, *Knowledge of Angels* (Cambridge: Green Bay Publications, 1994), foreword. All other quotations from this novel will be indicated by page number within the body of this essay.
3 Brian Moore, *Catholics* (1st pub. 1972; paperback edn, London: Vintage, 1992), p. 53. Sources of all further quotations from this novel will be given by paperback page number in the body of the essay.
4 John Fuller, *Flying to Nowhere* (1st pub. 1983; paperback edn, London: Vintage, 1992), p. 102. Sources of all further quotations from this novel will be given by paperback page number in the body of this essay.

5 R. F. Foster, *Modern Ireland: 1600–1972* (1988; Harmondsworth: Penguin, 1989), p. 56.
6 Gerald of Wales, *The History and Topography of Ireland*, trans. and ed. John O'Meara (Harmondsworth: Penguin, 1982), p. 61.
7 This passage is from a lecture delivered in 1912 by Joyce in Italian in Trieste. The lecture is translated in 'Daniel Defoe', *Buffalo Studies*, 1 (1964), pp. 24–5.

The Uses of Impurity: Fiction and Fundamentalism in Salman Rushdie and Jeanette Winterson

Mark Wormald

Wedged between a grocery stall and the fishmonger on the edge of the market square in Cambridge, not far from the second-hand bookseller whose rare-book Thursdays attract academics like flies, a man sells white Aran sweaters and confronts the end of the millennium. The awning directly above his head tells prospective customers: 'JESUS IS LORD OVER THIS BUSINESS', and must either bore straight into or go straight over the head of the baked-potato man who has the pitch nearly opposite. It also provokes another sort of competition. A potato's throw away, members of the Socialist Workers' Party stand rather forlornly selling their newspapers. One Saturday in November 1995, shoppers could not help noticing a couple of tables set up just over the way, forcing them to run a more forbiddingly metaphysical gauntlet as they headed for The Gap. The tables, manned by smiling young men, were laid with a cloth announcing: 'ISLAM: THE ONLY IDEOLOGY FOR HUMANITY'.

These two rival slogans invite two observations. 'We stand at a moment in history in which, as we look around the planet, it appears that God – or, rather, formal religion – has begun once again to insist on occupying a central role in public life.'[1] This from one novelist, writing in an essay titled as intriguingly as it is dated: 'In God We Trust', '1985, 1990'. In 1992 another novelist, and a self-proclaimed 'secularist', predicted: 'it is Islam that will, in the next few decades, come to play the role of communism as a rival to the ideological power of the West.'[2] The observations are, of course, linked. The first is Salman Rushdie's, and in historical terms straddles an event – the publication of *The Satanic Verses* in September 1988 – that in turn unleashed what has become known as the 'Rushdie Affair', and prompted the second, by Daniel Easterman, his carefully chosen *nom de plume* suggesting the peculiar form of resurrection that a career in fiction can offer to an academic orientalist.

Between them, these two pairs – the two religious advertising jingles, the two measured critical responses to the global phenomenon of religious revival those jingles represent – evoke a compelling and deeply serious confrontation. Secular authorship versus religious authority, fiction against fatwa, profit against prophet, big money advances against a still-mounting price on the novelist's head: such soundbites and headlines are the stuff of the Rushdie Affair. Yet, as the terms and aspects of this opposition have proliferated, it has become clear that the confrontation contains a danger for its witnesses as well as for its victim. The danger is of interpretation, of balance. Readers brought up within a Western humanist tradition of literature and criticism may find it increasingly difficult to balance competing elements of their own culture as they determine their response to a series of diverse, sometimes contradictory and even by definition irreconcilable polarities. In order to interpret and evaluate the terms of the opposition, and to establish their necessary distinctness, such readers compare them; yet such a comparison is never objective. The frame of reference, the horizon of expectations, involved in undertaking such a comparison dictates the outcome of the judgements it produces. Mario Vargas Llosa's recent observation written in the shadow of the Rushdie Affair, that 'Men do not live by truth alone'[3] demonstrates what it argues: that a sensitivity to nuance and linguistic register, a painstakingly acquired if rarely examined intuition about the availability of scripture to fondly heretical variation, and the ability to distinguish the bread of historical fact or inherited formulas of wisdom from the more intoxicating substances of less familiar narrative and metaphor, are precisely the skills which skew our readings of banners and phrases obviously outside our own tradition. Armed with these skills, we find it easy to deprecate clumsy attempts to appropriate the discourse of secularized spirituality and liberal humanism for other ends. They are clumsy because they so obviously betray their authors' failed mastery of the codes we are used to. Those who wrote 'ISLAM: THE ONLY IDEOLOGY FOR HUMANITY' may well have read Easterman on Islam's growing rivalry to the ideological power of the West, and may well have envisaged themselves, standing a hundred yards or so from Rushdie's Alma Mater King's College, as a part of the Rushdie Affair. But they still stand outside the field of measured debate and tolerant conversations that students and defenders of literature and culture identify as their own stock-in-trade. 'In ordinary conversation,' as Terry Eagleton observes, 'to claim that someone is thinking or speaking "ideologically" is normally to suggest that their view of things is skewed by a set of rigid preconceptions.'[4]

Yet to identify the apparent ignorance of those young Muslims, to react to their almost comic discomfort in the midst of a marketplace crowded with the produce of postmodernism, is not to take proportionate comfort in our own position as consumers and commentators. It is rather to expose the frailty of postmodernism's wares, and to challenge the assumptions of its more vocal peddlers. As Eagleton also concedes: 'Postmodernism is an "end of ideology" world, just as it has been declared to be the end of history. But this, of course, is true only for postmodern theorists. It is hardly true for American Evangelicals, Egyptian fundamentalists, Ulster unionists or British fascists.'[5]

In what follows I take two lessons from that rueful admission. Both are lessons about language and its reach. First, if the Rushdie Affair raises questions about the relationship between literary fiction and religious fundamentalism, these questions need to be addressed in an appropriately measured manner, and within a field of reference broad enough to reflect varieties of religious experience beyond as well as within Islam. If we are indeed to go on comparing and reaching judgements about secular writing and holy scripture, we need to acknowledge and investigate the terrain of the comparisons we employ, and ensure that they are sufficiently robust and sufficiently vivid to reflect our experience of our subject. In particular, such comparisons should emulate the manner in which competing forms of fundamentalism continue to coexist alongside and against other discourses of postmodernism. As that scene in Cambridge market reminds us, the juxtapositions involved can sometimes be too close for comfort.

The second lesson lies in Eagleton's hint about the partiality of postmodern theory. The 'ordinary conversations' of postmodern and other recent theorists are less likely to provide us with these terms and techniques of comparison than the writings of novelists whose lives and work have been devoted to confronting and comparing the experiences of religious faith and secular fiction. Here I propose a route out of the stark and unsatisfactory oppositions of the Rushdie Affair by acknowledging, and attempting to emulate, the perspectives and strategies adopted within the writings of two such novelists, Salman Rushdie and Jeanette Winterson. Both have suffered (and have with varying degrees of irony and anguish protested against the misrepresentation involved) from the application to their work of 'rigid preconceptions', whether by fundamentalists of religion or cultural theory. Both novelists have resisted this misrepresentation by resorting to a common, and curiously recognizable, terrain, a landscape composed of familiar metaphors variously redeployed.

As we will see, the terrain of metaphor in Rushdie and Winterson extends well beyond the Rushdie Affair; but one effect of *The Satanic Verses* and the terrible consequences of its publication was to force Rushdie to declare his motives for exploring it, and thus to provide an unusually clear view of its features. This declaration took time. In the immediate aftermath of the Ayatollah Khomeini's fatwa, the rhetoric of opposition within his own novel seemed to have supplied the best means of defence, as Rushdie came to occupy the desperate position faced by his namesake Salman the Persian, satirist in *The Satanic Verses*. Charged by the prophet Mahound with a crime he has already admitted to another satirist, Baal, that of introducing alterations into the transcription of the prophet's revelations, and 'actually writing the Book, or re-writing, anyway, polluting the word of God with my own profane language,' Salman has only one defence against Mahound's accusation of unforgivable blasphemy, that he has 'set your words against the Words of God'.[6] And that is to stick, defiantly, to the terms of the offence: 'It's his word against mine' (p. 368). In the first two defences he wrote of his work, both in 1990, Rushdie seemed to espouse his character's defiance, and deliberately appropriated a vocabulary resembling that of his pursuers: he had written 'In Good Faith', and when he asked 'Is Nothing Sacred?' he seemed to answer himself by making the novel, as a genre, his own secular scripture, his own 'anti-Qu'ran', as Easterman described *The Satanic Verses*.[7] By 1991, however, Rushdie's tactics seem to have changed. He acknowledged that his previous statements of faith in fiction had alienated or confused 'even moderate Muslims', and that they had done so because they remained confined within the polar oppositions of the Rushdie Affair's relentlessly extending variation on 'that evergreen favourite, the Balloon debate' about the fate of *The Satanic Verses* and its author. In such a debate, 'the assembled company blithely accepts the faintly unpleasant idea that a human being's right to life is increased or diminished by his or her virtues or vices', and rationalizes this collective brutality by arguing that 'it's only make-believe, after all'.

Rushdie's response to this formulation of his position in that debate is revealing, because it suggests the other form of defiance he had by then brought to his own defence, and which, well before and since *The Satanic Verses*, his fiction's variety of 'make-believe' has consistently enlarged. We glimpse a larger terrain, metaphorical rather than discursive, to which he is drawn in response to a crisis, and the rhetorical means by which this terrain has been constructed.

I have now spent over a thousand days in just such a balloon; but, alas, this isn't a game . . . Trapped inside a metaphor, I've often felt the need to redescribe it, to change the terms. This isn't so much a balloon, I've wanted to say, as a bubble, within which I'm simultaneously exposed and sealed off. The bubble floats above and through the world, depriving me of reality, reducing me to an abstraction . . .

It's ridiculous – isn't it? – to have to say, But I *am* a human being, unjustly accused, unjustly embubbled. Or is it I who am being ridiculous, as I call out from my bubble, *I'm still trapped in here, folks; somebody, please, get me out?*

Out there where you are, in the rich and powerful and lucky West, has it really been so long since religions persecuted people, burning them as heretics, drowning them as witches, that you can't recognize religious persecution when you see it? . . . The original metaphor has reasserted itself. I'm back in the balloon, asking for the right to live.[8]

'Trapped inside a metaphor', Rushdie's impulse is not to abandon it as a vehicle, but to 'redescribe it, to change the terms': that is, he remains doggedly faithful to the essential and necessary fluidity of metaphor as a cognitive and imaginative technique. He converts balloon to bubble complete with Warner Brothers cartoon speech, and then uses this dangerous fluency in two customarily distinct idioms to return to the rhetoric of the debating chamber and the elements of Western history with an intensified awareness of their premises. Only then can he make his Western addressees re-imagine what happens once 'the original metaphor has reasserted itself'. '[The] balloon is over the chasm again; and it's still sinking.' Only then can he persuade them of the qualities of the richly and dangerously ambiguous element of which his vantage point in the balloon affords one vivid view.

Obviously, a rigid, blinkered, absolutist world-view is the easiest to keep hold of, whereas the fluid, uncertain, metamorphic picture I've always carried about is rather more vulnerable. Yet I must cling with all my might to that chameleon, that chimera, that shape-shifter, my own soul; must hold on to its mischievous, iconoclastic, out-of-step clown instincts, no matter how great the storm. And if that plunges me into contradiction and paradox, so be it; I've lived in that messy ocean all my life. I've fished in it for my art. This turbulent sea was the sea outside my bedroom window in Bombay. It is the sea by which I was born, and which I carry with me wherever I go.[9]

That sea is capacious, accommodating, if also curiously confused. (How can he carry with him something into which he seems about to be plunged?) As such, it may provide a means of resolving the paradox that all these quotations from Rushdie seem to raise: the relationship between a defence of fiction as 'sacred' and a notion of its process as one of pollution, the introduction by profane scripture of wounding

impurity into territory and traditions of reading that claim inviolabil-
ity, exclusiveness, immobility. Almost a decade since the publication
of *The Satanic Verses* – the apotheosis of challenging literary fiction
that was for many untrained or unliterary readers an unreadable,
offensively polluting reconstruction of the very origins of one of the
world's holy books – it is salutary to reflect again on this conflict of
Word and word, sacred scripture and profane text, from a perspective
which that distance allows.

Both before and after *The Satanic Verses*, Rushdie's fiction has
aspired to such distance, and been at pains to free itself from an exclusively hostile tone to the religion he grew up with. Obviously, a
concern for Islam, whether in the melting-pot of suburban Bombay or
the disputed but unpolluted Kashmir, the politicized puritanism of
Pakistan, or its early and disputed history, did consume much of
Rushdie's energies as a novelist in the first half of his career (and *The
Satanic Verses* now stands at that career's midpoint). But even in the
trilogy he regarded *The Satanic Verses* as completing, Rushdie has been
careful not to confine such treatment to a single religion, nor to the
politics of any one form of religious extremism or fundamentalism:

> I have talked about the Islamic religion because that is what I know the
> most about. But the ideas about religious faith and the nature of relig-
> ious experience and also the potential implications of religious experi-
> ence and also the political implications of religious extremism are
> applicable with a few variations to just about any religion.[10]

His fiction confirms this. When Tavleen, the beautiful but deadly Sikh
extremist, detonated her own grenade-encumbered breasts on board
The Satanic Verse's own vehicle, the Bostan, Air India flight 420, one
of the victims dispatched with most relish was the aptly named Eugene
Dumsday, the American Christian creationist; while the portrayal of
Mainduck Fielding in *The Moor's Last Sigh* turns the same lampoon-
ing satire on a contemporary figure of militant Hinduism. And that
same novel opens with its hero, Moraes Zogoiby, nailing instalments
of his narrative to Spanish doors, and so aligning himself with an
Andalusian Martin Luther. He even records how his beloved, 'a self-
professedly godly un-Christian Indian, joked about Luther's protest at
Wittenburg to tease her determinedly ungodly Indian Christian lover:
how stories travel, what mouths they end up in!'[11]

Pausing over the moral of such a moment, along with the order of
Rushdie's observations about religion, we might conclude that an emphasis on the politics of religious fundamentalism in Rushdie's work
before or since *The Satanic Verses* still risks underplaying the impulses

and affiliations and the sheer experience of reading such material, the experience of reading it closely, watching how it moves from mouth to mouth. Indeed, when Rushdie's narrator intervenes in *Shame* to make his most explicit observation about 'so called Islamic fundamentalism', his complaint about it is precisely that it is not fundamental at all, not an organic, developing, dynamic part of the history of the people on which it has been imposed. And imposed from above. With force. He counts it as a mythology, 'rammed down people's throats'.

> Few mythologies survive close examination. And they can become very unpopular indeed if they're rammed down people's throats.
>   What happens if one is force-fed such outsize, indigestible meals? – One gets sick. One rejects their nourishment. Reader: one pukes.
>   So-called Islamic 'fundamentalism' does not spring, in Pakistan, from the people. It is imposed on them from above.[12]

The criticism implies its own imperative for the novelist. Give your own readers something that *is* so rooted, that springs from history in the way that people do, messily, richly, chaotically. Give them an indecent meal they want to swallow. That is what Rushdie has always tried to do, and is still doing. In the name and genealogy of Moraes Zogoiby, Rushdie is still purging the false, shallow purism of Islamic heritage from his work by presenting us with the polluted, hybrid, half- or quarter-caste *par excellence*, with Catholic Portuguese-Indian blood on his hero's maternal side, and Jewish-Moorish on the other. He is still presenting us with it tastily. Here is Moraes: 'I was raised neither as Catholic nor as Jew. I was both, and nothing: a jewholic-anonymous, a cathjew nut, a stewpot, a mongrel cur. I was – what's the word these days? – *atomised*. Yessir: a real Bombay mix' (p. 104). Moraes is writing from Spain, about India, with a hint of classical Lucretian cosmology and maybe a flourish in the direction of twentieth-century particle physics thrown in for good measure. He is relishing it. And we should be. Rushdie's English readers are comfortable with all that Bombay mix, because we can buy it all here. In our own market stalls. Where other slightly more modest Christian banners hang, alongside the stalls that stock all the other raw materials – the books, the fruit, the spices – which Jeanette Winterson as well as Rushdie has enjoyed adding to fundamentally impure fictions.

We might expect to find Winterson admiring, and talking to, Rushdie, and doing so in a marketplace. For they have much in common. She too has written protestant fictions, works that reimagine autobiographical origins by reimagining the elements that a single childhood shares with the origin of an idea or a faith. Like Rushdie, her literary reputation owes much to the relish with which she has communicated the clashes within the culture of her youth. Her early fiction shows what happens when a fundamentalist faith struggling to control the material world meets the powerful temptation of that world. Where in *Midnight's Children* (1981) Saleem Sinai is born in the same year and city as Rushdie, the narrator of *Oranges are not the Only Fruit* (1985) shares a first name, a Christian name, and the discovery of a sexual orientation, with her creator. As with Rushdie, Winterson's determination to keep tapping these sources of fiction, her insistence on the reality of the imagination and the necessarily imaginary status of reality, has landed her in trouble with readers impatient with the sophisticated ironies involved in the blurrings of such distinctions. And, following Rushdie's precedent, she has been driven as a result of what she takes to be wilfully reductive misreading, a literalism of the sort she is herself charged with, to launch some forthright but theoretically problematic defences of her work and her intention.[13] In doing so, she has confirmed the degree to which both novelists have responded to an impatience with the servants of God by discovering an alternative channel for their faith. Wintersons's book of essays *Art Objects* (1995) – the pun is integral – stands with *Imaginary Homelands* as a hymn to books, paintings, and high culture, High Modernism in particular, as articles of writerly faith, totems and lifebelts to clutch at in times of fire or flood.

This raises yet more vivid, graphic connections between Rushdie and Winterson. These are best conveyed in terms of images, because they concern the images I have just raised, fire and flood. Fire, first: Rushdie was not the only one to provoke a book-burning. In the Lancashire town of her childhood, as Winterson is fiercely determined to tell us in *Art Objects*, Winterson's adoptive mother burned the books she kept hidden under her mattress (p. 154).

For a conjunction of fire and flood, we need to turn from essay to fiction. Though to exactly what sort of fiction remains in doubt. *Boating for Beginners*, Winterson's second book, was published, like the more famous *Oranges*, in 1985, and since downgraded, by Winterson herself. Though it was launched as 'her second novel', and still described as such on the endpapers of the 1990 paperback edition, Winterson herself has since revised its status. In the bibliographies of her work included in her other recent works, it is advertised as 'Comic Book'. We can see why: the sheer frivolity of the linguistic detail of the writing emerges from a summary of the plot. Gloria Munde and her mother Mrs Munde take part in a Cecil B. De Millennarian remake of Genesis and the Flood, in which Noah is the director and God's omnipotence an accident that happens when Noah plays at being

Frankenstein. Winterson's writing is more than usually anarchic, min-
ing headlines and slogans from the literary culture of Shelley and since
with an apparently random vigour, and applying the paraphernalia of
late twentieth-centuy consumerism to a decadent Nineveh with gay
abandon. Structurally, too, there is nothing like the systematic appropriation of the books of the Old Testament that *Oranges* performs in
charting Jeanette's growth out of her childhood's straitened Land of
the Pure into a world of secular literature and literary sexuality.

Just because of this, however, the development of metaphor in *Boating for Beginners* and the little metanarrative commentary that it contains are both more startlingly arresting than their equivalents in the
better-known book. Because in these respects *Boating for Beginners*
reveals just what writers like Winterson, or Rushdie, for that matter,
both of them Oxbridge graduates sensitive to the evolution of literary
and historical tradition, find stimulating in the appeal of still better-
known books – in Rushdie's case the Qu'ran; for Winterson, the amal-
gamated text of the Bible. The following passage from *Boating for
Beginners* explores the motivations of the Bible's many writers, and
the enduring appeal of the 'faith' that drove them. Winterson's narrator observes, 'Just as a point of interest', that 'the Bible is probably
the most anti-linear text we possess, which is why it's such a joy' –
and also why it has inspired her own anti-linear fiction:

> Maybe Genesis is less important than it was, but we still like flood stories
> – whether they're Plato's Atlantis or yarns about the Loch Ness monster.
> Freud says we are preoccupied with deluges as a safeguard against bed-
> wetting. That may or may not be true; what remains is the potency of the
> myth. Myths hook and bind the mind because at the same time they set
> the mind free: they explain the universe while allowing the universe to go
> on being unexplained; and we seem to need this even now, in our twenti-
> eth-century grandeur. The Bible writers didn't care that they were bunch-
> ing together sequences some of which were historical, some preposterous,
> and some downright manipulative. Faithful recording was not their busi-
> ness. Faith was. . . . Every believer is an anarchist at heart. True believers
> would rather see governments topple and history rewritten than scuff the
> cover of their faith. For them, all things are possible. They are poets,
> insomuch as poetry expands, whereas prose defines. Believers are danger-
> ous and mad and may even destroy the world in a different deluge if they
> deem it necessary to keep the faith. They are fanatics, and reasonable
> people will never deal with their excesses until reasonable people find a
> counter-myth in themselves and learn to fight fire with fire.[14]

Apart from 'the Romantics', who 'didn't need it because they found
their own fire', the Bible, she argues, has been an inevitable recourse

for 'almost every other quasi-revolt':

> because when the heart revolts it wants outrageous things that cannot possibly be factual. Robes and incense and larger-than-life and miracles and heroes. It's all there, it's heart-food, and the more we deprive ourselves of colours and folly, the more attractive that now legitimate folly will become.
>
> But read it; read it for its arrogance, its sleight of hand. It's very beautiful, and it's a pointer for living. The mistake is to use it as a handbook. That way madness lies. (pp. 66–7)

We need to follow her narrator's advice when learning the art of *Boating for Beginners*. We are not allowed to take its plot too seriously; indeed, Winterson's narrative is less important as 'plot' than as illustration of her aesthetics of metaphor. Gloria's mother Mrs Munde shares with several of Rushdie's matriarchs, from *Midnight Children*'s Reverend Mother to *Shame*'s Bilquis Hyder, a vivid and dangerous weakness for metaphor, an inability to understand it for anything but literal truth. This inability is sympathetically described as the product of despair with the contemporary world, a despair Winterson shares: 'When Mrs Munde delivered herself into the everlasting hands of the Almighty, she did so because her heart was too loud for this muffled world' (p. 67). But her dislocation from that world, her heart's loudness, ensures that her own refuges are solipsistically inadequate. An amateur in astronomy and addicted to romances, she is satisfied by neither. As a result, and from her inability to be 'free-thinking in a sense that would have allowed her to question the institutions that made her moody: her family, her marriage, her career prospects', she is equally closed to the possibility of amending or appropriating the means by which such institutions create their own myths. Employed in the 'comic-book' world of Noah's family enterprise as a cook charged by Noah's son Ham with developing the Hallelujah hamburger, Mrs Munde is nevertheless appealingly blind to any ulterior motives for such applications and rearrangments of material, whether on the part of her creator or of her employer. The appeal of Noah's remake of Genesis passes her by. Deciding to 'stay up and read *Genesis* again':

> 'The film won't be as good as the book,' she sighed. 'They never are.'
>
> Gloria just smiled. She didn't care about the film. It was a means to an end as far as she was concerned – her own ends, her own development. (p. 67)

The central relationship of *Boating for Beginners* deals at some length with the tension of attitudes to interpretation revealed here. As Noah starts filming, Gloria hears 'one of the art people' say: 'I see a lot of similarities here to *Macbeth*, don't you?' (p. 52). In such a world, where the sequences of history and myth, contemporary consumerist culture, literary traditions and biblical archetypes are so mischievously confused – where Gloria can buy Northrop Frye at a railway book stall and mistake his critical prose for a romance – the interpretation of metaphor becomes an indispensable means of guiding characters and readers through the intricacies of Winterson's imagined territory. This often has surprising results. A vivid but primitive perception of metaphor both comforts and impels Mrs Munde; an 'impressionable and earnest girl' who 'had spent nearly all her youth gazing out of the window, wondering about the nature of the cosmos and how she could truly be part of it', she had with time and the continuing frustration of her astronomical ambitions 'persuaded herself that this early impulse was really a metaphor for something else, and when she heard about the Unpronounceable she knew her instinct had been correct' (p. 19). Yet she remains instinctual. Gloria, on the other hand, has been the lucky and random recipient of Frye's schema of

> the development of language through three stages: the metaphoric, where persons and matter share a common energy and are described as an inseparable unit; the didactic, where persons and matter are separable and the inner life (intellectual) assumes ascendancy; and finally the prosaic, where we describe what we see and feel without recourse to imagery because we think imagining gets in the way. (p. 44)

Gloria, we read, had 'begun to table her own life according to its premises', and had by the time of her introduction to Noah, his family and their film of the flood 'clearly reached stage two'. But Gloria's own analysis of her development is comically incomplete. Engaged on a task of collecting animals for the ark and the impending flood, she tells one new friend, with unconscious irony, 'about Northrop Frye and her own present state of probing curiosity which she had exchanged for her previously inchoate state and would, if all went well, trade in for an understanding of the world which was both fluent and fluid. Continuous Prose' (pp. 98–9). In a world heading ominously for total immersion, total fluency, total fluidity is hardly to be desired. Instead, as that intervention of Winterson's narrator on the writers of the Bible had suggested, with her insistence that their mad jumbled poetry *expands*, where prose *defines*, 'there are advantages to being in the first, or metaphoric, stage of development. Her mother made no distinction between thinking things and objects of thought, and so appeared to maintain an extraordinary degree of control over her environment' (p. 48). And when she demolishes the lower storey of their house, the bedrooms nevertheless stay up because, Mrs Munde explains, of her 'Willpower . . . If I want the bedrooms to stay up, they stay up. I built them, they're part of my life' (p. 47).

It is a mark of the priorities and prominences of Winterson's imaginative agenda, and evidence of her desire to make this agenda central to the older, larger cultural myth-system she is working within, that she incorporates Mrs Munde's wisdom into her own narrative, and converts an outrageous metaphor for her own juicily fluid practice into the substance of the book's own 'counter-myth'. *Boating for Beginners* prepares the reader for this gambit in its abundant provision of religious paraphernalia, whose tones recall the banners in Cambridge market. Thus God's dayglo cloud, a neon display, descends proclaiming 'GOD IS LOVE, DON'T MESS WITH ME' (p. 14); Noah has a businessman's commitment to selling the miracle of his suspiciously cosy relationship with God on a 'Glory Crusade': 'Noah told them that only when the time is ripe can miracles happen' (p. 13). But Winterson's comic book also demonstrates how the comic can appropriate, and literalize, and subvert, these clichés of faith. For instance, Winterson plays with the notion of these 'ripe' miracles, and of the forbidden fruits they stand under. In the play and the film Noah is directing, Eden has not an apple but an orange tree, not one creeping serpent but three seductive goddesses; in Winterson's book of the film, the orange itself becomes 'a bright orange demon', whose confidences and instructions come to her young heroine obscurely, as in a dream, and then with increasing explicitness as a counterweight to the merely theoretical perspectives supplied by Gloria's reading of Northrop Frye. The orange demon, appearing to Doris, one such theoretically sophisticated friend of Gloria's, announces that its role in Gloria's life will be 'teaching her to be poetic while she teaches herself to be analytic'; to 'give her something real to worship'. To Doris's reply that this fastidious irruption of poetry may well get in the way of her own role in the film, the demon reveals: 'Doesn't matter about the film . . . We're not interested in plot, are we?' To Doris's grumblingly postmodern rejoinder – 'I am . . . I may never occur in another novel. You appear all the time; you can afford to be relaxed' – it is Winterson's own turn to agree:

> It was true. The orange Thing turns up everywhere, as a demon, a sprite, omnipotent author, flashes of insight. It is there in *Jude the Obscure*, *The Little Foxes*; it probably impersonated Scarlett O'Hara in most of *Gone with the Wind*. Whenever something other than the plot drops in, it is really the orange demon adding an extra dimension.
>   The demon did a twirl and sailed back to where Doris was standing. . . .

'We're going to have trouble with this flood myth stuff. I know it's supposed to have happened a long time ago – if it happened at all – and I know we're only making a movie, but have you ever known someone to have the power and not use it?' and with a bright flash, the creature was gone.

'I hate them elementals,' spat Doris. 'Always popping up being cryptic and pretending they're doing you a favour. "Flood myths", what's all that about anyway?' (pp. 71–2)

We have already seen one answer Winterson's narrator has given to that question in her disquisition on the power of the flood myth in ancient scriptures, ancient myths. And the arrogance and sleight of hand of the passage I have just quoted suggests how more recent, secular scriptures may be seen to be continuing the good work. It is, of course, one such and here unnamed secular scripture that the orange demon has come from, with its message of liberating but confusing anti-realism, of counter-myth speaking from within the furniture of an old myth. It is *Oranges are not the Only Fruit*, and Jeanette's own orange demon; it is also – in the form of a literary tradition that spins narratives from narratives, and interrupts them, demolishes them, with a Mrs Mundean wilfulness – the fairy-tale realms to which, in *Oranges*, Jeanette is led and in which she is transformed. It is the city of wells and libraries in which, at the end of that novel, she becomes an independent reader of poetry and prose, and from which, and in her own latest stage of development, she draws her metaphorical archetypes, the crusading knight Sir Perceval, and Winnet Stonejar.

It is, then, ultimately the palimpsest of patterns undercut, undermined, fluencies and fluidities interrupted by other fruits, from within a local literary history and from its outer reaches, which Winterson's own fiction becomes. The single, unitary, orginary source of knowledge, and its old symbol, the fruit, the biblical apple, or the orange Jeanette's adoptive mother prefers, opens onto a plurality as fluent as its own segments. Only as a consequence of this plurality can its own elements be sifted, squeezed, suppressed, swallowed, or redesignated, as *Boating for Beginners* has been, by the author, the manufactured or compromised creator on the receiving end of a literary tradition.

Rushdie too provides his own positive answers to Doris's gloomy question about 'all them elementals' and the elements of 'flood myths'. And he does so with the same potent and expansive use of metaphor. His fiction contains a number of crucial moments when myths or points of origin are plumbed to the point at which illusions of foundations explode or are swept away; what destroys them is a metaphorical logic which has bewildered those critics concerned, like Gloria, only to analyse. Here, briefly, are three of these locations.

Two are in *The Satanic Verses*, and represent instances where Rushdie adopts Salman the Persian's technique of 'polluting', rewriting the Book, playing with names, registers, foundations of fundamentalism just as Winterson did too. When Gibreel Farishta, one of the novel's two heroes and a late twentieth-century Bollywood filmstar, dreams the sections of the novel that have landed his creator in such terrible trouble, he dreams precisely the period of early Islamic history that Rushdie studied for a Part II History dissertation as an undergraduate at Cambridge.[15] Gibreel dreams it, that is, with the benefit of someone else's carefully acquired, carefully disguised, historical detail. He dreams the controversy Salman the Persian admitted to having a hand in, of verses of the Qu'ran that had to be altered, revised, tampered with, because, as first transcribed to the Prophet, they seemed to suggest granting a kind of tolerance to three local goddesses, Laz, Manat and Uzza, the daughters of Shaitan or another ancient fallen angel. Gibreel's dreams give him unique access to the locality implied by that controversy, an Arabian desert, an Arabian city called Jahilia, or, in English, 'State of Ignorance', built entirely of sand, and so uniquely vulnerable to the radical but canny businessman Prophet and his followers, whose power over the ignorant and decadent citizens of Jahilia derives ultimately from the secret the Prophet has learned from his own family history, his own family stories: his power over a water, a source, that can destroy the foundations of Jahilia but sustain the life of its people. 'Water is the enemy in Jahilia', and 'comes from underground streams and springs, one such being the fabled Zamzam'; it is just this fabled source that the 'businessman' acquires a powerful knowledge of through stories much older than he:

> before the businessman there are other stories, here he is, Archangel Gibreel, revealing the spring of Zamzam to Hagar the Egyptian so that, abandoned by the prophet Ibrahim with their child in the desert, she might drink the cool spring waters and so live. And later, after the Jurhum filled up Zamzam with mud and golden gazelles, so that it was lost for a time, here he is again, pointing it to that one, Muttalib of the scarlet tents, father of the child who fathered, in his turn, the businessman. The businessman: here he comes. (pp. 91–2)

This bafflingly detailed tissue of fiction and history, environment and genealogy, ancient legend and emphatically contemporary language, extends still further. Abu Simbel, the grandee of Jahilia, for whom, we are told, the name of the businessman Mahound spells 'crisis', is also the name of an Egyptian village swamped and flooded by the construction of the Aswan dam in the mid-1960s. How do we interpret this odd fusion of ancient and modern, this almost indecipherable metaphor for the contradictory interaction of faith and technology in the twentieth century's own Islamic revival? D. J. Enright sounded a note of analytical despair in his review of the novel: 'Questions of this kind raise their heads everywhere, and if the reader stops to puzzle out the answers he will never finish the book.' The only option, if also the unsatisfactory one, was to settle for a 'first, fluent reading' that confined itself to 'pure story', which might never resolve such questions.[16] A purity, a story, whose fluency, whose power, depends precisely on containing and blending these textual and historical impurities.

Enright may have found one answer to his questions, a source for the water that flows through the sand structures of analysis, in *Midnight's Children*, and in the very passage at which those 420 marvels are introduced.

> Midnight's children! . . . from Kerala, a boy who had the ability of stepping into mirrors and re-emerging through any reflective surface in the land – through lakes and (with greater difficulty) the polished metal bodies of automobiles . . . and a Goanese girl with the gift of multiplying fish . . . and children with powers of transformation . . . from the great watershed of the Vindhyas, a boy who could increase or reduce his size at will . . . from Kashmir, there was a blue-eyed child of whose original sex I was never certain, since by immersing herself in water he (or she) could alter it as she (or he) pleased . . . near Jalna in the heart of the parched Deccan I found a water-divining youth.[17]

Here as throughout the novel's intricate network of plots and blocked then unblocked nasal passages, the secular visions of Rushdie's magical realism and Saleem's experience depend not just on the concept of fluidity but on its element.

Since *The Satanic Verses*, however, and his enduring experience of that terrible balloon, Rushdie's texts have been more explicit on the subject of their dependencies. They identify how, why and which oceans and rivers of stories run through his fiction; revealing Rushdie's own equivalent of Winterson's Bible, the eleventh-century Sanskrit collection of 350 tales arranged in eighteen books known as the Kathascritsagara, or the 'Ocean of the stream of stories'. Now Rushdie himself only came clean, as it were, about this ocean-source in *Haroun and the Sea of Stories*; but little Haroun's attempt to undo the evil Khattam Shud's plugging and subsequent stagnation and pollution of the ocean of story has a resonance which converts the curious device on which it depends into an issue of much larger significance for all of

Rushdie's writing. Khattam Shud's plug, lowered from his own shadowy vessel of inexpressive intolerance, his 'ark' of shadows, has blocked 'a hole or chasm'. Once Haroun reveals it, by diving bravely down through the stench of stagnation, 'the glowing of pure unpolluted stories came bubbling up' again.[18]

Reflecting on this moment, Jean-Pierre Durix has drawn a conclusion which recalls Foucault's historical reflections on the 'never yet fulfilled tradition' to which Rushdie's writing, in the enduring effacement of Rushdie the man, may be seen to go on contributing. 'Taken metaphorically, nobody really invents anything absolutely new. This theory could be taken as a lost by-product of Modernism.'[19] Yet as soon as we compare such critical observations with Rushdie's own statements on the subject – 'Nothing comes from nothing. This is, to my surprise, called "postmodernism". It is impossible to believe that anything in history comes from no roots'[20] – an important difference emerges between the critic's writing and the novelist's. The critic is concerned to preserve categorical distinctions between the 'metaphorical' and 'theory', to distinguish between 'Modernism' and its 'by-products'; the novelist explains the critical concept, the abstraction, in terms of a metaphor. That apparently casual but richly rewarding turn towards metaphor is the method by which fiction preserves and renews its modernist inheritance. But that method, and the metaphors on which the work of Winterson and Rushdie depends, are best appreciated by revealing the uses that both writers have made of them, and by isolating the raw materials that they have mixed with the water of narrative to produce their own uniquely flavoursome preserves.

The most direct way of tasting those raw materials, and what the two novelists have made of the ingredients, is via roughly chopped and blended quotation. The method happens to be Winterson's. Even before the narrative of *Oranges are not the Only Fruit* begins, the novel's two carefully attributed epigraphs set the terms for what will follow, and describe the motive force behind it. The second, which is also the title, neatly evokes restoration and Restoration: it is restored to its source in Nell Gwynn, the Catholic Charles II's mistress and thus, historically, a colourful symbol of scandalous sexual excess and catholicity of taste that cast a rich shadow over the subsequent reign of Protestant William of Orange. It evokes, that is, the whole opposition of Puritan and Royalist, and suggests one historical source of Winterson's own sympathies and interest: the mischievous charm of a period explicitly opposed to Puritanism. The first epigraph suggests the locale and manner of the application of those sympathies, and the formal consequences of such rich ingredients. From Mrs Beeton's *The Making of Marmalade*, we read: 'When thick rinds are used the top must be thoroughly skimmed, or a scum will form marring the final appearance.'[21]

Winterson lets the artfully jumbled substance of Old Testament and new fairy tale in her text stand as evidence of the 'skimming' that has gone into its construction. Saleem Sinai's rich statement of his own method in the closing pages of *Midnight's Children* provides a more explicit commentary on the intimate and homely preserving work of creativity. Saleem sets down the ingredients and attitudes requisite for his 'chutnification' of history, and reveals himself to be engaged upon a strikingly similar project:

> What is required for chutnification? Raw materials, obviously – fruit, vegetables, fish, vinegar, spices. Daily visits from Koli women with their saris hitched up between their legs. Cucumbers (like his nose, for instance) aubergines mint. But also: eyes as blue as ice, which are undeceived by the superficial blandishments of fruit; which can see corruption beneath citrus-skin; fingers which, with featheriest touch, can probe the secret inconstant hearts of green tomatoes: and above all a nose capable of discerning the hidden languages of what-must-be-pickled, its humours and messages and emotions . . . At Braganza Pickles, I supervise the production of Mary's legendary recipes; but there are also my special blends, in which, thanks to the powers of my drained nasal passages, I am able to include memories, dreams, ideas. (p. 460)

But Saleem is no Mrs Beeton. Indeed, one thing that distinguishes this radical catholic mix from the early Winterson, and anticipates the directions her work took after her flirtations with the orange demon, is Saleem's relaxed and even welcoming attitude to the scum that Mrs Beeton was so keen to avoid: Saleem is happy to accommodate the unpredictable distortions that such impurities entail:

> There is also the matter of the spice bases. The intricacies of turmeric and cumin, the subtlety of fenugreek, when to use large (and when small) cardamoms . . . *not to mention the flavourful contributions of the occasional speck of dirt. In the spice bases, I reconcile myself to the inevitable distortions of the pickling process.* . . . The art is to change the flavour in degree, but not in kind; and above all (in my thirty jars and a jar) to give it shape and form – that is to say, meaning. (pp. 460–1; my emphasis)

Winterson's later narrators would agree with Saleem. *Sexing the Cherry* (1989), for instance, changes the flavour of her narration in degree, but not in kind: it returns both to the story of a foundling and to the period of Catholic, royalist England in order to carry Nell Gwynn's banner into darker territory. In the figure of the enormous, grotesquely filthy Dog Woman, the scum that floats to the surface when such vivid 'raw material' is stirred up is not skimmed but, on the contrary, given a voice and considerable power. The Dog Woman has a quasi-Adamic or prophet's power to name her young charge, Jordan:

> I call him Jordan and it will do. He has no other name before or after. What was there to call him, fished as he was from the stinking Thames. A child can't be called Thames, no and not Nile either, for all his likeness to Moses. But I wanted to give him a river name, a name not bound to anything, just as the waters aren't bound to anything. When a woman gives birth her waters break and she pours out the child and the child runs free. I would have liked to pour out a child from my body but you have to have a man for that and there's no man who's a match for me.
>
> When Jordan was a baby he sat on top of me much as a fly rests on a hill of dung. And I nourished him as a hill of dung nourishes a fly, and when he had eaten his fill he left me.
>
> Jordan . . .
>
> I should have named him after a stagnant pond and then I could have kept him, but I named him after a river and in the flood-tide he slipped away.[22]

Yet Winterson's text does not yet let Jordan slip away: instead, it finds a neat way of transcending the limits of the Dog Woman's power over her fluid element. Where the Dog Woman's narrative ends, *Sexing the Cherry* provides Jordan with another voice and with a life of his own. Given the other vessel evoked by his name, the chamber-pot, the novel closes with a fitting vision of Jordan under a late twentieth-century bridge beside a polluted Thames. The irony with which the Dog Woman embarked on her passage above has thus been refreshed if not renewed.

This anxiety to exploit but then also to rise above the perspective of any one narrator is one that Winterson and Rushdie share. It has driven them both to experiment with a device that often threatens to violate the horizons of their own metaphorical terrain, or at the least to populate the margins of their fiction. Throughout their careers, both have inserted metafictional commentary and commentators into their narratives: the effect can be disconcerting, invigorating, or even sufficient to raise doubts as to their own faith as writers in the power of story. Winterson's orange demon we have already discussed; and in *Shame* Rushdie needed to rely upon a writer-narrator to structure his thoughts on religious fundamentalism. But Rushdie's own most plausible teacher about plural reality has only recently proved her longevity and flexibility. One of *The Satanic Verses*'s most reliable and endearing voices was that of the art historian Zeeny Vakil. What made Zeeny's views on the hybridity and multiplicity of Indian art and life convincing was that, unlike the writer-narrator of *Shame*, and many of Winterson's narrators, she did not need to transcend the narrative to explain it; she was, instead, a character within it, a part of its world. Rushdie's own sense of Zeeny's value may be inferred from her reappearance in *The Moor's Last Sigh*. Readers may value her in part for her sophisticated interpretations of the way Indian art represents its country's myths – when Moraes seeks out her 'usual sardonic take' on the troubled turbulence of Bombay, for instance, she turns almost Foucauldian, blithely blames the violence of the parties to its competing myths of origin: 'I blame fiction. The followers of one fiction knock down another popular piece of make-believe, and bingo! It's war. . . . So, OK. I'd rather die fighting over great poets than over gods' (p. 351).

But Rushdie's commentator is more useful still because she has a more vividly defined role in that element of the novel's 'pure story', that fundamental element in which Rushdie has always, I suspect, been more richly inventive than Winterson. In *The Moor's Last Sigh*, Zeeny Vakil has found herself a job. Her presence as the curator of 'the Zogoiby bequest' (p. 363) indicates that Rushdie has found more particular instances of his old theme for her to look after and to be defined against. For although this new role ends suddenly, and brutally – Zeeny dies in the violent destruction of the exhibition housing many of the works painted by Moraes's mother Aurora – she has done enough to confer a mark of characteristically hybrid fictional-critical approval on the power of Aurora's images, and their place within Rushdie's career. It is the function of Moraes's extended first-person narrative, co-extensive with the novel rather than contained within it, to ensure that the power endures, and thus to argue a larger case: that such mingled images, confused but familiar metaphors of creativity, are capable of renewing perspectives on the future and the past not just of any one novel or novelist's world but of fiction itself.

Moraes's commentary on the outpourings of his mother's Moorish imagination doubles, then, as a comment on the principles of the novelist's own practice, in which, attempting ' "not Authorised Version but Aurorised Version", as she told me', the artist 'began to explore the idea of placing a re-imagining of the old . . . story . . . in a local setting, with me playing a sort of Bombay remix.' In the works that result:

> the creatures of Aurora's imagination began to populate [local territory] – monsters, elephant-deities, ghosts. The water's edge, the dividing line between two worlds, became in many of these pictures the main focus of her concern. She filled the sea with fish, drowned ships, mermaids, treasure, kings; and on the land, a cavalcade of local riff-raff – pickpockets, pimps, fat whores hitching their saris up against the waves – and other figures from history or fantasy or current affairs or no-

where, crowded towards the water like the real-life Bombayites on the beach, taking their evening strolls. At the water's edge strange composite creatures slithered to and fro across the frontier of the elements. Often she painted the water-line in such a way as to suggest that you were looking at an unfinished painting which had been abandoned, half-covering another. But was it a waterworld being painted over the world of air, or vice versa? Impossible to be sure.

'Call it Mooristan,' Aurora told me. 'This seaside, this hill, with the fort on top. Water-gardens and hanging gardens, watchtowers and towers of silence too. Place where worlds collide, flow in and out of one another, and washofy away. Places where an air-man can drowno in water, or else grow gills; where a water-creature can get drunk, but also chokeofy, on air. One universe, one dimension, one country, one dream, bumpo'ing into another, or being under, or on top of. Call it Palimpstine. And above it all, in the palace, you.' (p. 226)

Aurora's words serve to situate her creator as well as her son. Her dangerous, bewilderingly fictionalizing 'aurorized version' sketches a territory that has always been central to Rushdie's imagination, and indeed to the project of revisionary postmodernist story-telling on which Rushdie and Winterson have both been engaged. Rushdie's Moraes appropriates and represents this territory when he asserts, of the Bombay that is Rushdie's *locus classicus*:

Bombay was central, had been so from the moment of its creation: the bastard child of a Portuguese–English wedding, and yet the most Indian of Indian cities . . . Bombay was central; all rivers flowed into its human sea. It was an ocean of stories; we were all its narrators, and everybody talked at once. (p. 350)

He also, perhaps, thus neatly represents the sources on which and from which two of fiction's most garrulous story-tellers continue to draw.

Notes

1 Salman Rushdie, 'In God We Trust', in *Imaginary Homelands: Essays and Criticism 1981–1991* (1991; London: Granta/Penguin, 1992), p. 376.
2 Daniel Easterman, *New Jerusalems: Reflections on Islam, Fundamentalism and the Rushdie Affair* (London: Grafton, 1992), p. 9.
3 Mario Vargas Llosa, 'The Truth of Lies', in his *Making Waves*, ed. and tr. John King (London: Faber and Faber, 1996), p. 330.
4 Terry Eagleton (ed.), *Ideology* (Harlow: Longman, 1994), p. 1.
5 Ibid., p. 18.
6 Salman Rushdie, *The Satanic Verses* (London: Viking, 1988), pp. 367, 374. Further references are to this edition and appear in the text.

7 Easterman, *New Jerusalems*, p. 122. He is summarizing and endorsing the argument of Malise Ruthven, in *A Satanic Affair: Salman Rushdie and the Wrath of Islam* (London: Hogarth Press, 1991). Richard Webster, *A Brief History of Blasphemy: Liberalism, Censorship and The Satanic Verses* (Southwold: Orwell Press, 1990), pp. 58–9, mounts a different argument about the status of Rushdie's novel: 'the furore which [*The Satanic Verses*] has caused is not a simple battle between fundamentalism and freedom. It is a battle between two factions of the same religious tradition – the Judaeo-Christian tradition to which, ultimately, Islam itself belongs. It is a clash not between religious authoritarianism and freedom but between two kinds of rigidity, two forms of fundamentalism.' While this represents a useful broadening of the terms of debate, Webster's book has no room to develop its argument by comparing Rushdie's work with that of other contemporary novelists.

8 Rushdie, 'One Thousand Days in a Balloon', in *Imaginary Homelands*, pp. 430–1.

9 Ibid., pp. 438–9.

10 Interview with *India Today* marking the publication of *The Satanic Verses*, in Lisa Appignanesi and Sara Maitland (ed.), *The Rushdie File* (London: Fourth Estate, 1989), p. 39.

11 Salman Rushdie, *The Moor's Last Sigh* (London: Jonathan Cape, 1995), p. 3. Further references are to this edition and appear in the text.

12 Salman Rushdie, *Shame* (London: Jonathan Cape Ltd, 1983), p. 250. Further references are to this edition and appear in the text.

13 See Jeanette Winterson, *Art Objects* (1995; London: Vintage, 1996), p. 103. Further references are to the Vintage edition and appear in the text.

14 Jeanette Winterson, *Boating for Beginners* (1985; London, Minerva, 1990), pp. 65–6. Further references are to the 1990 edition and appear in the text.

15 Appignanesi and Maitland, *The Rushdie File*, pp. 3, 41.

16 Quoted, ibid., pp. 16–17.

17 Salman Rushdie, *Midnight's Children* (1981; London: Picador, 1982), p. 198. Further references are to the Picador edition and appear in the text.

18 Salman Rushdie, *Haroun and the Sea of Stories* (London: Granta, 1990), p. 167.

19 Jean-Pierre Durix, ' "The Gardener of Stories": Salman Rushdie's *Haroun and the Sea of Stories*', in M. D. Fletcher (ed.), *Reading Rushdie: Perspectives on the Fiction of Salman Rushdie* (Amsterdam, 1994), p. 348.

20 Interview in the *Observer*, 3 May 1994, p. 54; quoted in Catherine Cundy, 'Through Childhood's Window: *Haroun and the Sea of Stories*', in Fletcher, *Reading Rushdie*, p. 339.

21 Jeanette Winterson, *Oranges are not the Only Fruit* (London: Pandora Press, 1985), p. vi. Further references are to this edition and appear in the text.

22 Jeanette Winterson, *Sexing the Cherry* (1989; London: Vintage, 1990), p. 11. With the publication of her novel *Gut Symmetries* (London: Granta, 1997), Winterson makes an explicit return to the muddy aquatic landscapes of her imagination, not least by naming her heroine 'Alluvia'.

12 Sex, Violence and Complicity: Martin Amis and Ian McEwan

Kiernan Ryan

Over the last twenty-five years Ian McEwan and Martin Amis have established themselves as two of the most accomplished, and most controversial, writers of their generation. A new novel by either man is an event, the occasion for full-page reviews, interviews, profiles and heated debates about the importance of their work. The chief factor that guarantees such intense scrutiny is the reputation for outrageousness that both writers acquired early on, a reputation which has barnacled their books ever since, whether they have merited the melodramatic epithets attached to them or not.

The caricature still haunting McEwan is that of a novelist obsessed with the perverted, the depraved and the macabre, an inscrutable voyeur who describes abjection and obscenity with chilling detachment. His characters and their quandaries are dissected with the clinical precision of a pathologist, and in a prose style equally appropriate to that profession. The idiom is deliberate, exact and impersonal, purged of emotive resonance and immune to empathy or agitation. It is not so much McEwan's soft spot for the gruesome that has fostered the antipathy of his detractors as his freezing of his moral faculties and his refusal to react as decency demands to the shocking scenes staged by his own morbid imagination. Amis's notoriety stems, by contrast, from his rapt absorption in the sordid realities of the ruthless and selfish. Greed and lechery, addiction and abuse, beat out the deep, recurrent rhythms of his fiction. His narratives habitually revolve around insufferable egotists and moronic dupes, heartless bastards and their helpless prey, tangled up in lethal webs of mutual manipulation and psychological torment. But what alienates readers from Amis is not the tacit acquiescence imputed to McEwan's reserve. Where Amis is found irksome, it is because of his exuberant immersion in the cheap, cruel world that he has conjured up. The suspicion is that Amis relishes being nasty. He seems to delight in investing the subhuman and vicious, the mean and degenerate, with a charismatic energy and turbo-charged eloquence which sanction and protract their modern sway.

The problem with settling for these images of Amis and McEwan is that they prevent us from engaging with the full scope and the complexity of what they are trying to do. Both novelists set out to vex and disturb. They repeatedly run the risk of antagonizing or offending their readers, and of attracting the charge of compliance with everything from which they should recoil. But the risk, it seems to me, is well worth taking, because it is the price of their unnerving honesty about the secret ubiquity of depravity and its seductive appeal, both to them and to us. Whether taunting or flouting the acceptable moral response, McEwan and Amis refuse to enlist the stock responses and routine pieties, and the consequences for the reader can be perplexing, especially when our noses are being thrust into what actually motivates and gratifies us, as distinct from what we would prefer to think makes us tick.

In interviews both authors have proved keen to contest, or at least complicate, the assumptions that might shackle or distort their readers' perceptions of their work. Amis is happy to admit that, as an author, he is 'not free of sadistic impulses'. He enjoys 'a sort of horrible Dickensian glee' when devising excruciating predicaments and fatal booby traps for his protagonists. Nor is he averse to playing up to his persona of callous aesthete and true heir of Vladimir Nabokov. Asked by one earnest interviewer, 'are you ever conscious of surrendering human insight for the sake of stylistic sheen?', Amis replies: 'I would certainly sacrifice any psychological or realistic truth for a phrase, for a paragraph that has a spin on it: that sounds whorish, but I think it's the higher consideration.' Nor has the realization that his fiction may be in cahoots with the very corruption he chronicles escaped him: 'In my writing, yes, I am fascinated by what I deplore, or I deplore what fascinates me: it's hard to get it the right way round.'[1]

But as his deployment of the word 'deplore' intimates, the Amis who frolics with Nabokov in the amoral surf of pure style cohabits with a fierce, frank twin, who believes without embarrassment in innocence, corruption and the pure evil of money. 'I don't offer alternatives to what I deplore,' concedes Amis; but he does insist that a moral dimension, a moral design, is obliquely involved in his work, and precisely at the level of style, because in fact 'Style is not neutral; it gives moral directions.'[2] The brazen contradiction voiced by Amis's rival selves is only apparent, however. For what he is doing is keeping at bay the obligation to subscribe to approved moral attitudes, while retaining a less reassuring commitment to fiction as an unpredictable art of moral discovery:

> I would say that the point of good art is remotely and unclearly an educative process, a humanising and enriching process. If you read a good novel, things must look a little richer and more complicated, and one feels that this should eat away at all ills. The only hope is education, and one is vaguely – though not centrally – involved in the process of education.[3]

McEwan has a much more claustrophobic sense of being cabined and cribbed by first impressions of his writing which are either unwarranted or way out of date. In an interview in 1983 he complained of having been 'labelled as the chronicler of comically exaggerated psychopathic states of mind or of adolescent anxiety, snot and pimples',[4] but a decade later it was clear that the label had stuck:

> Once this set of expectations is set up round my work, people read it in this way. And even when, as in *The Child in Time*, there isn't this element, then *all* people write about is the absence of it. So, yes, I have a problem with my reputation and I give readings to try to oppose it, because I think that my work is not a monochrome of violence and horror.[5]

The success of McEwan's campaign to revamp his reputation may be judged by the headline stamped above the interview he gave to *The Times* to publicize his novel *Enduring Love* (1997): 'The Prince of Darkest Imaginings'.[6] In reality, most of McEwan's fiction since *The Child in Time* (1987) has shown him moving away from the sealed-off, suffocating worlds of childhood trauma, teenage alienation and secret adult obsession. As *The Innocent* (1990) and *Black Dogs* (1992) make plain, he has been opening his novels out to embrace wider public and political issues, to explore the state of the nation and the post-war history that has steered us into the quicksand of nuclear proliferation, ecological catastrophe and sexual bewilderment. His outspoken criticism of Thatcher's Britain, his public campaigning for nuclear disarmament, and his equally open support for feminist causes had already found direct expression in his film and TV scripts of the early 1980s – most memorably in *The Imitation Game* (1980) and *The Ploughman's Lunch* (1983). But these affiliations inevitably bolted McEwan into yet another stereotype, and left him rightly wary of inviting a crude equation of his politics with his fiction: 'It's a minefield, politics and the novel. If you set about writing fiction with a clear intention of persuading people of a certain point of view, you cramp your field, you deny yourself the possibility of opening up an investigation or free inquiry.'[7]

Amis would doubtless say Amen to that, sharing with McEwan as he does a belief that the deeper springs of fictions are unconscious, and that much of what really matters in one's writing is out of one's hands. To quote McEwan again:

> I am aware of the danger that in trying to write more politically, in the broadest sense – trying to go out more into the world, because it is a world that distresses me and makes me anxious – I could take up moral positions that might preempt or exclude that rather mysterious and unreflective element that is so important in fiction . . . So I hope that moral concerns will be balanced, or even undermined, by the fact that I still don't have complete control. Some element of mystery must remain.[8]

McEwan has written of the 'contradictory fantasies and aspirations' that govern his fiction; and what he has to say echoes what Amis suggests about the paradoxical obligation of his narratives to be self-validating, responsible to nothing beyond their own formal precinct, yet obscurely propelled by a subliminal urge to enlighten and exhort without prescribing or preaching. 'I prefer a work of fiction to be self-contained,' says McEwan, 'supported by its own internal struts and beams, resembling the world, but somehow immune from it.' At the same time, 'Against all this, I value a documentary quality, and an engagement with a society and its values; I like to think about the tension between the private worlds of individuals and the public sphere by which they are contained.' And he concludes:

> Perhaps I can reconcile, or at least summarise, these contradictory impulses in this way: the process of writing a novel is educative in two senses; as the work unfolds, it teaches you its own rules, it tells how it should be written; at the same time it is an act of discovery, in a harsh world, of the precise extent of human worth.[9]

It is only when the writer is let off the hook of moral responsibility, of conscious educative intent and political decorum, that he or she is apt to push back the frontiers of moral understanding by bringing us up to date on what we are really doing and feeling, however ideologically unsound we may unfortunately turn out to be. This is what the fiction of Amis and McEwan endeavours to do, and what makes it hard for some readers to swallow. Their books seek to unseat our moral certainties and sap our confidence in knee-jerk judgements by making us recognize our involvement in what we are reading. They force us to face the dishonesty of dividing ourselves from the imaginary populace of their fiction and disavowing our kinship with the authors who imagined such beings for our diversion.

Amis relates a revealing anecdote about his father, Kingsley, in the Introduction to *Einstein's Monsters* (1987), a collection of stories fuelled by his consuming horror of nuclear weapons and the prospect of global annihilation. It is not hard to spot where Amis *fils* picked up his penchant for the diabolical:

> Anyone who has read my father's work will have some idea of what he is like to argue with. When I told him that I was writing about nuclear weapons, he said, with a lilt, 'Ah. I suppose you're . . . "against them", are you?' *Épater les bien-pensants* is his rule. (Once, having been informed by a friend of mine that an endangered breed of whales was being systematically turned into soap, he replied, 'It sounds like quite a good way of *using up* whales.' Actually he likes whales, I think, but that's not the point.)[10]

Épater les bien-pensants (outraging the righteous, appalling the politically correct) could happily serve as the watchword of Martin Amis's own novels and a key to their perverse, provocative logic. The strategy is to espouse the despicable standpoint of the least enlightened and exemplary members of the human community, and proceed to promote their version of things with an energy and conviction which presuppose its self-evidence. The adopted stance slyly assumes the implied reader's assent to what is offered, after all, as no more than the plainest common sense or, at worst, an undeluded realism.

Yet it is not simply a matter of Amis's pretending to the reverse of what he really feels. The irony is more intricate and barbed than that. It is more like an act of demonic possession than of sedate ventriloquism. The delinquent, the demented, the vain, the lecherous and the vile are *authorized* in a manner that confers normality upon them and compels us to wonder whether they may not be the rule rather than the exception. The author is seized by a self who licenses a blissful indulgence in what one is not supposed to feel and think and want – an indulgence which the reader is invited to share. The writer's and the reader's deepest pleasure consists less in their sense of ironic superiority to the benighted narrator than in the vicarious delight of identification, which is rooted in finding the scandalous secretly seductive and its apologists convincing. This is pandering to people's worst instincts without a doubt, but always in a manner which candidly concedes their hold over the author, and which leaves honest readers little choice but to come clean about the scale of their own capitulation.

For both novelists what really turns the screw on our moral condition is the mood of imminent catastrophe in which we have learned to live. Amis's and McEwan's militant loathing of nuclear weapons and the climate of barely quelled terror they breed is a matter of more than merely anecdotal interest. It is inseparable from the atmosphere of sustained apprehension that suffuses their fictional worlds and defines the distinctive feel of their narratives. Much of their most powerful work to date was written before the defrosting of the Cold War, and at the height of popular protest at the insane military doctrine of Mutually Assured Destruction. But the warheads have not ceased to proliferate since the fall of the Wall in 1989, and it is worth pausing before dismissing Amis's anxiety in *Einstein's Monsters* as obsolete. For if Amis is right, the sheer existence of these weapons in the world has already changed us irreversibly, and the depth at which we have buried their presence in our subconscious is the exact measure of our subjection to their silent terror:

> If you give no thought to nuclear weapons, if you give no thought to the most momentous development in the history of the species, then what *are* you giving them? In that case the process, the seepage, is perhaps preconceptual, physiological, glandular. The man with the cocked gun in his mouth may boast that he never thinks about the cocked gun. But he tastes it, all the time.[11]

This apocalyptic sense of ripening global violence and deferred destruction seeps down into the souls of everyone, subtly warping our personalities, cramping our expectations and infecting our morale. For Amis and McEwan this plight is indivisible from the sensation of being trapped in time, which is explored and fought in *The Child in Time* and Amis's novel *Time's Arrow* (1991). Here is Amis again in *Einstein's Monsters*:

> Our time is different. All times are different, but our time is *different*. A new fall, an infinite fall, underlies the usual – indeed traditional – presentiments of decline . . . something seems to have gone wrong with time – with modern time; the past and the future, equally threatened, equally cheapened, now huddle in the present. The present feels narrower, the present feels straitened, discrepant, as the planet lives from day to day . . . What we are experiencing, in as much as it can be experienced, is the experience of nuclear war. Because the anticipation . . . the anxiety, the suspense, is the only experience of nuclear war that anyone is going to get.[12]

The latent capacity for holocaust is enough to lock us all into the same looming, catastrophic teleology, which exerts a constant proleptic pressure on the pulse. It puts us under daily strain in areas of our lives which seem utterly remote from those familiar film-clips of mushroom clouds on the horizon. Amis's novel *London Fields* (1989) milks every drop of black humour from this revelation. It unmasks the deadly reciprocity of domestic violence and the atomic violence escalating in the international public sphere: the two realms feed off each other in a suicidal mockery of symbiosis. Guided only by the obscene plausibility of its thesis, *London Fields* tracks the fearful symmetries that link pornography, TV addiction and child abuse, and these in turn with nuclear targeting and the emergence of the dartboard as the supreme icon of yob culture and symbol of the evolutionary triumph of Tabloid Man on his junk diet of simulated sex and death.

Entropy, apocalypse, Judgement Day: the world winding down, time running out and the guilt stacking up. The overwhelming suspicion that modern life is the life of a lemming, with the cliff-edge only yards away, goes a long way towards explaining Amis's characteristic style and tone: the swaggering verbal exorbitance and figurative overkill, the urgent italicized insistence, the sustained, speeding note of desperate excess. This compulsive riff finds relief only in the company of its elegiac sibling, when Amis's prose relaxes to savour the pathos of our predicament, and its rhythms rely on cadenced refrains, on dying falls, to wring grief from the heart and flood the novel with the poignancy of belatedness and valediction.

'He felt the urgency of contracting time,' writes McEwan of the central character of *The Child in Time*.[13] But the same apprehension of time about to terminate, of skidding towards the precipice, already informs the atmosphere of McEwan's earliest fictions, *First Love, Last Rites* (1975), *In Between the Sheets* (1978) and *The Cement Garden* (1978). The protagonists are frequently housed in some suburban dead-zone and sealed inside a situation from which the oxygen of emotion has been pumped. This is what creates the obscure sense of menace: the expected evocation of anguish, compassion, shame or elation is suppressed by the rational objectivity of the dispassionate observer. This is McEwan's way of responding to the same reality as Amis confronts – with a spare, fastidious restraint at times so numb as to seem cataleptic, yet so exact as to border on hallucination. The austere style is in fact electric with tension, taut with the strain of excluding what it cannot trust itself to say, but which seethes nevertheless beneath the surface of each word. 'I like precision and clarity in sentences,' McEwan has said, 'and I value the implied meaning, the spring, in the space between them.'[14]

McEwan and Amis write in a fashion which presupposes our common implication in the same 'event horizon' (to hijack a grim euphemism from the nuclear phrase-book). This horizon is defined by the universal stranglehold of nuclear and market forces, which have turned Eros and Thanatos, love and death themselves, into commodities to be screened and narrated, watched and consumed. Violence has bled through into sexuality with a vengeance, as what once lurked in the shadows as pornography has crept into the cultural limelight; while violence, conversely, has been eroticized to a degree even de Sade might be dismayed by, acquiring an aesthetic aura which confrontation with the reality of its effects finds it ever harder to dispel. The scope for resistance or refusal, let alone transformation, seems to shrink geometrically as capitalist technology invades our very cells to programme our appetites and fantasies, to install the structures of addiction – to food, to sex, to drugs, to money, to violence, to voyeurism – which the market needs to survive. The pornographic and the cataclysmic waltz arm in arm through the novels of both these writers, who know that they are marketing flesh and fear to feed the habits in themselves and us, habits which are as corrosive as they are compulsive.

First Love, Last Rites commits us to the clammy embrace of three tales that turn on the sexual abuse of children. In 'Homemade' the adolescent narrator recounts with shameless cynicism how he finally dispatched his virginity by forcing himself on his tearful little sister. 'I had a connoisseur's taste', he muses, 'for violence and obscenity.' 'Butterflies' voices a solitary male's recollection of the day he slid imperceptibly into molesting and murdering a neighbour's nine-year-old daughter: 'My mind was clear, my body was relaxed and I was thinking of nothing . . . I lifted her up gently, as gently as I could so as not to wake her, and eased her quietly into the canal.' And in 'Disguises' a young schoolboy submits to the transvestite fantasies of his deranged theatrical aunt: 'dressed like somebody else and pretending to be them you took their blame for what they did.'[15] The title tale of *In Between the Sheets* couples the incestuous and the paedophile motifs once more, as a divorced father recalls the night he barely resisted the fantasy of his own daughter's desire for him: 'Was she awake, was she innocent? . . . But she was asleep and almost smiling, and in the pallor of her upturned throat he thought he saw from one bright morning in his childhood a field of dazzling white snow which he, a small boy of eight, had not dared scar with footprints.' The volume opens with a story expressly billed as 'Pornography'. In this, two nurses take an exquisitely apt revenge on the seedy pornographer's apprentice who has been two-timing them, and who has generously shared his latest genital infection with them both. 'We'll leave you a pretty little stump to remember us by', they promise, as the sterilizer hisses beside the bed to which they have strapped him, for what he thought would be a less complete masochistic treat. And the concluding tale, 'Psychopolis', located in Los Angeles, kicks off with the teller chaining his girlfriend to the bed – at her own request – and keeping his word to ignore all her pleas for release: 'I was not at all excited. I thought to myself, if I unlock the chain she will despise me for being weak. if I keep her there she might hate me, but at least I will have kept my promise . . . I closed my eyes and concentrated on being blameless.'[16]

In *The Comfort of Strangers* (1981) the sadomasochistic mind-games take a still more vicious turn. A listless young English couple, Colin and Mary, are on holiday in Venice, cocooned in that state of dreamy distraction to which so many of McEwan's characters fall prey. They find themselves slipping, as if mesmerized, into the sinister orbit of the charismatic Robert, a pathologically virile, proudly patriarchal native of the city. Driven at once by an obsessive desire for the androgynous Colin and by a guilty abhorrence of such a travesty of masculinity, Robert lures the strangely compliant couple into a trap and, with the connivance of his wife, calmly kisses and kills the object of his fascination: ' "See how easy it is," he said, perhaps to himself, as he drew the razor lightly, almost playfully, across Colin's wrist, opening wide the artery. His arm jerked forward, and the rope he cast, orange in this light, fell short of Mary's lap by several inches.'[17]

Amis needs no lessons from McEwan when it comes to spinning paranoid plots around violators and victims, murderers and murderees. *The Rachel Papers* (1973) records a self-absorbed adolescent's stalking of his eponymous female prey, whom he discards without compunction once he has used her up. The *Dead Babies* (1975) of his second novel are a bunch of bored, hell-bent hedonists in their twenties, who gather for a weekend feeding-frenzy of sex and drugs and wind up slaughtered by the homicidal maniac lurking in their midst, the suave and spellbinding host of their jaded debauchery. *Other People* (1981) and *London Fields* forge intricate fables about a woman worn out by using and being used, a woman who has '*got to the end* of men'.[18] In each case the protagonist is sucked into the whirlpool of her own demise at the hands of a brooding male figure, whom she senses to be waiting for her at the end of the book. Amis's most acclaimed novel, *Money* (1984), offers a frenetic, headlong study in self-destruction by the spirit of the 1980s incarnate, the transparently named John Self. Self is a ruthless advertising man with wet dreams of more wealth from movies in America and a self-confessed addict of 'swearing, fighting, hitting women, smoking, drinking, fast food, pornography, gambling and handjobs'.[19] An accomplished hustler and predator with a trail of cast-off dupes behind him, he nevertheless finds himself targeted and undone by the motiveless malignity of an unhinged actor and inspired con-man. This protean nemesis taps straight into Self's secret hunger for dissolution and ingeniously expedites his doom.

It is the preoccupation with complicity, however, that gives Amis's and McEwan's fiction its most distinctive twist: complicity not merely as a theme, but as a condition of writing and a consequence of reading. McEwan opens *The Cement Garden* with a frisson of Oedipal guilt as a father drops dead face-down in the wet cement with which he has covered the garden, at the exact moment when his pubescent son climaxes for the first time while masturbating indoors: 'I did not kill my father,' states the first sentence of the novel, 'but I sometimes felt I had helped him on his way.'[20] The sleazy Soho Romeo who incurs the unkindest cut of all in 'Pornography' ends up melting with masochistic desire for the impending mutilation. He has invited it, as surely as the LA woman in 'Psychopolis' invites the narrator to chain her up and wrestle with his conscience. Still more unnervingly, Colin in *The Comfort of Strangers* seems to seek out his killer. He surrenders to some dreadful subliminal logic, whose necessity he can neither comprehend nor question. McEwan has spoken of this novel's concern with 'the extent to which people will collude in their own subjection': 'There is something about Colin's behaviour which suggests from the beginning that he is a victim; he goes along with Robert and is easily manipulated, which suggests an unconscious contractual agreement. I think such a contract can exist between oppressor and victim.' The tragic persistence of that contract in people's lives may be due to the unpalatable fact that 'there might be desires – masochism in women, sadism in men – which act out the oppression of women or patriarchal societies but which have actually become related to sources of pleasure.'[21]

The same fraught issue crops up in Amis too. It is only by acknowledging the power of this involuntary contractual bond that we can make sense of the otherwise intolerable assertions by the narrators of *London Fields* and *Other People* that their female leads were *asking for it*: 'And the worst thing was that she had wanted that violence done to her. She had brought it about. And she had wanted more.'[22] Nicola Six, the *femme fatale* of *London Fields*, scripts and directs her own death. She dupes the murderer into murdering her, choreographing his every step down to the final, brutal blow. 'The girl will die,' warns the narrator at the outset. 'It's what she always wanted. You can't stop people, once they *start*. You can't stop people once they *start creating*.'[23] Of the photograph of a man about to be hanged, Amis writes in *Other People*: 'there was something desperate and triumphant in his stare, almost a snigger of complicity in this terrible act he had goaded the world into. It was as if he were the punisher and they the punished.'[24]

The Cement Garden, *Black Dogs*, *Enduring Love* and all but a handful of McEwan's stories are first-person narratives. Every one of Amis's novels except *Dead Babies* and *The Information* (1995) is likewise related in the first person, or takes the form of a third-person account enclosed and disrupted by a first-person narrator, who maintains a running conversation with us about how the novel is going. The adoption of a first-person narrative voice is hardly an innovation in itself. But Amis and McEwan exploit to an unusual degree the confessional possibilities built into the novel as a form since its inception. (I am thinking in particular of its well documented debts to spiritual autobiography and the diary.) The first-person narrator creates an illusion of unmediated intimacy which the third-person perspective is obliged to forgo or insinuate by other means. All the surrogates, voice-overs and body-doubles hired by both novelists prove to be 'compulsive monologuists' (to filch a phrase from 'Psychopolis').[25] They are all itching to bend our ear and spill the beans. Each has something to hide which they are bent on divulging *to us*, their secret sharers and *hypocrites lecteurs*. McEwan's child-molesters and real or wishful murderers of wives and fathers are owning up to us; and that act of confession casts us in the corresponding role of the confidant expected to share their point of view or even shoulder their burden of shame. It is McEwan's cunning effacement of his presence, of all signs of ulterior authorial intent, that compels our identification with his estranged soliloquists. By allowing the confession of the child-killer in 'Butterflies' to proceed unchecked by commentary or judgement, McEwan implicates himself and us through our confinement to the vision of this isolated voice. To read such narratives demands, after all, a kind of acquiescence, which may pave the way for our own admission of affinity.

The books of both authors are full of furtive couplings, killings and concealments in which we are made to feel as embroiled as the novelist. In 'In Between the Sheets' the author is fingered as an accomplice by the fact that the narrator is himself a writer, who makes no bones about the voyeuristic, leech-like qualities he displays both as a man and as an author. His sexuality meets its match in his profession, which obliges him to raid his most intimate imaginings for material to transform into fictional products he can sell. The narrator's fastidious habit of entering his daily word-count in a ledger unearths, moreover, the buried economic implications of *giving an account* of something. It reminds us of the market force-field that underpins McEwan's act of writing, and our act of reading, the fetishized commodity between our hands. While reading Amis too, we are rarely allowed to forget the bizarre transaction that we have entered into: paying someone for inventing a story in which these poor souls are put through all this grief for our amusement, to pass the time. As the author's persona in *Other People* remarks, putting the plot on hold to address us directly: 'You sell something, don't you, I'm sure? I know I do . . . Selling time, time sold: that's the business we're all in.'[26]

An Amis plot exploits to the full the conspiratorial connotations of the word *plot*. From his first novel Amis has been turning his readers into Keyhole Kates and Peeping Toms. The title of *The Rachel Papers* assigns the book the status of a diary discovered, of private documents brought to public light. *London Fields* turns out to be the posthumous papers of the terminally ill narrator, who has taken his own life. And *Money* advertises itself openly in the subtitle as *A Suicide Note* directly addressed, as Amis's preface insists, to us, the dear and gentle readers of John Self's frantic autobiography. One of the many points about the protagonist's surname is that the Self to whom we are listening is also *our* self and, of course, the author *himself*. Amis amplifies his involvement by brazenly including one 'Martin Amis', contemporary novelist, as a pivotal figure in the plot. Indeed the novel is thickly populated with his proxies and deputies, such as the barely veiled Martina Twain, all of whom aid and abet Amis in trapping and torturing the hapless narrator with our connivance. 'I get the sense', observes John Self to us at one point, 'that everything is ulterior. And you're in on it too, aren't you. You are, aren't you. I don't know how. I'll find out in the end.'[27]

The dying narrator of *London Fields* discovers the fated murderer of the female protagonist to be none other than himself. The novel's posthumous 'Endpapers' include a letter to Amis's *Doppelgänger*, Mark Asprey, to whom he commits the manuscript of the novel we have just read: 'On your desk in the study you will find a full confession.' But he rightly suspects that he is as much a fall-guy as the culprit, adding 'PPS. You didn't set me up. Did you?' And he signs off with an even shrewder, eerie intuition: 'I feel seamless and insubstantial, like a creation. As if someone made me up, for money.'[28] Yet it will not do simply to foist all the guilt onto the tyrannical author, whom the act of writing about reality, about the way he finds the world, can transform from the spider into the fly. The 'Prologue' to *Other People* begins:

> This is a confession, but a brief one.
>   I didn't want to have to do it to her. I would have infinitely preferred some other solution. Still, there we are. It makes sense, really, given the rules of life on earth . . . and my most sacred duty is to make it lifelike. Oh, hell. Let's get it over with.[29]

But where does that leave us, the readers, if, as the Martin Amis character in *Money* claims, we too 'have something of the authorial power to create life'? It leaves us with what the narrator of *London Fields* calls 'Giddiness and a new nausea, a moral nausea, coming from the gut, where all morality comes from (like waking up after a disgraceful dream and looking with dread for the blood on your hands)'.[30]

In their quest for a way out of this maze of mutual incrimination both novelists cling to recollections of original innocence, displaced anticipations of release, which may at least console us that what we are is what we have become, rather than what we are doomed to be from the start. McEwan and Amis lead us to the threshold of extrication by leading us back to birth and babies, children and childhood. They return us to that phase in the individual's development where we can watch the unblemished self being absorbed into the adult universe of blame. The self's capacity for innocence is vindicated by the reminder that complicity is not innate but acquired, as the constraints of language and gender escort the infant into the prisonhouse of history. Hence McEwan's fixation on children or adolescents who are about to leave the haven of infancy behind, whom we witness at some climactic or epiphanic moment of initiation (*First Love, Last Rites*) after which things will never be the same. In the same spirit *The Rachel Papers* tails Charles Highway through his sexual rite of passage, as he topples from the brink of blamelessness into the sink of resigned culpability; while the wilfully brutal title of *Dead Babies* provides the perfect image of pure vulnerability violated, of embryonic innocence poisoned in the womb.

Conversely, both writers are captivated by acts of withdrawal and regression. The grisly eccentricity of the orphaned children in *The Cement Garden*, who preserve their deceased mother's body in the cellar, makes grotesque sense as part of their protracted endeavour to keep the bubble of childhood intact and the toils of adulthood at bay. The bubble is eventually burst by the police arriving just as the narrator's virginity is departing in a rapturous act of incestuous coition with his sister. But for a while the spell holds, and otherwise forbidden impulses can be indulged. The younger brother Tom, for instance, has his craving to be turned into a little girl and coddled like a helpless toddler eagerly gratified by his sisters. Tom's blissful retreat from masculinity and maturity finds arresting parallels elsewhere in McEwan. The most poignant instance occurs in *The Child in Time*, when the glamorous publisher and politician Charles Darke abruptly abandons his irresistible rise and buries himself in a rural sanctuary. There he dresses, acts and speaks like the carefree schoolboy he yearns to be once more. The futility of dwelling in this sad simulacrum of a *Boy's*

Own world ultimately kills him: one icy winter's day he sits down at the foot of his tree-house and calmly freezes himself to death.

The mind-bending metaphysical conceit of Amis's *Other People* allows a once vicious woman to be reborn through her death and live life again as an adult innocent, a holy fool called Mary Lamb. Mary's guileless incomprehension of the most banal human habits and social customs is conveyed through an ironic child's-primer prose that chimes with her nursery-rhyme name. This grants us a violently estranged view of what passes for normality. The cruel absurdities of daily living strike us afresh through the eyes of a woman uncontaminated by what almost everyone blindly accepts. Predictably enough, survival gradually obliges Mary to internalize the divisive conventions of gender and class, and ultimately merge back into the hard-bitten bitch she had been in her previous life. Mary is killed off at the end, but this dazzling metempsychotic fiction leaves the sacrificial Miss Lamb incarnate once more, given yet another crack at starting from scratch and getting it right this time round.

The reversed entropy of *Time's Arrow* pulls off a similar miracle of redemptive defamiliarization. An equally pristine, naive narrative voice relates the biography of a Nazi war criminal *backwards*, from extinction to conception. The life and times of Odilo Unverdorben, one of the surgical butchers of Auschwitz, unravel in reverse. 'Unverdorben' means 'unspoiled' in German: as the present speeds into the past like a video rewinding, Unverdorben grows up into the purified child his name conceals, sloughing off the scales of relinquished guilt. His death-camp victims spring back to life and return to liberty, their mutilated bodies made magically whole again. More recent scenes of commonplace male brutality are rewound too, sharpening our awareness of what these acts entail, the appeal for affection they betray and the fragile trust they violate:

> The women at the crisis centres and the refuges are all hiding from their redeemers. . . . The welts, the abrasions and the black eyes get starker, more livid, until it is time for the women to return, in an ecstasy of distress, to the men who will suddenly heal them. Some require more specialised treatment. They stagger off and go and lie in a park or a basement or wherever, until men come along and rape them, and then they're okay again.[31]

No doubt Amis and McEwan lay themselves open to the charge of sentimentality by nourishing our nostalgia for the lost Eden of infancy. Perhaps there is some truth too in the view that the sentimental impulse and a taste for violence are actually Siamese twins rather than the separate selves we might suppose them to be. But sometimes sentimentality is the closest we can afford to get to compassion. And sometimes it is the only piece of wreckage left to cling to. At the close of *London Fields* the bloodstained, suicidal narrator writes his last letter to the woman whom, he hopes, the battered baby he has rescued will one day grow up to be. He fears that she will have forgotten who he was and what she meant to him, that what he feels for her as he writes will not survive:

> Of course you were far too young to remember. But who says? If love travels at the speed of light then it could have other powers just on the edge of the possible. And things create impressions on babies. . . .
>
> So if you ever felt something behind you, when you weren't even one, like welcome heat, like a bulb, like a sun, trying to shine right across the universe – it was me. Always me. It was me. It was me.[32]

The last chapter of *The Child in Time* concludes with the startling birth of a new baby to a couple hitherto sundered by the harrowing loss of their first-born, the three-year-old daughter one day stolen from them, never to return. Caught off-guard by its precocious arrival in a remote retreat, the couple bring the child into the world all on their own. For one ecstatic moment, mother, child and father are transfixed beyond time, marooned in a trance of untarnished hope. Then the pitiless tide of history floods in and sweeps them on again, as their discovery of the child's sex confers on it the gender that will shape its destiny and snare it in the net of complicity no human being can escape:

> It was a beautiful child. Its eyes were open, looking towards the mountain of Julie's breast. Beyond the bed was the window through which they could see the moon sinking into a gap in the pines. Directly above the moon was a planet. It was Mars, Julie said. It was a reminder of a harsh world. For now, however, they were immune, it was before the beginning of time, and they lay watching planet and moon descend through a sky that was turning blue.
>
> They did not know how much later it was they heard the midwife's car stop outside the cottage. They heard the slam of its door and the tick of hard shoes on the brick path.
>
> 'Well?' Julie said. 'A girl or a boy?' And it was in acknowledgement of the world they were about to rejoin, and into which they hoped to take their love, that she reached down under the covers and felt.[33]

Notes

1 John Haffenden, *Novelists in Interview* (London: Methuen, 1985), pp. 12, 16, 3.

2 Ibid., pp. 14, 23.

3 Ibid., p. 24.
4 Ibid., p. 173.
5 Rosa González Casademont, 'The Pleasure of Prose Writing vs Pornographic Violence: An Interview with Ian McEwan', *European English Messenger*, 1: 3 (1992), p. 41.
6 'The Prince of Darkest Imaginings', *The Times*, 6 Sept. 1997, 'The Directory', p. 9.
7 Casademont, 'Pleasure of Prose Writing', p. 44.
8 Haffenden, *Novelists*, pp. 173–4.
9 Damian Grant and Ian McEwan, *Contemporary Writers: Ian McEwan* (London: the Book Trust and the British Council, 1989), n.p.
10 Martin Amis, *Einstein's Monsters* (1987; Harmondsworth: Penguin Books, 1988), p. 12.
11 Ibid., p. 5.
12 Ibid., p. 17.
13 Ian McEwan, *The Child in Time* (1987; London: Picador, 1988), p. 47.
14 Grant and McEwan, *Contemporary Writers*.
15 Ian McEwan, *First Love, Last Rites* (1975; London: Picador, 1976), pp. 12, 73, 125.
16 Ian McEwan, *In Between the Sheets* (1978; London: Picador, 1979), pp. 93, 26, 103.
17 Ian McEwan, *The Comfort of Strangers* (1981; London: Picador, 1982), p. 121.
18 Martin Amis, *London Fields* (London: Jonathan Cape, 1989), p. 126.
19 Martin Amis, *Money: A Suicide Note* (1984; Harmondsworth: Penguin Books, 1985), p. 293.
20 Ian McEwan, *The Cement Garden* (1978; London: Picador, 1980), p. 9.
21 Haffenden, *Novelists*, pp. 181, 178.
22 Martin Amis, *Other People: A Mystery Story* (1981; Harmondsworth: Penguin Books, 1982), p. 28.
23 Amis, *London Fields*, p. 1.
24 Amis, *Other People*, p. 197.
25 McEwan, *In Between the Sheets*, p. 108.
26 Amis, *Other People*, p. 23.
27 Amis, *Money*, p. 285.
28 Amis, *London Fields*, pp. 468, 470.
29 Amis, *Other People*, p. 9.
30 Amis, *London Fields*, p. 3.
31 Martin Amis, *Time's Arrow* (London: Jonathan Cape, 1991), p. 39.
32 Amis, *London Fields*, p. 470.
33 McEwan, *The Child in Time*, p. 220.

13 Can Fiction Swear? James Kelman and the Booker Prize

Geoff Gilbert

James Kelman's *How late it was, how late* won the Booker Prize in 1994. The prize yokes aesthetic and market values uneasily together: 'it makes an annual declaration about values that transcend the best-seller lists. It can turn the winning fiction into a best-seller and a film';[1] and previous winners of the prize *had* experienced both legitimation as aesthetically valuable and considerably enhanced sales. As Richard Todd states, summarizing the unstable and various data relating to the sales of Booker Prize winners,

> Whatever the truth of claims that by the mid 1980s a Booker winner might expect up to 80,000 extra hardback sales as a direct result of the prize itself, the point such claims illustrate is the fact that at some stage between the late 1970s and the mid 1980s the Booker laureate's dividends, direct or indirect, came dramatically to exceed the monetary value of the prize itself.[2]

Every winner between 1979 and 1996 – with one exception – appeared in Alex Hamilton's annual list of the top hundred 'fastselling' paper-backs for the year after it was awarded the prize.[3] Booksellers, particularly Waterstone's, have come to use the Booker Prize – the debates that precede it, the media coverage, the selection of the shortlist and the winner – to structure their marketing of contemporary 'quality' fiction. That is, the prize has become a reliable machinery of legitimation, defining a particular kind of cultural value to a particular market-place with relatively predictable results.[4]

Kelman's novel interrupted this process. Booksellers asserted that it had been 'a catastrophic flop'. Todd, more calmly, suggests that 'it will have proved the least commercially successful Booker winner since before 1980.'[5] It is a remarkable moment, I think. A market had been created, not for a particular *kind* of writing – there is little stylistic or thematic overlap between A. S. Byatt and Roddy Doyle, Kingsley Amis and Arundhati Roy – but for The Booker Winner. It is clear that there was something about the terms in which Kelman was discussed that interfered with the closed circuits of consecration and commodification. While the prize has always been surrounded by controversy – the decision is always, for some critics, *wrong* – this disagreement has generally been turned to account, generating a valuable interest. Kelman's contentment with the anger his novel generated, remarking in one interview that 'I'm very glad that it wasn't a unanimous decision . . . Very pleased indeed, you know. If it had been, I would have to examine what I was doing',[6] may look disingenuous, a calculated pleasure in the kind of commodified oppositional status that Irvine Welsh occupies so successfully. But I think that something resonant has happened here; that there is something about Kelman's novel which is aptly reflected both in the debates that surrounded the 1994 Booker Prize and in the failure to transform that debate into a marketable interest. The relative failure of this machinery opens up a place where the aesthetic can appear, not only as something disinterested in economic interest, but as something which is capable of making something happen. This chapter is an attempt to tell a story which accounts for this significant glitch; the story of how Kelman's novel managed to swear at the Booker and the model of cultural production it embodies.

There is some evidence that Kelman was theoretically prepared for such an intervention into the industries of contemporary culture. The novel can be understood as driven by the same animus that informs his essay 'Art and Subsidy, and the Continuing Politics of Culture City'. It concerns the hugely prestigious, and hugely expensive, year that Glasgow spent as European City of Culture in 1990. Kelman's argument is grounded in two positions. He argues first that the money (around £50 million) was ill directed. The presentation of a city to which private investment could be attracted in the name of art and culture was paid for by cuts in the hitherto-existing cultural life of the city; cuts in the public funding of museums, public libraries, swimming pools, public parks and halls. There were attempts to close the People's Palace, a museum that documents and celebrates the diversity of Glasgow working-class life, and to sell off Glasgow Green, the traditional stage for Glasgow countercultural life. 'What has been presented as a celebration of art in all its diversity is there to behold, a quite ruthless assault on the cultural life of the city.'[7] And Pat Lally, the leader of the Labour District

Council, perhaps unsurprisingly, blamed the cuts on poll-tax protesters.

It is not that traditional and local values and forms of expression were being suppressed in favour of 'modern' and international forms; rather that the messy and contested field of a descriptive and participatory culture was subjected to a generalized myth of Culture – Culture with a capital C and a smiley face (the logo for Glasgow during and after the City of Culture year was a yellow 'Mr Happy' face with the slogan 'Glasgow's miles better'). And, like the Booker Prize (run by a peculiar hybrid entity, uniting Booker plc, a food-processing corporation, with representatives of the literary, bookselling and academic worlds), this particular model of culture assumes the 'health', the 'soundness' of a partnership between profit-making organizations and artistic production, in directing what Kelman calls 'a mythical general good which if it doesn't exist has at least found a name, "Culture"'.[8]

This 'mythical general good', the Smithsian imaginary resolution of potentially conflicting interests, masks the activities of power which, for Kelman, characterize the 'real world'. He suggests that free creative endeavour is necessarily pitted against this expensive misrecognition:

> in present day Scotland, as elsewhere in Britain and most of the so-called 'free-world', it isn't art and big business that are close allies, it's art and subversion; the notion that creative endeavour has a right to public – let alone private – subsidy is not a paradox, it is a straightforward contradiction. It's much more consistent that people engaged in the field as an end in itself should be attacked, in one way or another, for this is a time of punishment, out there in the real world.[9]

How late it was, how late opens with a dramatization of this scene, where punishment and the real world are brought into a glancing relation to Culture City. Sammy Samuels has woken up strange after a long session drinking. He is not wearing his own shoes; has his best trousers on rather than his jeans. Unstable both to himself and as a fictional character (it is not clear whether this mysterious if relatively trivial metamorphosis will attract a realist explanation), he comes upon a group of tourists, maybe a party of businessmen being shown investment opportunities. He smiles at them out of what is described as 'municipal solidarity':

> so fair enough, ye play yer part and give them a smile, so they can tell ye know a life different to this yin where what ye are is all
>   where what ye are, that it's part of another type of whole, that they know well cause they've been telt about it by the promotional events' organisers.[10]

The smile of municipal solidarity – ghosting the logo of Culture City, 'Glasgow's miles better', 'Glasgow smiles better' as well as the significant verbal formulation 'Samuel Smiles', the Victorian ideologue of self-help – transposes Sammy, for this group, from someone defined restrictively but particularly in the truncated phrase 'what ye are is all' stumblingly into a limb of the mythical general body of 'Culture': 'where what ye are, that it's part of another type of whole'. Smiling, he becomes part of the city as defined by 'the promotional events' organisers'; enters the space defined by Culture City and the Booker Prize.

As he feels himself increasingly uncomfortably looked at, the group of businessmen-tourists undergo their own metamorphosis: 'He caught sight of the tourists again. Only they werenay tourists, no this time anyway they were sodjers, fucking bastards, ye could smell it; even without the uniforms' (p. 3). They are policemen, sodjers, in plain clothes. Here, as in many places, the text is insistently bilingual. 'Sodjers' both places Sammy in a geographical and class location, and resonates through standard English ('soldiers'). It can't merely be translated into a standard English concept – 'police' – because it also indicates a critical knowledge: that from the position of the particular, the law is manifest as force. This force and this critical knowledge are masked by the ideal of a single language which might harmoniously subtend and translate particular instances. Dialect does not just 'place' Sammy, but understands him as a place from which 'standard English' is revealed as sociolect.

The appearance of the police provokes a decision: 'But he had decided. Right there and then. It was here he made the decision. And he was smiling; the first time in days. Know what I'm saying, the first time in days he was able to smile. Fuck them. Fuck them all' (p. 3). The decision he makes is to provoke the sodjers into beating him up, which they do. He is arrested, beaten up again in the police station, and goes blind. This is the minimally realist version of the opening of the novel, and it is important to register that, while the novel 'settles down' into a largely realist mode, depicting the movements, speech, and thought of Sammy Samuels as he negotiates the city, his blindness, and various state institutions, it settles through this hazy opening. While we may tend to accept the plausible aetiology of his blindness – that it happens as a result of being beaten up – there is a problem of vision that the writing insists upon which predates this moment. When he wakes up and 'edg[es] back into awareness', there is already something strange with his eyes: he sees 'all kind of spots and lights' (p. 1). The gaze of the tourists who become the police is experienced as a 'Terrible brightness and he had to shield his own cause of it, like they were godly figures and the light coming from them was godly or something but it must have been just the sun high behind them' (p. 2).

Again, the realist rationalization stands, and is meant to stand, I think, but it is doubled by a creative capacity in writing and of writing to figure a state which representation shadows: 'like what was happening was something he had known for a while, he just hadnay registered the fact, as if it was some kind of bad dream running side-by-side with his life' (p. 10). His gathering blindness reminds him of an intense act of reading:

> And then his fucking eyes as well, there was something wrong with them, like if it had still been daylight and he was reading a book he would have had double-vision or something, his mind going back to a time he was reading all kinds of things, weird things, black magic stuff and crazy religious experiences and the writing started to get thick, each letter just filled out till there was nay space between it and the next yin. (pp. 9–10)

This very material writing, rather than standing outside Sammy, in a narrating position imagined separate from him, is associated with him, with a *presentation* of him which accompanies the representation of him as a character. So in the short section quoted above the shift, from 'he had decided. Right *there* and *then*' (where the specificity of the decision is associated with the representational distance of 'had decided', 'there', and 'then') to 'It was *here* he made the decision', indicates the present of the writing – 'here' – and at the same moment aligns that present with Sammy's presence.[11]

It is a presence which is severely limited. The novel finishes with this limitation completed as disappearance: 'that was him, out of sight' (p. 374). Before that, Sammy has figured it as a truncation: 'ye would be as well being a torso, an upper trunk just'. The inert body of this fantasy is what is reserved from cultural and political mediation; the little held back as properly *his*:

> so even for an upper trunk, ye could still do yerself in, if ye wanted, ye would find ways, ways only known to folk in that exceptional circumstance. The average person wouldnay know cause they wouldnay know – the circumstance; naybody would know it, except yerself and them other yins that had formed yer self-help society, then the ones ye got yer support off for yer lobbies, the MPs or whatever, the famous names. Naybody would know yer possibilities; except yerself and them like ye, the totally dysfunctional; except ye wouldnay be totally dysfunctional else ye would be dead so it would have to be the almost totally dysfunctional; yez would all meet to discuss it at yer meeting place, getting yer living conditions improved, yer quality of life, start yer petitions to parliament and the town council and sending yer man to Brussels although ye would have to post the cunt if it was a torso, except if ye couldnay

talk and ye couldnay see then how could ye set out yer wants to the foreign delegates cause ye would be fuckt, even having yer wee discussions with the members, yez would all be fuckt, yez wouldnay even know yez were there, except listening for sounds; sounds of scuffling and breathing and sniffing and muttering, sneezes and coughs, which ye couldnay hear if ye were deaf, ye would need folks to listen for ye and translate, to represent ye, yer interests, except ye couldnay tell them what yer interests were so they would just have to guess, what it was ye wanted, if ye wanted something, they would have to guess it. (pp. 316–17)

As control over representation is ceded – as the mediation of the torso by representation is understood to be outwith its control – control over expression is asserted (here the involving vocation of the generalizing second-person and the breathless cadencing of a bleakly comic torrent). The value and presence of character is locked helplessly before representation, impaired in its ability to work in the world; at the same time this position is recuperated as powerful, affective writing. In an earlier novel, *The Busconductor Hines,* the busconductor is imagining ways in which he can pass on some kind of agency or power to his son. He resolves to educate him and to take him swimming, to build up analytical and physical power:

you'll be able to take care of yourself anywhere anytime anyfuckingbody you'll be able to do it son, control, take control, of the situation, standing back, clear sighted, the perspective truly precise and into the nub of things, no tangents, just straight in with an understanding already shaped that that which transpires shall do so as an effect of the conditions presented; there will be no other course available; you shall know what to do and go and fucking do it, with none of that backsliding shite. The backsliding shite; there can be reasons for it. Things arent always as clear as they sometimes appear. You can have a way of moving which you reckon has to be ahead in a definite sense and then, for some reason what happens is fuck all really, nothing, nothing at all, nothing at all is happening yet there you are in strangely geometric patterns wherein points are arranged, have been arranged, in a weird display of fuck knows what except it is always vaguely familiar, whatever that means, though this is what it seems like . . . they were stealing the bread out your mouth son and if they couldn't reach it you were opening the mouth wider son the eyelids shut that you didn't offend son that you didn't see son in case you actually saw son that you had to actually do, because one thing you didn't want was to do son so the eyelids shut you put forward the mouth with head lowered while the slight stoop or curtsey and forefinger to eyebrow the sign of the dross, we do beg kindly sir we do beg you kindly, for a remaindered crust of the bread we baked.[12]

The imagined capacity to 'do', to cause something to happen, take control, is bled out. The muscular body approaches the torso; agency disappears as the same old structures are reproduced: 'nothing at all is happening yet there you are in strangely geometric patterns wherein points are arranged, have been arranged, in a weird display of fuck knows what except it is always vaguely familiar, whatever that means, though this is what it seems like'. But as this capacity to do slides back – until it becomes mere expletive, a periphrastic do that fills out the cadence of the prose: 'we do beg kindly sir' – attention shifts towards the writing: 'whatever that means, although *this* is what it seems like'.

Alongside the representation of the powerless body the in-turning prose. This movement, where a recognition of the absolute negligibility of certain agents in the face of the reproduction of social structures is recuperated as a resistant aesthetic autonomy, is characteristic of Kelman. A prose in control only of itself is an adequation and an answer to a 'time of punishment . . . in the real world'. I want to understand this as a sophisticated intervention into an argument about, to borrow the title of J. L. Austin's book *How to Do Things with Words*. Austin is interested in a class of utterances called 'performatives'. These kinds of utterance, unlike statements whose business is to 'describe a state of affairs' or 'state a fact', are best understood as actions. In the case of performatives, 'to *say* something is to *do* something; or . . . *by* saying something or *in* saying something we are doing something'.[13] He gives a variety of examples, of which one is the christening of a ship: the *Queen Elizabeth*. '[S]uppose that I have the bottle of champagne in my hand and say "I name this ship the *Queen Elizabeth*" . . . [I]t would be absurd to regard the thing that I say as a report of the performance of the action which is undoubtedly done – the action of . . . christening . . . We should say rather that, in saying what I do, I actually perform that action.'[14]

Austin's 'speech-act theory' understands that the relation between particular verbal forms and actions cannot be entirely formally internal to language: that the felicity of performatives depends upon a larger cultural ground.

> Suppose that you are just about to name the ship, you have been appointed to name it, and you are just about to bang the bottle against the stem; but at that very moment some low type comes up, snatches the bottle out of your hand, breaks it on the stem, shouts out 'I name this ship the *Generalissimo Stalin*', and then for good measure kicks away the chocks. Well, we agree of course on several things. We agree that the ship certainly isn't now named the *Generalissimo Stalin*, and we agree that it's an infernal shame and so on.[15]

The success or failure of performatives depends not only on utterance, but also on the authority conferred on the speaker by a culture; here a culture called up by the mere instatement of 'we agree of course'. 'Of course' this is right: in law, the ship is not named the *Generalissimo Stalin*. But this surely does not exhaust a description of the situation. Has *anything* been done with these words? Can the force which produces 'infernal shame' be understood systematically? In this example, written in 1956, we might suggest that 'shame' expresses the failure fully to authorize the imposition of liberal capitalism in response to posited alternatives; the necessary repressive actions involved in sustaining the 'we' that agrees, of course. This is more or less a paraphrase of part of Kelman's Booker acceptance speech, when he argued that nobody can logically deny the right of an individual or a culture to determine its own structures of meaning, but can only overpower it. It is the kind of situation that Kelman represents often in his fiction: the actions of a 'low type' that make 'nothing' happen, but which produce an unstable but predictable intensification of affect around the unveiling of power.

Because performatives make their final appeal to a set of assumptions which can never be completely articulated (Jürgen Habermas, in an extension of Austin's argument, notes that these 'background circumstances have a holistic nature; they cannot be exhausted by a countably finite set of speculations'[16]), failure attends every performative as a possibility. But both Austin and Habermas exclude failure – as exception – from a theoretical account of how performatives work. So while Habermas accepts that the theoretical account is governed by idealizing suppositions (centrally, that communicants are only communicating when they share an ideal of a possible future agreement), at the same time, this account is seen as sufficient for understanding the field of communicative practice. '[T]hese idealizations are not arbitrary, logocentric acts brought to bear by theoreticians on unmanageable contexts in order to give the illusion of mastery; rather, they are presuppositions that the participants themselves have to make if communicative action is to be at all possible.'[17] Disavowal of theoretical reduction is supported by a theoretical reduction that threatens to take the form of a policeable imperative ('presuppositions that the participants *have* to make').

The very model for the exclusion of 'exceptions' which are present to all performatives, but not to be taken into account in a theory of performativity, is the exclusion of fiction:[18]

> the performative utterance will . . . be *in a peculiar way* hollow or void
> if said by an actor on the stage, or if introduced in a poem, or spoken in

a soliloquy. . . . Language in such circumstances is in special ways –
intelligibly – used not seriously, but in ways *parasitic* upon its normal
use – ways which fall under the doctrine of the *etiolations* of language.
All this we are *excluding* from consideration. Our performative utterances, felicitous or not, are to be understood as issued in ordinary
circumstances.[19]

Fiction, here, is logically parasitical on ordinary circumstances; it
depends on an imagined real event prior to it, which it represents. In
Habermas's terms, fiction is generated when speech acts are 'impaired',
or when they 'maintain their illocutionary meaning only as in the
refraction of indirect repetition or quotation'.[20] Kelman's work
presents two kinds of objections to this. First, it marks and polit-
icizes the fact that 'ordinary circumstances' are not coherent: that
they are idealized and asserted, and that this assertion can be understood in certain circumstances as a repressive act. Secondly, his writing is aware of itself as a fiction that is not merely representational;
that does not depend for its internal logic on an imagined 'real' situation anterior to it. There is at least an aspect of the phrase 'this is
what it seems like', for example, which is second to nothing, which
refers only to the action in the present of reading the words on the
page. I have been suggesting that these two objections are related.
The representation of an impaired capacity to act in 'ordinary circumstances', where agents become hollowed, etiolated, disabled, is
doubled and recuperated in Kelman's work by a turn towards a non-
representational writing.

Swearing is synecdochical for this doubled objection. In order to
understand this, I want to articulate the way that swearing functions
within the novel, and then to relate that to the way the novel is received. In the act of swearing there is a particular grasping of the relation between individuals and 'ordinary circumstances' which, without
being fully comprehended, shaped responses to the novel in the British media. I shall trace a relation between three directions in which
Kelman's curse tends: a realist swearing, operating between characters in the novel; the way that swear words regulate a heightened intensity at certain moments of the prose, expletives in a lyric of truncated
autonomy; and the way that swearing informs a reductive but uneasy
characterization of the novel in debates that surrounded the Booker
Prize. An understanding of this complex – in which a low type snatches
the bottle from its legitimate operators with resulting infernal shame –
should allow us to grasp a significant relation between the particularity of the fiction and its mysterious behaviour in the marketplace.

Within the realist universe, a constant swearing defines Sammy's
sociolect (although it is wrong to assume that this is simply a class

marker), mildly underlining, functioning as a more or less neutral pro-noun. And then, coextensive with this but not necessarily so, it marks the boundaries between his position and the institutions with which he has to deal. As he is told in the police station, when a statement is being taken: 'Don't use the word "cunts" again, it doesnay fit in the computer' (p. 160). Or, when the DSS doctor is examining him in order to assess him for disability benefit:

> In respect of the visual stimuli presented you appeared unable to respond.
> So ye're no saying I'm blind?
> It isn't for me to say.
> Aye but you're a doctor.
> Yes.
> So ye can give me an opinion?
> Anyone can give you an opinion.
> Aye but to do with medical things.
> Mister Samuels, I have people waiting to see me.
> Christ's sake!
> I find your language offensive.
> Do ye. Ah well fuck ye then. Fuck ye! (p. 225)

It is clear that language is not being used to communicate here, but rather takes part in a contest of opposed positions. The anger which issues in Sammy's swearing is a recognition of this relation, and swear-ing functions to clarify it: to make manifest and to increase the oppo-sition between the positions the two speakers occupy. Here Sammy Samuels refuses to accommodate himself to the language of insti-tutions. Although at other moments he displays the ability pragmat-ically to switch codes,[21] the angry refusal here, concomitant with his 'decision' to get blinded, is part of the perverse self-definition which the representation adumbrates.

Perhaps this becomes clearest in Sammy's dealings with Ally, who offers to represent his case for compensation. He warns Sammy about his use of bad language.

> Right . . . Look eh pardon me; just one thing, ye're gony have to watch yer language; sorry; but every second word's fuck. If ye listen to me ye'll see I try to keep an eye on the auld words.
> . . .
> I'm no meaning nothing; it's just it's a good habit to get into for official purposes. Ye annoyed? Don't be. (p. 238)

Maybe this is a little heavy-handed, but it makes clear what is already evident: that the desire to improve Sammy's language is not about meaning, is not aimed at removing ambiguity or at excising obscenity, but that 'keeping an eye' on words is about engaging with official structures – whether to contest them or, as the syntax here suggests, at the risk of serving them – on their own terms.[22] As Sammy reminds Ally, 'There's a difference between repping somebody and fucking being somebody; know what I'm talking about, being somebody?' (p. 241), and it is the value of this difference – the distance between the torso and Brussels – that both the protagonist and the novel perversely maintain (it is not realistically in Sammy's interest to insist on it, nor in Kelman's interest in the marketplace).

It is maintained as a paranoid inwardness, a systematic mistrust that closes Sammy off from exchange with others. The reason why the police are so interested in Sammy, it seems, is that while drinking, he met up with Charlie Barr, an old acquaintance and political radical. Barr's presence – Sammy's thoughts revert to him regularly – offers the possibility of a redemptive political affiliation; a place where Sammy's self-help can open up to some form of community, can participate in a limited but resistant culture. The absent Helen, the girl-friend who has mysteriously disappeared as Sammy enters the fiction, offers the domestic version of this political possibility. Both possibilities are insistently negated. Thinking of Charlie Barr, hope flickers:

> Ye couldnay trust nay cunt but.
>   One guy he could trust
>   nah he couldnay. . . . That was it about life man there was nay cunt ye could trust. Not a solitary single bastard that ye could tell yer tale of woe to. So ye just blundered about the place bumping into walls and fucking lampposts and innocent members of the community out for a fucking stroll. (p. 251)

It is this gap – 'nay cunt' – that the expletive inhabits. It mimes the negation of escape:

> Stuff heavy on top of ye. Ye felt like pushing up the way, getting it to fuck off yer shoulders. Like that feeling ye get when ye stand at the edge of a cliff and ye look out to sea and the wind's blowing and a tanker's way out on the horizon and ye feel as if ye're really fucking out in the open and so christ almighty the opposite of hemmed in, the opposite
>   So what Sammy was feeling was the opposite of the opposite (pp. 132–3)

So, while standing in a queue at the DSS, Sammy thinks: 'It would be great if they all introduced themselves instead of this fucking' (p. 122). That is the end of the paragraph. 'Fucking' stands as a full stop, taking the place of the absence of the noun that would denote the absence of community and communication. 'Fucking' is the 'opposite of the opposite'. While it is probably best read as internal monologue, this (an unpunctuated paragraph break) is also clearly a place where the *author's* hand appears.[23] These moments of negation, where the expletive marks a gap by filling it with sociologically-specific animus, while they are attached to the represented character, then, are also the principle of the *writing* of Sammy.

The term is, quite precisely, 'expletive' (from Lation *explere*, to fill out). Probably a philological coinage denoting words introduced into prose or poetry merely in response to the demands of metre or cadence, without semantic content, it only later acquired the sense of 'oath' or swear word.[24] Kelman's swearing grasps this, holding the curse to the relatively autonomous demands of cadence. At the same time it implicates the history of swearing, the disenchanted history of secularization and atomization within which sanctioned performatives – swearing *on*, swearing *by* – are hollowed out, leaving the husk, the expletive, to fill the vacancy,[25] and by filling it with nothing but animus to register it as a gap. The convergence of the etiolated oath and the verbal filler marks the expletive as the sign of the intersection of impairment (bodies registered at the place where performative power has disappeared) and literature's excess over representation; the sense in which it is other than merely parasitical on 'normal' usage.[26]

It is this that drives response to the novel in the British media.[27] Reviewers who were unable accurately to recount the plot of the novel could tell you precisely how many times the words 'fuck' and 'cunt' appear in its pages. The intricate filling-out of the prose with expletives issues in a double response. The novel is both impossibly difficult, closed-off against 'the reader'; and it is reducible to a transparently indecorous body. So Kenneth Baker, 'former Home Secretary and literature lover' is quoted as saying, 'The winning book is impenetrable. I think the judges have retreated into a world of their own',[28] and a 'Booker executive' said that *How late it was, how late* was 'the only book on the shortlist which he had been unable to get through'.[29] The difficulty is opposed to other challenging novels. '[Alan Hollinghurst's short-listed novel *Folding Star*] also dealt bravely with the sort of topics which make people uncomfortable, yet it did so in a language of such richness that it wooed rather than alienated the reader.'[30] A bizarre piece in the *Daily Telegraph* compared Kelman himself with the prettified, postmodernized skyscrapers of Renfrew: 'It occurred to me that he would not look too bad with a bit of panelling here and there, a pagoda or a minaret on top of him. They might improve his manners, soften his outlook on life and persuade him to write something which some of us might wish to read.'[31]

The interiors need no attention; the failure of a modernist project (Kelman's insistent negation of the positive claims of modernism) should be simply transformed – re-presented for the benefit of 'some of us' – into a cheery postmodernism. What is startling here is how little in control this reviewer – these reviewers – are of what they mean to say, and how fully their positions are anticipated – almost dictated – by Kelman. These reviews, then, are possessed by a directed quality of the novel, the way that it holds itself back from subsumption into 'public' space, as repressively idealized by the Booker. One of the judges, Julia Neuberger, put it at its most simple: 'I am implacably opposed to the book. It's not a book which is publicly accessible.'[32]

But in the same movement in which the book is imagined to withhold something, it is penetrated. Neuberger continues: 'It's just a drunken Scotsman railing against bureaucracy.' The *Independent's* Booker Prize headline was simply: 'Foul Mouthed Booker Winner'. The novel has a body, it speaks, it has a foul mouth.[33] And, as I have suggested, this reduction ('it's *just*') is appropriate. It registers the impairment which is the shared condition of Sammy and of creative endeavour in a time of punishment: this is the world 'where what ye are is all' as opposed to that in which 'it's part of another kind of whole'. The novel comprehends this vision already; a vision which reduces Sammy to a mere effect of his position (most reviews hold him to his prison record, and to the drinking which he so patently does *not* do during the novel, with as much tenacity as the police.[34]) What it does is to force the stakes of this to become evident; to reveal the authority of the reviewer as a naked and sociologically particular assertion. So Simon Jenkins, in an involved and unpleasant fantasy, likened Kelman to 'an illiterate savage'. For him too the novel is best understood as a person. He describes the experience of reading it in terms of 'an encounter I once had in a no smoking compartment of a corridor train to Glasgow. An ambassador of the city lurched into the compartment and crashed down opposite me and subjected me to a three hour ordeal . . . ending by demanding money with menaces.' Against this fantasized threat, disrespectful of the proper distance at which fiction and most citizens should be kept, he asserts his power: 'If it comes to war, my Standard English will win.'[35] 'Fuck yez', says the low type to the Booker; and we all agree, it's an infernal shame.

Notes

1 *The Times*, 12 Oct. 1994.
2 Richard Todd, *Consuming Fictions: The Booker Prize and Fiction in Britain Today* (London: Bloomsbury, 1996), p. 101.

3 Ibid., pp. 315–18.
4 For a fuller exposition of the economic logic of 'the field of cultural production', see Pierre Bourdieu, *The Field of Cultural Production: Essays on Art and Literature*, ed. Randall Johnson (Cambridge: Polity Press, 1993), esp. ch. 3: 'The Production of Belief: Contribution to an Economy of Symbolic Goods'. Kelman's argument in 'Artists and Value', in *Some Recent Attacks: Essays Cultural and Political* (Stirling: AK Press, 1992), esp. pp. 11–13, is very different, but this defence of a resistant aesthetic standard is performed against an analysis of the reductive manipulation of the idea of aesthetic 'value' as a mere marker of sociological – and ultimately of socioeconomic – distinction.
5 Todd, *Consuming Fictions*, p. 20. Bookshop data suggest that Kelman sold around 'a quarter of the 1987–95 average' (p. 115 n.22).
6 Julia Llewellyn Smith, interview with Kelman, *The Times*, 13 Oct. 1994.
7 James Kelman, 'Art and Subsidy, and the Continuing Politics of Culture City', in *Some Recent Attacks*, p. 32.
8 Ibid., p. 33.
9 Ibid., p. 36.
10 James Kelman, *How late it was, how late* (London: Secker and Warburg, 1994), p. 2. Subsequent page references will be given in the text.
11 Cairns Craig has described the presentation of *being* as the centre of Kelman's earlier fiction, in 'Resisting Arrest: James Kelman', in Gavin Wallace and Randall Stevenson (eds), *The Scottish Novel since the Seventies: New Visions, Old Dreams* (Edinburgh: Edinburgh University Press, 1993), pp. 106–12.
12 James Kelman, *The Busconductor Hines* (1984; London: Phoenix, 1992), pp. 90–1.
13 J. L. Austin, *How To Do Things with Words: The William James Lectures Delivered at Harvard University in 1955* (Oxford: Oxford University Press, 1976), p. 12.
14 J. L. Austin, 'Performative Utterances', in *Philosophical Papers*, ed. J. O. Urmson and G. J. Warnock (Oxford: Oxford University Press, 1979), p. 235.
15 Ibid., p. 240.
16 Jürgen Habermas, 'Excursus on Levelling the Genre Distinction between Philosophy and Literature', in *The Philosophical Discourse of Modernity: Twelve Lectures* (1985; trans. Frederick Lawrence, 1987; Cambridge: Polity Press, 1990), p. 197.
17 Ibid.
18 For an extended critique of speech-act theory, beginning from this question, see Derrida's arguments (to which Habermas is responding) in 'Signature Event Context', and 'Limited Inc a b c . . .', in *Limited Inc* (Evanston, Ill.: Northwestern University Press, 1988). Derrida is cast, both by Habermas and by John R. Searle (whose response to 'Signature Event Context' provoked 'Limited Inc a b c . . .'), in the position of the 'low type': because he critiques the presuppositions on which communicative rationality is built, he is deemed not properly to have entered the field of

communicative rationality – the 'argument' – himself. Possibly the most striking thing about this debate is the temperature it produces: the kind of rising affect that surrounds swearing in Kelman's novel and its reception.

19   Austin, *How To Do Things with Words*, p. 22. Emphases in the original.

20   Habermas, 'Excursus', p. 201.

21   Caroline Macafee, in *Glasgow* (Amsterdam: John Benjamins, 1983), p. 23, notes that working-class men are less likely to 'code-switch' – to accommodate to the dialect of an interlocutor – than any other group in Glasgow.

22   In a different context, Robert Crawford demonstrates continuities between the process of 'improvement' – including the elimination of 'Scotticisms' from aspirant middle-class language – and the birth of 'English Literature' as a university subject. See *Devolving English Literature* (Oxford: Clarendon Press, 1992), ch. 1, 'The Scottish Invention of English Literature'.

23   The voice changes from third to second person across this break (as in the previous quote, the break after 'opposite' marks a shift from second to third person).

24   As far as I can ascertain, English is the only language within which this dual function of the word – and hence this particular productive possibility – operates. The *Oxford English Dictionary* gives 1815 as the earliest use of the word to mean 'oath'. There is also a rare sense (sense 3 in the *OED*) of 'tending or seeking to supply a loss, compensative', which takes the word close, perhaps not suprisingly, to Derrida's definition of the 'supplement' – see particularly 'That Dangerous Supplement', in *Of Grammatology* (1967; trans. Gayatri Chakravorty Spivak, Baltimore: John Hopkins University Press 1976).

25   For a history of swearing, see Geoffrey Hughes, *Swearing: A Social History of Foul Language, Oaths and Profanity in English* (Oxford: Blackwell, 1992). This pattern may explain another of Kelman's habitual subjects: the emptiness of work. The dialectical relation work might establish between humans and their environment is reduced to employment, to filling a vacancy within an inexorably reproducing structure.

26   Judith Butler has discussed the hasty and unsatisfactory resolution of the problematic status of performatives within debates about homosexual identity in the US military, and around issues of 'hate speech', in *Excitable Speech: A Politics of the Performative* (New York: Routledge, 1997).

27   The reviews I cite are from papers nominally British. The polity they represent, though, is revealed not to include Scotland.

28   Quoted by Peter Grosvener, *Daily Express*, 12 Oct. 1994.

29   Quoted by Mike Ellison, *Guardian*, 12 Oct. 1994.

30   Max Davidson, 'Critics View', *Daily Telegraph*, 13 Oct. 1994.

31   'Way of the World', *Daily Telegraph*, 17 Oct. 1994.

32   The reviews associate this difficulty with failure to sell. 'Kelman was not the choice of the man at the Bloomsbury bookshop', according to Mike Ellison in the *Guardian* (12 Oct. 1994). And '[a bookseller] whose Sloane Square branch in London sold precisely one copy of Kelman yesterday,

says: "I do feel someone ought to inject some practical experience of bookselling into the panel" ', quoted by Peter Grosvener, *Daily Express*, 13 Oct. 1994.

33 Robert Winder, *Independent*, 12 Oct. 1994.

34 So, for example, John Bayley, chairman of the judges, speaks of 'James Kelman's novel, set in Glasgow about a blinded ex-prisoner on the binge', in 'Why we chose James Kelman', *The Times*, 12 Oct. 1994; and Compton Miller calls it 'a weird novel about a drunken ex-convict', in 'This Week', *Daily Express*, 1st edn, 12 Oct. 1994.

35 Simon Jenkins, *The Times*, 12 Oct. 1994.

Bibliography

Abish, Walter, *Alphabetical Africa* (New York, 1974).
—— *How German Is It?* (London and Boston, 1979).
—— *Eclipse Fever* (New York, 1993).
Acker, Kathy, *Hello, I'm Erica Jong* (New York, 1982).
—— *Blood and Guts in High School* (London, 1984).
—— *Don Quixote, Which was a Dream* (London, 1986).
—— *Empire of the Senseless* (New York, 1988).
—— *Literal Madness* (New York, 1988).
—— *In Memoriam to Identity* (London, 1990).
—— *Hannibal Lecter, My Father* (New York, 1991).
—— *Portrait of an Eye* (London, 1992).
Ackroyd, Peter, *Hawksmoor* (London, 1985).
—— *Chatterton* (London, 1987).
—— *Dickens* (London, 1990).
—— *The House of Doctor Dee* (London, 1993).
Allen, P. G., *The Sacred Hoop: Recovering the Feminine in American Indian Traditions* (Boston, 1986).
Alvarez, A., *Beckett* (London, 1973).
Amis, Martin, *The Rachel Papers* (London, 1973).
—— *Dead Babies* (London, 1975).
—— *Other People* (London, 1981).
—— *Money* (London, 1984).
—— *Einstein's Monsters* (London, 1987).
—— *London Fields* (London, 1989).
—— *Time's Arrow* (London, 1991).
—— *The Information* (London, 1995).
Angelou, Maya, *I Know Why the Caged Bird Sings* (New York, 1969).
Appignanesi, Lisa, and Maitland, Sara (eds), *The Rushdie File* (London, 1989).
Atwood, Margaret, *Surfacing* (London, 1972).
Bakhtin, Mikhail, *The Dialogic Imagination*, ed. M. Holquist, trans. C. Emerson and M. Holquist (Austin, Texas, 1981).

—— *Problems of Dostoevsky's Poetics*, ed. and trans. C. Emerson (Manchester, 1984).

Ballard, J. G., *The Day of Creation* (1987).

Barker, Pat, *The Ghost Road* (London, 1995).

Barnes, Julian, *Flaubert's Parrot* (London, 1984).

Baudrillard, Jean, *The Mirror of Production* (St Louis, 1975).

—— *A Critique of the Political Economy of the Sign* (St Louis, 1981).

—— *In the Shadow of the Silent Majorities* (New York, 1983).

—— *Selected Writings*, ed. Mark Poster (Cambridge, 1988).

Beckett, Samuel, *The Beckett Trilogy* (1959; London, 1979).

—— *How It Is* (London, 1964).

—— *Proust* and *Three Dialogues* (London, 1965).

—— *Collected Shorter Prose 1945–1980* (London, 1984).

—— *Collected Poems 1930–1978* (London, 1984).

—— *The Complete Dramatic Works* (London, 1986).

—— *Nohow On* (London, 1989).

—— *As the Story Was Told* (London, 1990).

Bhabha, Homi K. (ed.), *Nation and Narration* (London, 1990).

Birch, Sarah, *Christine Brooke-Rose and Contemporary Fiction* (Oxford, 1994).

Bourdieu, Pierre, *The Field of Cultural Production: Essays on Art and Literature*, ed. Randal Johnson (Cambridge, 1993).

Bowen, Elizabeth, *The House in Paris* (London, 1935).

Bowie, Malcolm, *Lacan* (Cambridge, Mass., 1991).

Bowlby, John, *Loss: Sadness and Depression* (Hardmondsworth, 1980).

Bowles, Jane, *Two Serious Ladies* (New York, 1943).

Brooke-Rose, Christine, *Amalgamemnon* (1984).

—— *Xorandor* (1986).

—— *Verbivore* (1990).

—— *Textermination* (1991).

Brooks, Peter, *Reading for the Plot* (London, 1984).

Brownmiller, Susan, *Against Our Will: Men, Women and Rape* (New York, 1975).

Buchan, James, *Heart's Journey in Winter* (London, 1996).

Burn, Gordon, *Alma Cogan* (London, 1991).

Burroughs, William S., *The Naked Lunch* (Paris, 1959).

—— *The Wild Boys: A Book of the Dead* (London, 1972).

—— *Exterminator!* (London, 1974).

—— *Ah Pook is Here* (London, 1974).

—— *Junky [Junkie]* (Harmondsworth, 1977).

—— (with Brion Gysin), *The Third Mind* (London, 1978).

—— *Port of Saints* (Berkeley, 1980).

—— *Cities of the Red Night* (London, 1981).

—— *Early Routines* (London, 1982).

—— *The Place of Dead Roads* (London, 1983).

—— *The Burroughs File* (San Francisco, 1984).

—— *Queer* (London, 1985).

—— *The Adding Machine* (London, 1985).
—— *The Western Lands* (London, 1987).
—— *Interzone* (London, 1989).
—— *Tornado Alley* (Cherry Valley, NY, 1989).
Butler, Judith, *Excitable Speech: A Politics of the Performative* (New York, 1997).
Butler-Evans, E., *Race, Gender and Desire* (Philadelphia, 1989).
Byatt, A. S., *Possession* (London, 1990).
Calvino, Italo, *If on a Winter's Night a Traveller*, trans. William Weaver (London, 1981).
—— *Six Memos for the Next Millennium*, trans. Patrick Creagh (London, 1992).
Coe, Jonathan, *What a Carve Up!* (London, 1994).
Coetzee, J. M., *Foe* (London, 1976).
—— *Waiting for the Barbarians* (London, 1980).
—— *The Life and Times of Michael K.* (London, 1983).
Connor, Steven, *Samuel Beckett: Repetition, Theory and Text* (Oxford, 1988).
—— *The English Novel in History 1950–1995* (London, 1996).
Cooper, David, 'The Invention of Non-Psychiatry', *Semiotext(e)*, 3/2 (1978), p. 66.
Crawford, Robert, *Devolving English Literature* (Oxford, 1992).
Dearborn, Mary V., *Pocahontas's Daughters: Gender and Ethnicity in American Culture* (New York, 1986).
Deleuze, Gilles and Guattari, Felix, *The Anti-Oedipus*, trans. R. Hurley, M. Seem and H. R. Lane (New York, 1977).
DeLillo, Don, *Americana* (Boston, 1971).
—— *White Noise* (New York, 1984).
—— *Libra* (New York, 1988).
—— *Mao II* (New York, 1991).
—— *Underworld* (London, 1998).
Derrida, Jacques, *Of Grammatology*, trans. Gayatari Chakravorty Spivak (Baltimore, 1976).
Dipple, Elizabeth, *The Unresolvable Plot: Reading Contemporary Fiction* (London, 1988).
Eagleton, Terry (ed.), *Ideology* (Harlow, 1994).
Easterman, Daniel, *New Jerusalems: Reflections on Islam, Fundamentalism and the Rushdie Affair* (London, 1992).
Ellmann, Maud (ed.), *Psychoanalytic Literary Criticism* (London, 1994).
Erdrich, Louise, *Beet Queen* (London, 1986).
—— *Tracks* (London, 1988).
Fanon, Frantz, *Black Skin, White Masks*, trans. Charles Lam Markham (1952; New York, 1967).
—— *The Wretched of the Earth*, trans. Constance Farrington (1961; Harmondsworth, 1967).
Fleck, R. (ed.), *Critical Perspectives on Native American Fiction* (Washington, DC, 1993).
Fletcher, M. D., (ed.), *Reading Rushdie: Perspectives on the Fiction of Salman*

Rushdie (Amsterdam, 1994).

Forster, E. M., *A Passage to India* (London, 1924).

Foster, Hal (ed.), *Postmodern Culture* (London, 1985).

Freud, Sigmund, 'Mourning and Melancholia' (1917), *Standard Edition of the Complete Psychological Works* (London, 1953–74), vol. 14.

Friedman, E. G. and Fuchs, M., *Breaking the Sequence* (Princeton, 1989).

Friel, Brian, *Translations* (London, 1981).

Fuller, John, *Flying to Nowhere* (London, 1983).

Goffman, Erving, *Stigma: Notes on the Management of Spoiled Identity* (Englewood Cliffs, 1963).

Gordon, Giles, *Beyond the Words: Eleven Writers in Search of a New Fiction* (London, 1975).

Gorer, Geoffrey, *Death, Grief and Mourning in Contemporary Britain* (London, 1965).

Grant, Damian and McEwan, Ian, *Contemporary Writers: Ian McEwan* (London, 1989).

Habermas, Jürgen, 'Modernity versus Postmodernity', *New German Critique*, 22 (1981), pp. 3–14.

—— *The Philosophical Discourse of Modernity: Twelve Lectures*, trans. Frederick Lawrence (Cambridge, 1990).

Haffenden, John, *Novelists in Interview* (London, 1985).

Harvey, David, *The Condition of Postmodernity: An Enquiry into the Origins of Social Change* (Oxford, 1989).

Harvey, John, *The Plate Shop* (London, 1979).

—— *Coup d'Etat* (London, 1985).

—— *The Legend of Captain Space* (London, 1990).

Hassan, Ihab, *The Postmodern Turn* (Columbus, Ohio, 1987).

—— 'Making Sense: The Trials of Postmodern Discourse', *New Literary History*, 18 (1987), pp. 437–59.

Heller, Joseph, *Catch 22* (1961; London, 1983).

—— *Good as Gold* (New York, 1979).

Higgins, Lynn A. and Silver, Brenda R. (eds), *Rape and Representation* (New York, 1991).

Hirsch, Marianne and Keller, Evelyn Fox (eds), *Conflicts in Feminism* (London, 1990).

Hite, Molly, *Ideas of Order in the Novels of Thomas Pynchon* (Columbus, Ohio, 1983).

Hughes, Geoffrey, *Swearing: A Social History of Foul Language, Oaths and Profanity in English* (Oxford, 1992).

Hulme, Keri, *The Bone People* (London, 1986).

Hutcheon, Linda, *A Poetics of Postmodernism: History, Theory, Fiction* (London, 1988).

Huyssen, Andreas, *After the Great Divide: Modernism, Mass Culture, Postmodernism* (London, 1986).

Ingalls, Rachel, *Binstead's Safari* (London, 1983).

Iser, Wolfgang, *The Implied Reader: Patterns of Communication in Prose Fiction from Bunyan to Beckett* (Baltimore, 1974).

Jameson, Fredric, *The Political Unconscious: Narrative as a Socially Symbolic Act* (London, 1981).

—— *Postmodernism, or, the Cultural Logic of Late Capitalism* (London, 1991).

Jay, Martin, *Force Fields: Between Intellectual History and Cultural Critique* (London, 1993).

Jhabvala, Ruth Prawer, *Heat and Dust* (London, 1975).

Joyce, James, *Ulysses* (Paris, 1922).

—— 'Daniel Defoe', *Buffalo Studies*, 1 (1964).

Kelman, James, *The Busconductor Hines* (London, 1992).

—— *Some Recent Attacks: Essays Cultural and Political* (Stirling, 1992).

—— *How late it was, how late* (London, 1994).

Kingston, Maxine Hong, *Tripmaster Monkey, His Fake Book* (London, 1989).

Klein, Melanie, 'Mourning and its Relation to Manic Depressive States' (1940), in *Love, Guilt and Reparation and Other Papers, 1921–1946* (London, 1947).

Klinkowitz, Jerome, *Structuring the Void: The Struggle for Subject in Contemporary American Fiction* (Durham, NC, 1991).

Knowlson, James, *Damned to Fame: The Life of Samuel Beckett* (London, 1996).

Kristeva, Julia, *Black Sun: Depression and Melancholia*, trans. S. Roudiez (New York, 1989).

Lacan, Jacques, *Ecrits*, trans. Alan Sheridan (London, 1989).

Lee, Alison, *Realism and Power: Postmodern British Fiction* (London, 1990).

Ling, Amy, *Between Worlds: Women Writers of Chinese Ancestry* (New York, 1990).

Llosa, Mario Vargas, *Making Waves*, ed. and trans. John King (London, 1996).

Lydenberg, Robin, *Word Cultures* (Urbana, Ill., 1987).

Lyotard, Jean-François, *The Postmodern Condition: A Report on Knowledge*, trans. Geoff Bennington and Brian Massumi (Manchester, 1984).

McCaffrey, Larry, *Postmodern Fiction: A Bio-Bibliographical Guide* (Westport, Conn., 1986).

McEwan, Ian, *First Love, Last Rites* (London, 1975).

—— *In Between the Sheets* (London, 1978).

—— *The Cement Garden* (London, 1978).

—— *The Imitation Game* (London, 1980).

—— *The Comfort of Strangers* (London, 1981).

—— *The Ploughman's Lunch* (London, 1983).

—— *The Child in Time* (London, 1987).

—— *The Innocent* (London, 1990).

—— *Black Dogs* (London, 1992).

—— *Enduring Love* (London, 1997).

McEwan, Neil, *Perspective in British Historical Fiction Today* (London, 1987).

McHale, Brian, *Postmodernist Fiction* (London, 1987).

—— *Constructing Postmodernism* (London, 1992).

Macherey, Pierre, *A Theory of Literary Production*, trans. G. Wall (London, 1978).

McKay, Nellie Y. (ed.), *Critical Essays on Toni Morrison* (Boston, 1988).
McNab, Andy, *Bravo Two Zero* (London, 1993).
Mahfouz, Naguib, *Midaq Alley* (1947; London, 1992).
Mailer, Norman, *Oswald's Tale* (New York, 1995).
Minh-ha, Trinh T., *Woman, Native, Other: Writing Postcoloniality and Feminism* (Bloomington, Ind., 1989).
Moore, Brian, *Catholics* (London, 1972).
Morgan, Ted, *Literary Outlaw: The Life and Times of William S. Burroughs* (London, 1988).
Morrison, Toni, *The Bluest Eye* (New York, 1970: 1990).
—— *Beloved* (New York, 1987).
Murphy, Robert F., *The Body Silent* (London, 1987).
Naipaul, V. S., *A House for Mr Biswas* (London, 1961).
—— *Guerrillas* (London, 1975).
Nash, Christopher, *World Postmodern Fiction* (London, 1993).
Ngugi Wa' Thiong'o, *Petals of Blood* (London, 1977).
Nye, Robert, *Falstaff* (London, 1976).
O'Donnell, Patrick (ed.), *New Essays on The Crying of Lot 49* (Cambridge, 1991).
Okri, Ben, *The Famished Road* (London, 1992).
Ondaatje, Michael, *The English Patient* (London, 1992).
Ozick, Cynthia, *Cannibal Galaxy* (New York, 1983).
—— *The Messiah of Stockholm* (London, 1987).
Paton Walsh, Jill, *Knowledge of Angels* (Cambridge, 1994).
Pearce, Richard, *The Novel in Motion* (Columbus, Ohio, 1983).
Pefanis, Julian, *Heterology and the Postmodern: Bataille, Baudrillard and Lyotard* (Durham, NC, 1990).
Pynchon, Thomas, *The Crying of Lot 49* (London, 1966).
—— *Gravity's Rainbow* (London, 1973).
—— *Vineland* (London, 1990).
—— *Mason and Dixon* (London, 1997).
Quayson, Ato, *Strategic Transformations in Nigerian Writing: Orality and History in Rev. Samuel Johnson, Amos Tutuola, Wole Soyinka and Ben Okri* (Oxford and Bloomington, Ind., 1997).
Quin, Ann, *Berg* (London, 1964).
—— *Three* (London, 1966).
—— *Passages* (London, 1969).
—— *Tripticks* (London, 1972).
Richardson, Samuel, *Clarissa, or, The History of a Young Lady*, ed. Angus Ross (Harmondsworth, 1985).
Ricoeur, Paul, *Time and Narrative* (Chicago, 1984).
Robinson, S. *Engendering the Subject: Gender and Self-Representation in Contemporary Women's Fiction* (Albany, NY, 1991).
Ronell, Avital, *Crack Wars* (Lincoln, Neb., and London, 1992).
Rose, Gillian, *Mourning Becomes the Law* (Cambridge, 1996).
Roth, Philip, *My Life as a Man* (New York, 1974).
—— *Operation Shylock* (London, 1993).

Rushdie, Salman, *Midnight's Children* (London, 1981).
—— *Shame* (London, 1983).
—— *The Satanic Verses* (London, 1988).
—— *Haroun and the Sea of Stories* (London, 1990).
—— *Imaginary Homelands: Essays and Criticism 1981–1991* (London, 1991).
—— *The Moor's Last Sigh* (London, 1995).
Ruthven, Malise, *A Satanic Affair: Salman Rushdie and the Wrath of Islam* (London, 1991).
Ryan, Kiernan, *Ian McEwan* (Plymouth, 1994).
Saghal, Nayantara, *Rich Like Us* (London, 1987).
Said, Edward, *Culture and Imperialism* (London, 1993).
Scanlan, Margaret, *Traces of Another Time: History and Politics in Postwar British Fiction* (Princeton, 1990).
Schor, Esther, *Bearing the Dead: The British Culture of Mourning from the Enlightenment to Victoria* (Princeton, 1994).
Sedgwick, Eve Kosofsky, *Between Men: English Literature and Male Homosocial Desire* (New York, 1985).
Sidhwa, Bapsi, *The Ice-Candy Man* (London, 1989).
Siegle, Robert, *Suburban Ambush: Downtown Writing and the Fiction of Insurgency* (Baltimore, 1989).
Silko, Leslie Marmon, *Ceremony* (New York, 1977).
—— *Almanac of the Dead* (New York, 1991).
Sinclair, Iain, *White Chappell, Scarlet Tracings* (Uppingham, 1987).
—— *Downriver* (London, 1991).
—— *Radon Daughters* (London, 1994).
Sinfield, Alan, *Literature, Politics and Culture in Postwar Britain* (Oxford, 1989).
Slusser, G. and Shippey, Tom (eds), *Fiction 2000: Cyberpunk and the Future of Narrative* (Athens, Gia., 1992).
Smyth, Edmund J., *Postmodernism and Contemporary Fiction* (London, 1991).
Sollors, Werner, *Beyond Ethnicity: Consent and Descent in American Culture* (New York, 1986).
Sontag, Susan, *Illness as Metaphor* (New York, 1978).
Soyinka, Wole, *Collected Plays*, 2 vols (Oxford, 1973–4).
Spark, Muriel, *The Abbess of Crewe* (London, 1974).
—— *The Takeover* (London, 1976).
—— *Reality and Dreams* (London, 1996).
Storey, David, *A Temporary Life* (1973).
—— *Saville* (1973).
Suleiman, Susan, *Subversive Intent: Women, Men and the Avant-Garde* (Cambridge, Mass., 1990).
Sutherland, John, *Fiction and the Fiction Industry* (London, 1978).
Swift, Graham, *The Sweet Shop Owner* (London, 1980).
—— *Shuttlecock* (London, 1981).
—— *Learning to Swim and Other Stories* (London, 1982).
—— *Waterland* (London, 1983).
—— *Out of this World* (London, 1988).

—— *Ever After* (London, 1992).
—— *Last Orders* (London, 1996).
Thompson, Hunter S., *Fear and Loathing in Las Vegas* (Frogmore, Herts., 1972).
Todd, Richard, *Consuming Fictions: The Booker Prize and Fiction in Britain Today* (London, 1996).
Tomaselli, Sylvana and Porter, Roy (eds), *Rape* (Oxford, 1986).
Tremain, Rose, *Letter to Sister Benedicta* (London, 1979).
—— *The Cupboard* (London, 1981).
—— *Sacred Country* (London, 1992).
Unsworth, Barry, *Stone Virgin* (London, 1985).
Walker, Alice, *You Can't Keep a Good Woman Down* (New York, 1981).
—— *The Color Purple* (New York, 1982).
Wallace, Gavin and Stevenson, Randall (eds), *The Scottish Novel since the Seventies: New Visions, Old Dreams* (Edinburgh, 1993).
Warner, Alan, *Morvern Callar* (London, 1995).
Webster, Richard, *A Brief History of Blasphemy: Liberalism, Censorship and The Satanic Verses* (Southwold, 1990).
Wheeler, K. M., *Guide to Twentieth Century Women Novelists* (Oxford, 1997).
White, Hayden, *Metahistory: The Historical Imagination in Nineteenth Century Europe* (Baltimore, 1973).
—— *The Content of the Form: Narrative Discourse and Historical Representation* (Baltimore, 1987).
White, John J., *Mythology in the Modern Novel: A Study of Prefigurative Techniques* (Princeton, 1971).
White, Patrick, *The Vivisector* (London, 1970).
Whyte, Susan Reynolds and Ingstad, Benedicte (eds), *Disability and Culture* (Berkeley, 1995).
Winter, Jay, *Sites of Memory, Sites of Mourning: The Great War in European Cultural History* (Cambridge, 1995).
Winterson, Jeanette, *Boating for Beginners* (London, 1985).
—— *Oranges are not the Only Fruit* (London, 1985).
—— *Sexing the Cherry* (London, 1989).
—— *Art Objects* (London, 1995).
—— *Gut Symmetries* (London, 1997).
Wright, Richard, *Native Son* (New York, 1940).
Young, Marguerite, *Miss Mackintosh, My Darling* (1965).
Zamora, L. P. and Faris, W. B., *Magical Realism: Theory, History, Community* (Durham, NC, 1995).
Žižek, Slavoj, *Looking Awry: An Introduction to Jacques Lacan through Popular Culture* (Cambridge, Mass., 1992).

Index